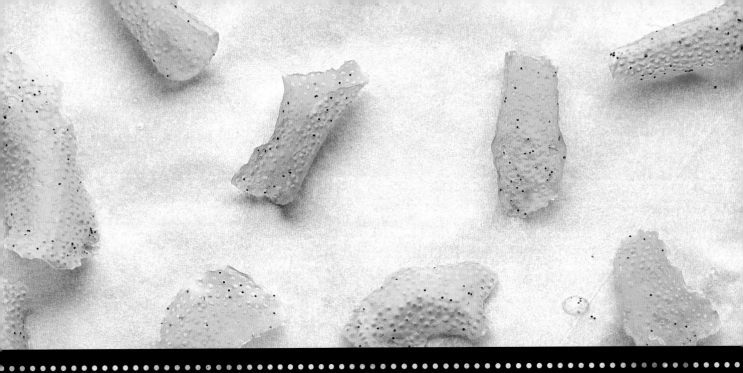

NOSTALGIC

jacqui
small

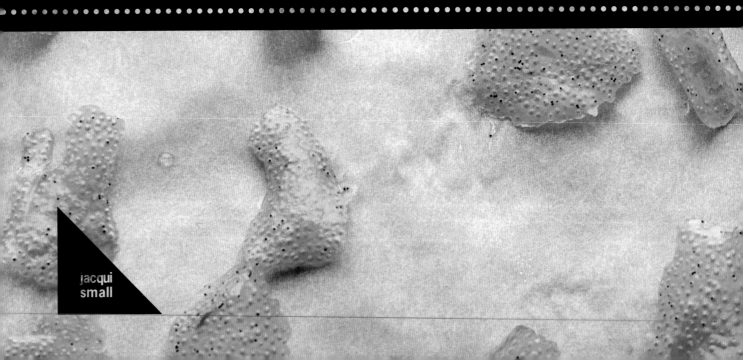

Delights

WILLIAM CURLEY

PHOTOGRAPHY BY KEVIN SUMMERS

First published in 2016 by
Jacqui Small LLP
74–77 White Lion Street
London N1 9PF

Publisher
Jacqui Small
Managing Editor
Emma Heyworth-Dunn
Project Editor
Abi Waters
Proofreader
Claire Wedderburn-Maxwell
Editorial Assistant
Joe Hallsworth
Designer
Robin Rout
Photographer
Kevin Summers
Culinary Assistant
Melissa Paul
Production
Maeve Healy

British Library
Cataloguing-in-Publication Data
A catalogue record for this book is
available from the British Library.

ISBN 978-1-910254-57-8

2018 2017 2016

10 9 8 7 6 5 4 3 2 1

Printed and bound in China.

Quarto is the authority on a
wide range of topics.

Quarto educates, entertains
and enriches the lives of
our readers – enthusiasts and
lovers of hands-on living.

www.QuartoKnows.com

CONTENTS

*To my father
'Big Bill', a Methil boy
through and through.
Without his support,
I would not have
achieved my goals.*

*And to my daughter
Amy-Rose –
I hope I can do the
same for you one day.*

FOREWORD

Nostalgic Delights. You can't avoid smiling as you say this seductive little phrase, and if you have an achingly sweet tooth like us, you will be rendered incapable in the face of William's glorious treats, stunningly revealed in pages dripping with the comfort of the familiar and excitement of the new. With his impeccable skills grounded in classic French haute cuisine, William teases with a fun, eclectic repertoire, brimming with surprises and entangled with fascinating memories that hint at their inspirations and resonate with all of us. Just reading the list of Delights, let alone sampling any, will instantly recall childhood. Here, we don't just taste, we feel the emotions of William's food.

In precise, meticulously researched recipes, the classics feature but with a refreshing, cleaner lightness that modernizes timeless icons such as Classic Millefeuille with its airy light layers and satiny fondant, along with others, such as Charlotte Royale and Charlotte Russe. All are brilliantly juxtaposed with cheeky innovations of childhood favourites such as Ice Cream Sandwich, Rout Biscuits, Fruit Pastilles and Marshmallows. Who could resist trying their hand at making a Curley Wurly, elegantly recreating a Walnut Whip or Snowballs with a tropical twist?

Over the years, we have observed and admired William's tenacious pursuit of his childhood vocation to excel as a pâtissier and chocolatier, steadily growing in confidence and skill to become one of Europe's most talented and lauded pastry chefs, achieving his place amongst the 100 best pastry chefs in the Relais Desserts International. Along the way,

we have mentored and even judged him as he has amassed an incredible list of prizes and awards including Master of Culinary Arts and the Academy of Chocolate's 'Britain's Best Chocolatier' four times.

As we read his latest, intensely personal book, we feel such pride, since it marks not only a progression in stature and maturity from his previous works, but a level of confidence in giving intimate, vivid insight to inspirations rooted in a happy childhood in Fife, worldwide travels and unforgettable apprenticeships served under culinary masters, such as Pierre Koffmann and Marc Meneau. William reveals how nostalgia can be profoundly grounding but also creatively inspiring, forming a true sense of identity.

In these days when attitudes towards food can swing between guilt and paranoia, the Roux family, in common with the French in general, still very much believes that food and eating is a glorious, positive source of pleasure that uplifts and draws people together. That is the essence of William's book. He invites us to join him in his humble and worthy pursuit to shamelessly celebrate pâtisserie, chocolate and all things sweet and delicious – whether beautifully simple or more elaborate in design. Enjoy the stunning photos, indulge in the mouthwatering confections and remember that it is the small, simple things in life that bind us together and often give the greatest pleasure and happiness.

Michel Roux, O.B.E., M.O.F.
Global Ambassador, The Waterside Inn

Alain Roux
Chef Patron, The Waterside Inn

MY JOURNEY OF *Nostalgic* MEMORIES

The definition of 'nostalgia' is *'A sentimental longing or wistful affection for a period in the past'*.
The word is thought to be derived from the Greek words *nostos*, meaning 'return home' and
algos, meaning 'pain', so it originally imparted the feeling of missing home.

Whether it be standing at Tannadice with my dad watching my beloved Dundee United taking on Europe's finest; playing my first record, *Sound Affects* by The Jam; eating too much of my mum's Black Forest gâteau at Christmas; or eating milk ice cream with my sister by the seaside on a warm summer's day on the east coast of bonnie Scotland – food plays a major part in my nostalgic memories, and my memories have also shaped my taste and style of cooking. Experiencing food throughout my life has had a vast impact on the path I have taken.

Some of my earliest and most influential memories of cooking come from visiting my granny on a Sunday afternoon. The smell of boiling jam and baking cakes still takes me back to the time spent with her. Peggy McHoul taught me not only to cook, but to understand the value of homemade food; an ethos that even today I try to embrace within my craft and pass on to the next generation of pâtissiers and chocolatiers. It was her influence that gave me the confidence, when I was fifteen, to enter a classroom full of girls baking cakes!

At college, I was very fortunate to be taken under the wing of a master baker, Dave Bryson, who encouraged me to take my passion forward. From college my journey continued, supported by people along the way who helped build a foundation and inspire me. In particular Scott Lyall and Willie Pike, who have both done so much for young chefs in Scotland, and remain good friends of mine today.

Arriving at Gleneagles Hotel as a 17-year-old apprentice opened my eyes to the historic grandeur of cooking – tall hats, huge copper pans, the smell of caramel and pots of cinder toffee bubbling and steaming. Even now, stepping into the kitchen of a great hotel encapsulates Escoffier's era. Auguste Escoffier brought the Golden Era of Marie Antonin Carême's haute cuisine from the mid-1800s into the 20th century. I was fortunate enough at Gleneagles to be taught by Ian Ironside, a very traditional chef who had previously

been the Head Pâtissier at The Savoy. He clearly had more influence than I had anticipated at the time, as later on I went to take on the same role at The Savoy.

Second to only my granny, my time with Pierre Koffmann has had the greatest impact on my relationship with food. Entering his kitchen and receiving his training at La Tante Claire opened the door for me into the fine food industry. His cooking is based on his memories and love of Gascony, from where he originally came. He taught me to be proud to cook from the heart.

My career took me to many incredible restaurants and hotels in Britain and France. Each helped to evolve my understanding and taught me something unique; whether it was being shown how to make the iconic Peach Melba by Anton Edelmann at The Savoy, Raymond Blanc's contagious enthusiasm for seasonal ingredients, or Marco Pierre White's search for perfection.

Nostalgia never leaves you and never stops. As with food, I may experience or create something tomorrow that will stay with me for life. Food evolves every day with new trends or fashions, but we always remember the past and always learn from it. Nostalgia will always continue to shape who we are and the past will always influence the future.

Within this book, I have aimed to capture different stages of my journey with food, beginning, of course in my family home and moving through my career to embrace history by way of a diversity of eras in pâtisserie and chocolate.

Every individual has their own interpretation of nostalgia, and of course their own fond memories of food. I hope that within the recipes I have created for this book there is going to be a little something enabling every reader to capture their own bit of nostalgia.

William Curley is a pâtissier and chocolatier as talented as he is audacious. He fully embodies the fundamental values of our Relais Desserts Association; the passion for his profession, openness towards others, the requirement for quality and innovation. It is always with great pleasure that I find our discoveries of the very best pâtisserie can be shared.

William Curley est un pâtissier chocolatier aussi talentueux qu'audacieux. Il incarne pleinement les valeurs fondamentales de notre Association Relais Desserts: la passion du métier, l'ouverture aux autres, l'exigence de la qualité, l'innovation. C'est toujours avec grand plaisir que je le retrouve pour partager nos expériences de la Haute Pâtisserie.

Frédéric Cassel
PRESIDENT, RELAIS DESSERTS

There is a remarkable history behind chocolate confectionery – Fry's, Rowntree's and Cadbury were all hugely pioneering in their day.

The concept – and original recipes – behind most of the famous bars is very clever. I have a lot of respect for the creativity of combining flavour and texture within a chocolate bar. Although manufactured bars have lost what they were once about with the tightening of profit margins – without high-quality chocolate and ingredients, even the best recipes will not taste good.

Most people have fond memories of traipsing along a confectionery aisle in a supermarket or choosing a selection of sugary snacks from a sweet shop.

CHOCOLATE
Confectionery

Within this section I wanted to recreate that sense of excitement when choosing from a variety of different types of chocolate bars.

I now find manufactured bars too sweet, but after encouragement from a good friend and mentor, Sara Jayne Stanes, I have created a 'grown-up' range, which is somewhat more balanced and sophisticated but far more decadent than the commercial counterparts. Sara is the authority on fine chocolate in the UK and has been at the forefront of driving the fine chocolate market forward and educating the nation for over 20 years.

TEMPERING CHOCOLATE

This is a great method as it requires no marble. All you will need is your porringer pot, double-boiler or bain-marie (water bath) and a thermometer. You will always need at least this amount of chocolate for dipping and moulding.

500g (1lb 2oz) dark (bittersweet) chocolate (65% cocoa solids), finely chopped (or use chocolate buttons)

1–2 Place two-thirds of the chopped chocolate into a porringer pot, double-boiler or over a bain-marie (water bath). Do not boil the water, as it may scald the chocolate. Stir regularly until the chocolate has completely melted and reaches 45–50°C (113–122°F) ensuring all the fat and sugars have melted evenly.

3–5 Gradually add the remaining chocolate – this is the seed. Stir vigorously and continue to stir until all of the chocolate has fully melted and the chocolate cools to 28–29°C (82–84°F) and thickens. Warm back up to 31–32°C (87–89°F). The chocolate is now tempered and ready to use. If the temperature drops below this, simply warm it up over the bain-marie again.

4

5

TEMPERING TIPS

When the chocolate reaches 31–32°C (87–89°F) this is known as the working temperature. The chocolate is tempered and ready to use. To test this manually, dip the end of a palette knife into the chocolate, then leave to set. If the chocolate is smooth and glossy when set (see below), you have successfully tempered your chocolate.

Be careful when using a bain-marie (water bath) that none of the water or steam gets into the chocolate. Chocolate is made up of cocoa solids, cocoa butter, sugar, vanilla and possibly milk powder. A small drop of water will moisten the ingredients and make the cocoa solids clump together and separate from the butter (in the same way that oil and water do not mix). You should never cover melting chocolate with a lid as the steam will condense and drop into the chocolate.

Over heating separates the cocoa solids and the other dry ingredients from the cocoa butter; it will begin to burn if over heated, the result being a dry, discoloured paste. There is no retrieving burnt chocolate so be careful when tempering and melting.

For milk chocolate, follow the same as above and melt to 45–50°C (113–122°F), cool to 26–27°C (79–81°F) and temper at 29–30°C (84–86°F). For white chocolate, follow the same as above and melt to 45°C (113°F), cool to 26–27°C (79–81°F) and temper at 29–30°C (84–86°F).

TEMPERED CHOCOLATE

UNTEMPERED CHOCOLATE

CASTING IN MOULDS

1 Temper your chosen chocolate as instructed on page 14. Fill the chocolate mould with tempered chocolate.

2 Scrape off excess chocolate with a scraper and also use the scraper to tap the sides of the mould to remove any air bubbles. Turn the mould upside down over a bowl and tap with the scraper again – the majority of the chocolate should fall out into the bowl underneath to leave a shell of chocolate coating each hole. Turn the right way up and scrape off the excess chocolate with the scraper. Place the mould upside down on a baking tray (sheet) lined with silicone (baking) paper. Leave it to set for 10–15 minutes in a cool, dry area.

3 Fill a piping (pastry) bag with your chosen filling and snip the end to make a small hole. Pipe the filling into each cavity until they are four-fifths full. To cap, pour more tempered chocolate over the top of the mould so that each hole is completely filled and level off with a scraper or palette knife. Leave the mould to fully set for at least 2–3 hours in a cool, dry area.

4–5 Once set, twist the mould to loosen the chocolates. Turn it upside down and tap gently so that the chocolates drop out of the mould.

1

2

3

4

DIPPING IN CHOCOLATE

1 Temper your chosen chocolate as instructed on page 14.

2 Use a dipping fork to lift the prepared confection from the tray and submerge it in the tempered chocolate.

3 Lift the dipped confection and remove any excess chocolate by gently tapping the dipping fork on the side of the porringer pot.

4 Place each dipped confection onto a tray lined with silicone (baking) paper. If necessary, use a small palette knife to carefully push the dipped confection off the dipping fork and onto the tray.

5 Leave to set in a cool, dry area for 1–2 hours.

Note: The minimum amount of chocolate to temper is 250g (9oz) – anything below this quantity becomes too difficult to work with. You may have leftover tempered chocolate with some of the recipes in this book that can then be stored in an airtight container and re-used.

5

3

1

2

3

4

DARK CHOCOLATE GANACHE

The word 'ganache' actually means 'fool' in French. There is a story that I often tell, which has become folklore in pastry kitchens, of how this delicious recipe earned its name. Long ago, in a grand kitchen in France there was a nervous young commis chef and a rather menacing head chef. On the day of a busy banquet everyone was rushing around. The young commis was carrying a heavy pan full of hot cream, while the head chef was walking the other way holding a big bowl of dark chocolate. In his haste, the young commis bumped into the head chef and accidentally sloshed hot cream into the bowl of chocolate. 'Ganache!' shouted the head chef, cursing the young commis. They looked at the mess of chocolate and cream in despair, but then noticed that the cream and chocolate had begun to combine. Carefully they mixed the bowl of chocolate and a smooth, glossy mixture began to form. After tasting their creation, they christened it 'ganache' and added it to their repertoire of recipes. Of course it was so good that the recipe spread far and wide and is adored all over the world to this day.

....

Makes 575g (1lb 5oz)

300ml (½ pint/1¼ cups) whipping (pouring) cream
250g (9oz) dark (bittersweet) chocolate
  (70% cocoa solids), finely chopped
25g (1oz/2 tablespoons) unsalted butter, softened

1 Put the cream in a saucepan and bring to the boil. Put the chopped chocolate in a mixing bowl. Pour the boiled cream over the chocolate.

2 Mix until emulsified and a ganache consistency is formed.

3–4 Add in the softened butter and mix well until fully incorporated. Leave to set at room temperature for about 1–2 hours.

Ideally use immediately. Once it starts to set, the ganache can be stored in the fridge for 2 days, but you will need to leave it to return to room temperature before using.

INFUSING/FLAVOURING

If infusing/flavouring, put the cream in the saucepan and bring to the boil. Remove from the heat, add the required ingredients (see flavour variations, right) and cover with cling film (plastic wrap). Leave for 30 minutes to infuse, then reheat to boiling point. Strain and continue with the ganache recipe as above.

FLAVOUR VARIATIONS

These variations on a basic chocolate ganache are used in many recipes. All of the variations below are made using the method opposite.

Milk Chocolate Ganache: use a mixture of 150g (5½oz) chopped milk chocolate (35% cocoa solids) and 135g (4¾oz) chopped dark (bittersweet) chocolate (65% cocoa solids).

Orange-infused Ganache: infuse 2g (½ teaspoon) finely grated orange zest with the cream as you boil it, then leave to infuse for 30 minutes. Strain the infused cream, return to the boil and continue with the method.

Rum Ganache: Make the ganache as instructed opposite using 350g (12oz) dark (bittersweet) chocolate (66% cocoa solids), 200ml (7fl oz/generous ¾ cup) whipping (pouring) cream, 80g (3oz/⅓ cup/¾ stick) unsalted butter. Once the butter is fully combined, add 65ml (2fl oz/¼ cup) dark rum.

Beurre de Sel Ganache: use 200g (7oz) chopped Toscano 65% chocolate, 150ml (5fl oz/⅔ cup) whipping (pouring) cream and 150g (5½oz) Sea Salt Caramel (see page 48).

Almond Praline Ganache: Make the ganache as instructed opposite and once the butter has been added, mix in 80g (3oz) Almond Praline Paste (see variation page 242).

Raspberry Ganache: use 250g (9oz) raspberry purée instead of the cream and increase the butter to 60g (2oz/¼ cup/½ stick).

Lemon Ganache: use a mixture of 125g (4½oz) chopped milk chocolate (35% cocoa solids) and 125g (4½oz) chopped dark (bittersweet) chocolate (65% cocoa solids). Pour 200ml (7fl oz/generous ¾ cup) boiled cream over the chopped chocolate. Add 100ml (3½fl oz) lemon juice and stir through. Lastly add 25g (1oz) butter and mix well.

HAZELNUT ROCHERS

This evokes memories of a tower of gold-wrapped chocolates, reserved only for special occasions. I can picture my mother presenting a plate of these on Christmas day, for them only to be devoured within minutes; it really was a luxurious treat. I have used Amedei Gianduja in the ganache for this recipe, which is made with the best Piedmont hazelnuts, giving the chocolates a lasting creaminess.

....

Makes 80 chocolates

For the Praline Ganache:
320ml (11fl oz/1⅓ cups) whipping (pouring) cream
1 vanilla pod (bean), split and scraped
40g (1½oz) invert sugar
300g (10½oz) Gianduja chocolate, finely chopped
160g (5½oz) dark (bittersweet) chocolate
  (70% cocoa solids), finely chopped
55g (1¾oz/3½ tablespoons) unsalted butter, softened

For the Nutty Chocolate:
500g (1lb 2oz) tempered milk chocolate
 (see page 15)
250g (9oz) roasted nibbed almonds

To finish:
100g (3½oz/⅔ cup) whole roasted hazelnuts
200g (7oz) feuillantine wafer, crushed
Edible gold leaf

You will also need:
• *piping (pastry) bag*
• *12mm (½ inch) nozzle (tip)*
• *dipping fork*

First, make the Praline Ganache:

1 Put the cream in a saucepan and scrape in the seeds from the split vanilla pod (bean). Bring to the boil, then remove from the heat and leave to infuse for 30 minutes. Strain the infused cream into a clean saucepan, add the invert sugar and bring to the boil.

2 Put the chopped chocolate in a mixing bowl. Pour the boiled cream over the chocolate and mix until emulsified and a ganache consistency is formed.

3 Add the softened butter and mix well until fully incorporated. Leave to set at room temperature for about 1–2 hours.

To assemble:

4 Put the Praline Ganache in a piping (pastry) bag fitted with a 12mm (½ inch) nozzle (tip). Pipe small bulbs of the ganache onto a silicone-lined tray (see pic on page 22).

5 Put a whole roasted hazelnut onto each bulb of ganache (see pic on page 23).

6 Pipe a larger bulb of ganache on top of each hazelnut (see pic on page 23) and leave to set for 1 hour in a cool, dry area.

Continue on page 22.

Next, make the Nutty Chocolate:

7 Temper the milk chocolate and add the nibbed almonds. If the chocolate thickens, warm it slightly.

To finish:

8 Roll each bulb into a sphere and coat in feuillantine wafer.

9 Use a dipping fork to dip each prepared chocolate sphere into the Nutty Chocolate (see page 17).

10 Place each chocolate on a silicone-lined tray to set for 1–2 hours in a cool, dry area.

11 Decorate with gold leaf to finish.

These chocolates will keep for 1 week stored in an airtight container in a cool, dry area.

4

5

6

8

9

MUSCADINES

Muscadines are a traditional French chocolate made using praline and orange liqueur, but I have stayed true to my Scottish roots in my version and used Drambuie. The drink is famous for being a prince's liqueur. During the Jacobite rebellion in the 1740s, Bonnie Prince Charlie was on the run. He was aided by the McKinnon Clan and as thanks to their bravery, he gave them a secret recipe for his own favourite drink, which today is known as Drambuie.

Makes 80 chocolates

350g (12oz) neige decor *(see Note)*
500g (1lb 2oz) tempered dark (bittersweet) chocolate (65% cocoa solids) *(see page 14)*

For the Drambuie Ganache:
160ml (5¼fl oz/⅔ cup) crème fraîche
160ml (5¼fl oz/⅔ cup) whipping (pouring) cream
50g (1¾oz) invert sugar
225g (8oz) dark (bittersweet) chocolate (65% cocoa solids), finely chopped
100g (3½oz) milk couverture chocolate, finely chopped
200g (7oz) Praline Paste *(see page 242)*
50g (1¾oz/3½ tablespoons) sea salt butter, softened
75ml (2½fl oz/⅓ cup) Drambuie

You will also need:
• *piping (pastry) bag*
• *12mm (½ inch) nozzle (tip)*
• *dipping fork*

First, make the Drambuie Ganache:

1 Put the crème fraîche, cream and invert sugar in a saucepan and bring to the boil.

2 Put the chopped chocolate in a mixing bowl. Pour the boiled crème fraîche mixture over the chocolate. Mix until emulsified and a ganache consistency is formed.

3 Add the Praline Paste and softened butter and mix until fully emulsified. When the butter is fully incorporated, add the Drambuie and mix well. Leave the ganache to firm, uncovered, in a cool, dry area for about 1–2 hours.

To assemble:

4 Line a baking tray (sheet) with silicone (baking) paper or a non-stick baking mat.

5 Spoon the firm ganache into a piping (pastry) bag fitted with a 12mm (½ inch) nozzle (tip). Pipe oblongs onto the lined baking tray (sheet) and leave to set for 2 hours in a cool, dry area.

6 Put the neige décor in a shallow tray or bowl and temper the chocolate. Use a dipping fork to dip each chocolate into the tempered chocolate (see page 17), then roll in the neige decor until evenly coated. Gently shake each chocolate in a sieve (strainer) to remove any excess powder, then leave to set in a cool, dry area for 1–2 hours.

These chocolates will keep for 1 week stored in an airtight container in a cool, dry area.

Note: Neige decor is a type of icing (powdered) sugar derived from cornflour (cornstarch) that does not dissolve in humid conditions.

VENUS NIPPLES

A very famous chocolate, traditionally named capezzoli de venere, which is Italian for 'nipples of Venus' and named after the Roman goddess of love. Traditionally they are made with marinated chestnuts, but I have used confit chestnuts and sesame in my recipe. These were one of the first things I made as a young apprentice on the chocolate section at Gleaneagles Hotel. At 17, I found the name very amusing, and I still do today!

Makes 50 chocolates

200g (7oz) confit chestnuts
500g (1lb 2oz) tempered dark (bittersweet) chocolate (65% cocoa solids) *(see page 14)*
250g (9oz) tempered white chocolate *(see page 15)*

For the Sesame Chocolate Discs:
25g (1oz) white sesame seeds
25g (1oz) black sesame seeds
250g (9oz) tempered dark (bittersweet) chocolate (65% cocoa solids) *(see page 14)*

For the Sesame Ganache:
200ml (7fl oz/generous ¾ cup) whipping (pouring) cream
30g (1¼oz) invert sugar
210g (7½oz) dark (bittersweet) chocolate (65% cocoa solids), finely chopped
30g (1¼oz) Gianduja chocolate
5g (1 teaspoon) shop-bought sesame paste
35g (1⅓oz/2¼ tablespoons) unsalted butter, softened

You will also need:
• *2cm (¾ inch) cutter*
• *piping (pastry) bag*
• *12mm (½ inch) nozzle (tip)*
• *dipping fork*
• *paper piping cornet (see page 250)*

First, make the Sesame Chocolate Discs:

1 Line a 20 x 30cm (8 x 12 inch) baking tray (sheet) with an acetate sheet or silicone (baking) paper.

2 Lightly toast the white and black sesame seeds in a frying pan over a moderate heat for a few minutes, then leave to cool. Temper the chocolate, then add the cooled sesame seeds to it and mix until evenly combined.

3 Use a step-palette knife to spread an even layer of the mixture onto the prepared tray. Leave to semi-set for about 30 seconds, then use a 2cm (¾ inch) cutter to cut out 50 discs – regularly wipe the cutter to ensure tidy discs. Place a sheet of acetate on top and weigh it down with a flat tray to prevent the sheet distorting. Leave to set in a cool, dry area for 30 minutes.

Next, make the Sesame Ganache:

4 Put the cream and invert sugar in a saucepan and bring to the boil.

5 Put the chopped dark chocolate and gianduja chocolate in a mixing bowl. Pour the boiled cream over the chocolate and mix continuously to form an emulsion. Add the sesame paste and the butter and mix until fully incorporated. Leave the ganache to firm in a cool, dry area for 1–2 hours.

To assemble:

6 Line a baking tray (sheet) with silicone (baking) paper and place the set chocolate discs on it.

7 Place the confit chestnuts on a wire rack set over a tray to drain any excess syrup away, then roughly chop into 1cm (½ inch) pieces. Place a piece of chestnut onto each sesame disc.

8 Spoon the firm ganache into a piping (pastry) bag fitted with a 12mm (½ inch) nozzle (tip) and pipe a bulb of ganache (about 8g/¼oz) onto each sesame disc, covering the piece of chestnut. Leave to set in a cool, dry area for 2 hours.

To finish:

9 Temper the dark (bittersweet) chocolate. Use a dipping fork to coat each chocolate disc with tempered chocolate, then carefully place them on the prepared tray (see page 17).

10 When the chocolates are all coated, temper the white chocolate and spoon it into a paper piping (pastry) cornet. Snip a small hole in the end and pipe a small bulb of white chocolate onto the tip of each chocolate. Leave to set for 1–2 hours in a cool, dry area.

These will keep for 1 week stored in an airtight container in a cool, dry area.

7

7

8

9

ALPINE CHOCOLATES

These are inspired by Toblerone bars. The combination of nougat, almonds and chocolate is timeless, and the shape of the bar representing the Alps mountain range is unique. The giant Toblerones that can be bought in duty-free at airports are still to this day hugely exciting to any child, despite being virtually impossible to eat!

Makes 20 chocolates

1 quantity of **Caramelized Almond Nibs**
(see variation page 243)
250g (9oz) tempered white chocolate
(see page 15)
500g (1lb 2oz) tempered dark
(bittersweet) chocolate
(70% cocoa solids) *(see page 14)*

For the Almond Nougat:
100g (3½oz/¾ cup) icing (powdered)
sugar, for dusting and rolling
50g (1¾oz/½ cup) nibbed almonds,
lightly roasted
40g (1½oz) egg whites (about 1–2 eggs)
100g (3½oz/scant ½ cup) honey
170g (6oz/generous ¾ cup) caster
(superfine) sugar
50g (1¾oz) liquid glucose
60ml (2fl oz/¼ cup) water

You will also need:
• *twenty 7.5 x 10.5cm (3 x 4 inch)
rectangles cut from OHP paper
(thick, clear plastic available in most
stationery shops)*
• *small paintbrush*
• *2cm (¾ inch) cutter*
• *piping (pastry) bag*

First, make the Caramelized Almond Nibs:

1 Make the Caramelized Almond Nibs as instructed on page 243.

Next, make the Almond Nougat:

2 Preheat the oven to 100°C (212°F/ Gas ¼). Line a baking tray (sheet) with a non-stick baking mat and dust with a little icing (powdered) sugar to prevent the nougat from sticking.

3 Spread the nibbed almonds out on a baking tray (sheet) and place in the preheated oven to keep warm.

4 Begin whisking the egg whites in the bowl of an electric mixer fitted with a whisk attachment on a slow speed.

5 Put the honey in a saucepan and begin to cook over a medium heat.

6 At the same time, put the sugar, glucose and water in a separate saucepan and begin to cook.

7 When the honey reaches 121°C (250°F), gently pour it into the whisking egg whites and continue whisking on a medium speed.

8 When the sugar syrup reaches 145°C (293°F), pour it onto the whisking egg white mixture. Continue to whisk on a medium speed for about 5 minutes until light.

9 Take the warm nuts from the oven and fold them through the meringue mixture.

10 Dust a work surface with icing (powdered) sugar and use a rolling pin to spread the nougat into a thin layer – about 5mm (⅛ inch) thick. Place on the prepared tray (sheet) and leave to set for at least 2 hours in a cool, dry area.

To assemble:

11 Make cone shapes with the prepared OHP rectangles and use tape to hold them together.

12 Temper the white chocolate. Use a paintbrush to carefully brush the inside tips of the cones with the tempered white chocolate, then leave to set for 30 minutes.

13 Cut the nougat into twenty 2cm (¾ inch) discs.

14 Temper the dark (bittersweet) chocolate and mix it with the prepared Caramelized Almond Nibs in a bowl. Spoon it into a piping (pastry) bag, snip the end to make a small hole and pipe each cone four-fifths full with chocolate.

15 Place a nougat disc in each cone and gently press into the chocolate to create a flat surface. Leave to set in a cool, dry area for 2–3 hours, before de-moulding by cutting the tape and carefully removing the plastic.

These will keep for 1 month stored in an airtight container in a cool, dry area.

12

13–14

CARTWHEEL

This is my take on a 1940s classic confection from Australia. Anyone who has eaten a Wagonwheel as a child must have the nostalgic memory of it being bigger than your hand! I have adapted the original style to include apricot in the marshmallow and also as a jam. This adds acidity and cuts through the sweetness.

Makes 12 cartwheels

½ quantity of **Hazelnut and Almond Pastry** *(see page 228)*
1 quantity of **Apricot Jam**
  (see variation page 241)

For the Apricot and Vanilla Marshmallow:

10g (¼oz) leaf gelatine
110g (3¾oz) apricot purée
½ vanilla pod (bean), split and scraped
225g (8oz/1 cup plus 2 tablespoons) caster (superfine) sugar
135ml (4¾fl oz/½ cup) water
38g (1½oz) egg white (about 1–2 eggs)
1g (a pinch) cream of tartar

To finish:
500g (1lb 2oz) tempered dark (bittersweet) chocolate
  (65% cocoa solids) *(see page 14)*
25g (1oz) freeze-dried apricot

You will also need:
• *6.5cm (2½ inch) pastry cutter*
• *piping (pastry) bag*
• *12mm (½ inch) nozzle (tip)*
• *dipping fork*

First, make the Hazelnut and Almond Pastry and Apricot Jam:

1 Prepare the pastry dough as instructed on page 228. Turn the dough out onto the work surface, shape it into a block and wrap it in cling film (plastic wrap). Put the dough in the fridge to rest for 2–3 hours.

2 Prepare the jam as instructed on page 241. Pour into a shallow tray to cool.

Now, bake the pastry biscuits:

3 Roll the pastry to 3mm (⅛ inch) thick and cut into 24 discs using the 6.5cm (2½ inch) cutter. Place on a baking tray lined with silicone (baking) paper and rest in the fridge for at least 30 minutes. Preheat the oven to 180°C (350°F/gas 4). Bake for 10–12 minutes or until golden in colour, then leave to cool.

Finally, make the Marshmallow:

4 Soak the gelatine in a bowl of ice-cold water for a few minutes to soften. Squeeze the gelatine to remove the excess water.

5 Put the apricot purée in a saucepan over a medium heat, add the seeds of the split and scraped vanilla pod (bean) and bring to the boil. Remove from the heat and stir in the soaked gelatine until dissolved.

6 Put 215g (7½oz/1 cup) of the caster (superfine) sugar and the water in a saucepan over a medium heat and cook to 130°C (266°F).

7 Simultaneously whisk the egg whites with the cream of tartar and the remaining sugar in a clean bowl to a soft peak.

8 Gradually pour the sugar syrup into the whisking egg. Add the apricot mixture and increase the speed. Continue to whisk until the marshmallow reaches a full peak and cools slightly. Spoon the marshmallow into a piping (pastry) bag fitted with a 12mm (½ inch) nozzle (tip).

To assemble and finish:

9 Once the pastry discs have cooled, place 12 discs on a tray. Pipe a ring of marshmallow around the edge of each. Spoon the apricot jam into a piping (pastry) bag and snip the end to make a small hole. Pipe a bulb into the centre of each marshmallow ring, then place another disc of pastry on top and gently push them together.

10 Temper the chocolate. Dip each biscuit in tempered chocolate (see page 17) and carefully place them on a tray (sheet) lined with silicone (baking) paper. Use a clean dipping fork to finish by imprinting the 3 prongs into the centre of each cartwheel and sprinkle with freeze-dried apricot. Leave to set for 1–2 hours in a cool, dry area.

These will keep for 5 days stored in an airtight container in a cool, dry area.

WALNUT WHIP

As a wee laddie, I always saw walnut whips as being a grown-ups choice of confectionery,
so I felt it was rather fitting to develop an elegant version for this book.

Makes 12 walnut whips

1 quantity **Walnut Feuillantine**
(see *Praline Feuillantine, page 136*) –
replace the Praline Paste with
50g (1¾oz) **Walnut Paste**
(see *variation page 242*) and add
30g (1¼oz) roasted walnuts
½ quantity **Dark (Bittersweet)**
Chocolate Ganache (see *page 19*)
1 quantity **Caramelized Walnuts**
(see *variation page 243*)
500g (1lb 2oz) tempered dark
(bittersweet) chocolate
(65% cocoa solids) (see *page 14*)

For the Coffee Marshmallow:
10g (¼oz) leaf gelatine
140ml (4¾fl oz/ ⅔ cup) water
6g (⅛oz/1 teaspoon)
  instant coffee granules
½ vanilla pod (bean), split and scraped
225g (8oz/generous 1 cup)
  caster (superfine) sugar
38g (1½oz) egg white (about 1–2 eggs)
1g (a pinch) cream of tartar

You will also need:
• *twelve 52 x 48mm (2 x 2 inch)*
  chocolate cone moulds
• *piping (pastry) bag*
• *plain and C8 star nozzle (tip)*

First, make the Walnut Feuillantine
and the Ganache:

1 Make the Walnut Feuillantine as
instructed on page 136. Line a baking
tray (sheet) with silicone (baking) paper.
Spread the mixture out thinly onto the
tray and leave to set for 30 minutes.

2 Prepare the ganache as instructed
on page 19. Leave to set at room
temperature for about 30 minutes.

Next, make the Caramelized
Walnuts and temper the chocolate:

3 Prepare the nuts as instructed on
page 243. Spread the nuts out in an
even layer so that they are all separated.

4 Temper the chocolate. Line the cone
moulds with the tempered chocolate
and leave to set for 30 minutes.

Now, make the Coffee Marshmallow:

5 Soak the gelatine in a bowl of ice-
cold water for a few minutes to soften.
Squeeze the gelatine to remove the
excess water.

6 Boil 30ml (2 tablespoons) of the
water in a small pan. Add the coffee
granules and vanilla seeds and mix well.
Remove from the heat and stir in the
soaked gelatine until dissolved.

7 Put 215g (7½oz/1 cup) of the caster
(superfine) sugar and the remaining
water in a pan over a medium heat and
cook to 130°C (266°F).

8 Simultaneously whisk the egg
whites with the cream of tartar and
the remaining sugar in a clean bowl
to a soft peak.

9 Gradually pour the sugar syrup
into the whisking egg. Add the
coffee mixture and increase the
speed. Continue to whisk until the
marshmallow reaches a full peak
and cools in temperature. Spoon the
marshmallow into a piping (pastry)
bag fitted with a plain nozzle (tip).

To fill the cones and finish:

10 Pipe the marshmallow into the
chocolate-lined cone moulds so that
they are two-thirds full. Cut the walnut
feuillantine into small pieces and push
them into the marshmallow.

11 Cap the filled moulds with dark
(bittersweet) chocolate (see page 16)
and leave to set in a cool, dry area for
1–2 hours.

12 De-mould the chocolates from
the moulds (see page 16). Spoon the
Dark (Bittersweet) Chocolate Ganache
into a piping (pastry) bag fitted with a
C8 star nozzle (tip) and pipe a rosette
of ganache onto the top of each
chocolate. Top with a Caramelized
Walnut on top of each ganache rosette.

These will keep for 5 days stored in an
airtight container in a cool, dry area.

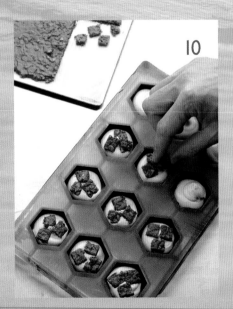

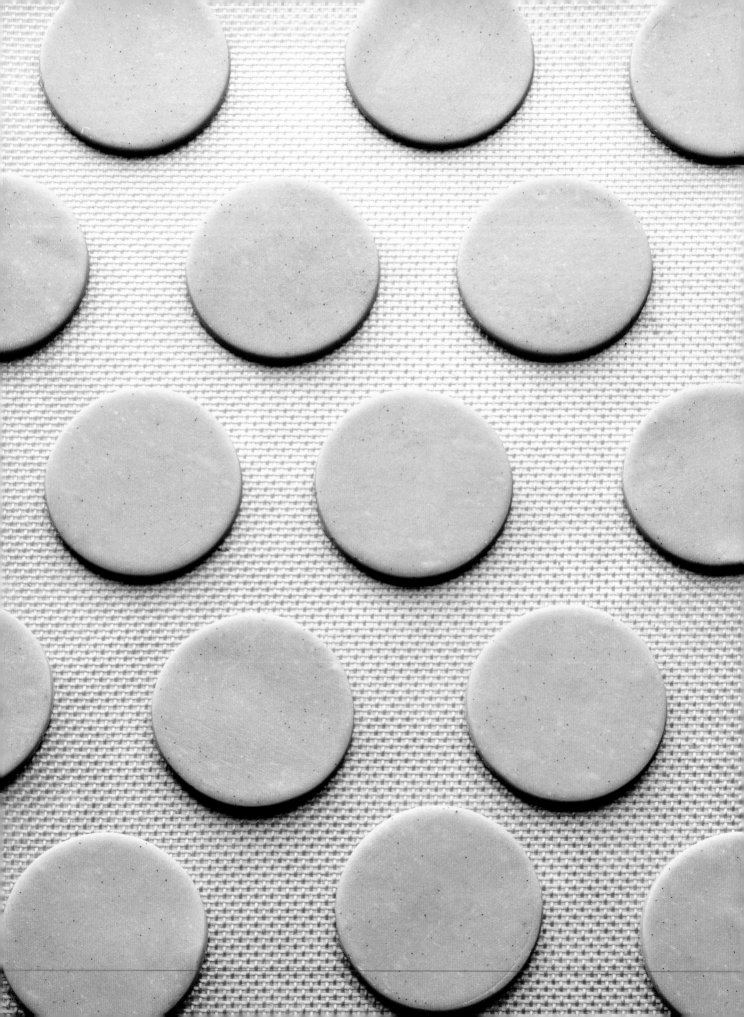

MATCHA & YUZU TEACAKES

*Tunnock's was formed in 1890 in Lanarkshire and still operates there today.
They are an institutional Scottish confectionery company – generations of children in Scotland will
have grown up enjoying a Tunnocks teacake or caramel bar as a treat.
The classic teacake is made of marshmallow with a shortbread biscuit base, dipped in either milk
or dark (bittersweet) chocolate. I thought that my take on it should be a bit unusual so used
Japanese flavours – matcha and yuzu – which are both colourful and interesting to taste.*

Makes 20–25 teacakes

1 quantity of **Matcha Pâte Sablée**
 (see variation page 229)
1 quantity of **Marmalade** *(see page 242),*
 but make with the same amount of
 yuzu instead of oranges
500g (1lb 2oz) tempered dark
 (bittersweet) chocolate
 (65% cocoa solids) *(see page 14)*
Matcha powder, for sprinkling

For the Matcha Marshmallow:
10g (¼oz) leaf gelatine
110g (3¾oz) yuzu purée
5g (⅛oz) matcha powder
145ml (5fl oz/⅔ cup) water
225g (8oz/1 generous cup)
 caster (superfine) sugar
1g (a pinch) cream of tartar
38g (1½oz) egg white (about 1–2 eggs)

You will also need:
• *5cm (2 inch) pastry cutter*
• *piping (pastry) bag*
• *15mm (¾ inch) nozzle (tip)*
• *dipping fork*

First, make the Matcha Pâte Sablée:

1 Make the Matcha Pâte Sablée as
instructed on page 229 and leave to
rest in the fridge for 2–3 hours.

Next, make the Yuzu Marmalade:

2 Make the marmalade, using yuzu
instead of oranges, following the
instructions on page 242.

Now, bake the pastry:

3 Line a baking tray with a non-stick
baking mat. Roll out the pastry to
4mm (⅛ inch) thick on a lightly floured
surface. Use the 5cm (2 inch) pastry
cutter to cut out 20–25 discs. Place
them on the prepared tray and leave
to rest in the fridge for 30 minutes.

4 Preheat the oven to 180°C (350°F/
gas 4). Bake the discs for 10–12
minutes until golden, then leave to cool.

Then, make the Matcha Marshmallow:

5 Soak the gelatine in a bowl of ice-
cold water for a few minutes to soften.
Squeeze the gelatine to remove the
excess water.

6 Put the yuzu purée in a saucepan
over a medium heat and warm.
Remove from the heat and stir in the
soaked gelatine until dissolved.

7 In a separate bowl, mix the matcha
powder with 10g (2 teaspoons) of the
cold water.

8 Put 215g (7½oz/1 cup) of the
caster (superfine) sugar and the water
in a saucepan over a medium heat and
cook to 130°C (266°F).

9 Simultaneously whisk the egg whites
with the cream of tartar and the
remaining sugar in a clean bowl to a
soft peak. Gradually pour the sugar
syrup into the whisking egg. Add the
yuzu mixture and matcha mixture and
increase the speed. Continue to whisk
until the marshmallow reaches a full
peak and cools in temperature.

To assemble:

10 Spoon the marmalade into a piping
(pastry) bag and snip the end to make
a small hole. Pipe a generous bulb of
marmalade into the centre of each disc.

11 Spoon the marshmallow into a
piping (pastry) bag fitted with a 15mm
(¾ inch) nozzle (tip). Pipe a large bulb
on top of the marmalade to cover the
disc. Leave to set for about 2 hours in
a cool, dry area.

12 Line a baking tray (sheet) with
silicone (baking) paper and temper
the chocolate. Use a dipping fork to
dip the teacakes into the tempered
chocolate (see page 17) and carefully
place them on the prepared tray.
Lightly sprinkle the tops with matcha
powder. Leave to set in a cool, dry
area for 1–2 hours.

*These will keep for 5 days stored in an
airtight container in a cool, dry area.*

NOUGATINE BOUCHÉE

In 1850, nougatine was created by Louis-Jules Bourumeau in the city of Nevers in Central France. Empress Eugenie visited in 1862 and was presented with a box of nougatine, and from then on the popularity of this confection spread throughout Europe. Traditionally, nougatine can be made into lots of different shapes, like baskets or croquembouche stands. I simply cut nougatine discs and assemble with spiced pâte de fruits and whipped ganache to create a seasonal bouchée.

Makes 20 bouchée

1 quantity **Cherry Pâte de Fruits**
(see page 220)
500g (1lb 2oz) tempered milk chocolate
(see page 15)

For the Nougatine:
200g (7oz/1 cup)
   caster (superfine) sugar
50g (1¾oz) liquid glucose
25g (1oz/1½ tablespoons)
   unsalted butter
75g (2¾oz/1 cup) lightly roasted
   flaked almonds

For the Spiced Whipped Ganache:
250ml (9fl oz/generous 1 cup)
   whipping (pouring) cream
30g (1¼oz) invert sugar
½ cinnamon stick
Pinch of nutmeg and ground ginger
250g (9oz) dark (bittersweet) chocolate
   (70% cocoa solids)
100g (3½ oz/½ cup/1 stick)
   unsalted butter, softened

To decorate:
Freeze-dried cherry powder
Edible silver leaf

You will also need:
• *18cm (7 inch) square metal mould*
• *5cm (2 inch) metal ring*
• *2cm (¾ inch) cutter*
• *piping (pastry) bag*
• *F7 large star nozzle (tip)*

First, make the Pâte de Fruits:

1 Place an 18cm (7 inch) square metal mould on a tray lined with silicone (baking) paper. Make the Cherry Pâte de Fruits as instructed on page 220 and pour it into the prepared mould. Leave to set for 2 hours.

Next, prepare the Nougatine.

2 Heat an empty heavy-based saucepan over a medium heat. When it is hot, add one-third of the sugar and all the liquid glucose. Heat slowly until it forms a light caramel and the sugar crystals have dissolved. Add the remaining sugar and continue to cook to an amber caramel. This can take up to 10 minutes but there are lots of variables so you must be vigilant and keep watch while it is cooking.

3 Add the butter and then the almonds and stir until combined.

4 Place a heatproof baking mat on a flat work surface (alternatively, lightly oil your work surface). Pour the nougatine mixture onto the prepared surface and leave to firm slightly for 1 minute.

5 Top with another baking mat to protect the nougatine while rolling.

6 Begin rolling the nougatine out.

7 Keep rolling until the nougatine is an even 3mm (⅛ inch) thick. If it becomes too firm to work with, it can be placed on a metal tray lined with a non-stick baking mat and into a warm oven for 1 minute until it softens.

8 Once the nougatine is rolled to the required thickness, use a 5cm (2 inch) metal ring to cut out 20 discs. Tap the top of the ring with a rolling pin to help cut through the nougatine.

9 Place the cut discs on a tray lined with silicone (baking) paper. Ideally use within an hour of preparation. If not, layer between sheets of and store in an airtight container.

Now, prepare the infused ganache:

10 Use the ingredients to prepare the Spiced Whipped Ganache following the instructions on page 19 (but without adding the butter). Leave to cool and thicken slightly but not set – this will take about 10–15 minutes.

To assemble and finish:

11 Use a 2cm (¾ inch) pastry cutter to cut the Cherry Pâte de Fruits into 20 discs and place one in the centre of each nougatine disc.

12 Put the thickened ganache mixture in a mixing bowl. Whisk until it becomes aerated, then gradually add the softened butter and whisk until it begins to hold its shape. Be careful not to overmix as it can become granular in texture. Spoon the ganache into a piping (pastry) bag fitted with a F7 large star nozzle (tip). Pipe a tall rosette onto each nougatine disc, ensuring that the Cherry Pâte de Fruits is covered. Leave to set for 1–2 hours in a cool, dry area.

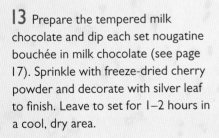

13 Prepare the tempered milk chocolate and dip each set nougatine bouchée in milk chocolate (see page 17). Sprinkle with freeze-dried cherry powder and decorate with silver leaf to finish. Leave to set for 1–2 hours in a cool, dry area.

These will keep for 1 week stored in an airtight container in a cool, dry area.

CINDER TOFFEE

This is also known as honeycomb and is a fun recipe to make as it is a great example of chemistry in cooking. The reaction when you add the bicarbonate of (baking) soda is very dramatic – you can imagine it being a part of some exciting experiment in a laboratory! The origin of cinder toffee goes back to the 1800s, but the 'Crunchie Bar' that we all grew up with was created by Fry's in 1929.

Makes 20–30 pieces

500g (1lb 2oz) tempered dark (bittersweet) chocolate (65% cocoa solids) *(see page 14)*
500g (1lb 2oz) tempered milk chocolate *(see page 15)*

For the cinder toffee:
190g (6½oz/1 scant cup) caster (superfine) sugar
50g (1¾oz/¼ cup) soft brown sugar
150g (5½oz) liquid glucose
50ml (2fl oz/scant ¼ cup) water
50g (1¾oz/scant ¼ cup) honey
10g (¼oz) bicarbonate of (baking) soda, sieved

You will also need:
• 20 x 20 x 6cm (8 x 8 x 2½ inch) metal frame

1 Line one deep baking tray (sheet) and another normal tray (sheet) with silicone (baking) paper.

2 Mix both sugars, the glucose, water and honey together in a saucepan and boil to 144°C (291°F). When the temperature is reached, remove immediately from the heat.

3 Slowly add the sieved bicarbonate of (baking) soda, stirring whilst adding – the mix will start to rise to the top of the saucepan.

4 Pour the mixture into the deep tray (sheet), then leave to cool and set for about 2 hours in a cool, dry area.

5 Use a sharp knife to break the cinder toffee into 20–25 chunks.

6 Temper the dark (bittersweet) chocolate. Use a dipping fork to coat half the pieces of cinder toffee in tempered chocolate (see page 17) and carefully place the pieces on the lined tray (sheet). Temper the milk chocolate and repeat this process to coat the remaining cindertoffee. Leave to set in a cool, dry area for 1–2 hours.

These will keep for 1 month stored in an airtight container in a cool, dry area.

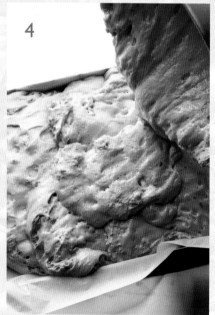

MARZIPAN ORANGE BAR

When I was an apprentice, my mum gave me a book called Belgian Chocolates *by Roger Geerts. The book was very inspirational to me; I still use it to this day. Despite my style being based on traditional French techniques, I think that every chocolatier is influenced by Belgian chocolates. Roger Geerts was a master of his craft, and his work optimizes the essence of Belgian chocolates.*

Makes 14 bars

½ quantity of **Orange-infused Ganache**
 (see variation page 19)
500g (1lb 2oz) tempered dark
 (bittersweet) chocolate
 (65% cocoa solids) *(see page 14)*

For the Confit Orange:
(this must be made in advance)
3 large oranges
375g (13oz/2 scant cups) caster
 (superfine) sugar
500ml (18fl oz/2 cups) water
1 vanilla pod (bean), split and scraped

For the Cinnamon Marzipan:
300g (10½oz) marzipan
2.5g (½ teaspoon) ground cinnamon

You will also need:
• *18cm (7 inch) square metal frame*

9

First, make the Confit Orange (this must be done at least 2 days before you want to serve):

1 Score around the outside of the oranges into quarters. Gently take off each quarter of the peel and cut it in half. Put the peel in a saucepan and fill with enough water to just cover the peel. Bring to the boil, then drain the peel and discard the water. Refresh the peel under cold water. Repeat this process 4 more times.

2 Put the sugar and water in a saucepan. Scrape the seeds from the split vanilla pod (bean) into the saucepan and drop in the empty pod too. Bring to the boil. Add the orange peel, reduce the heat to low and continue to cook for a further 30 minutes. Remove the saucepan from the heat and leave it to cool slightly. Cover with a lid and leave to cool completely overnight.

3 Return the saucepan to the hob and bring to the boil. Reduce the heat to low and cook for a further 2 hours, until the orange is soft and candied. Leave to cool overnight.

4 Drain off any excess syrup (the syrup can be saved and re-used) and discard the vanilla. Put the orange confit on a wire rack. Leave to dry for 3–4 hours.

Next, make the Cinnamon Marzipan:

5 Mix the ingredients together in a bowl until fully incorporated.
To assemble:

6 Line a tray with silicone (baking) paper and place the metal frame on it. Roll out the marzipan to 1cm (½ inch) thick. Trim the edges and place it into the metal frame on the prepared tray.

7 Make the Orange-infused Ganache following the instructions on page 19. Pour the ganache into the metal frame on top of the marzipan layer. Gently tap to ensure the ganache is evenly spread. Leave to set in a cool, dry area for at least 2 hours.

8 When the ganache is fully set, remove it from the metal frame. Use a hot knife to cut into fourteen 2.5 x 8cm (1 x 3¼ inch) bars.

9 Cut each piece of confit orange in half and trim to size if necessary. Place a piece of Confit Orange onto the centre of each bar.

10 Prepare the tempered chocolate and use a dipping fork to coat each bar in chocolate (see page 17). Place on a tray in a cool, dry area and leave to set for 1–2 hours.

These will keep for 1 week stored in an airtight container in a cool, dry area.

Tip: Alternatively, confit oranges can be bought online or from high-quality food stores.

CARAMEL BAR

Caramel is very nostalgic for many people. The smell of the cooking sugar takes me back to my days as an apprentice working at Gleneagles Hotel, where there would often be a huge pan filled with deep amber caramel sending up clouds of sweet aroma.

Makes 24 bars

500g (1lb 2oz) tempered dark (bittersweet) chocolate (65% cocoa solids) *(see page 14)*

For the Sea Salt Caramel:
120ml (4½fl oz/½ cup) whipping (pouring) cream
1 vanilla pod (bean), split and scraped
250g (9oz/1¼ cups) caster (superfine) sugar
40g (1½oz) liquid glucose
200g (7oz/generous ¾ cup/1¾ sticks) salted butter, cubed

You will also need:
• *four 6-hole chocolate bar moulds, with 115 x 22 x 10mm (4¼ x 1 x ½ inch) cavities (patterned or plain)*
• *piping (pastry) bag*

First, make the Sea Salt Caramel:

1 Put the cream in a saucepan. Scrape the seeds from the split vanilla pods (beans) into the cream and drop in the empty pods (beans) too. Bring to the boil. Take off the heat and leave to infuse for 30 minutes.

2 Heat an empty heavy-based saucepan. When it is hot, add one-third of the sugar with the liquid glucose and heat slowly until it forms a light caramel and the sugar crystals have dissolved.

3 Gradually add the remaining sugar and continue to cook until you get an amber caramel. This will take up to 10 minutes, but there are lots of variables so you must be vigilant and keep watch while it is cooking.

4 Gradually add the cream to the caramel (discarding the vanilla as you do). Mix well, then take off the heat.

5 Add the butter, cube by cube. Pour into a shallow tray and leave to cool.

Tip: the Sea Salt Caramel will keep for 1 month if stored in an airtight container in a cool, dry area

To assemble:

6 Temper the chocolate and use it to line the moulds (see page 16). Leave to set for 30 minutes.

7 Spoon the cooled caramel into a piping (pastry) bag and snip the end to make a small hole. Pipe the caramel into the lined moulds until they are about four-fifths full.

8 Cap with the remaining tempered chocolate (see page 16) and leave to set for 1–2 hours in a cool, dry area before de-moulding each bar as instructed on page 16.

These will keep for 1 month stored in an airtight container in a cool, dry area.

3

4

5

5

CHOCOLATE MINT BAR

Fry's is the original iconic British chocolate brand. Joseph Fry was the first person to create a chocolate bar by mixing together cocoa mass, cocoa butter and sugar. As the brand evolved Fry's also become pioneers in the chocolate and confectionery market and went on to develop the first filled bar – the Fry's Chocolate Cream. It is still available to buy today, as is the peppermint version. My take on this historical bar uses a fresh mint infusion and a white chocolate ganache, instead of fondant with peppermint oil. Using fresh infusions is very much a part of my ethos in cooking. It allows the complexity of the flavour of the herb used to be fully appreciated.

Makes 18 bars

500g (1lb 2oz) tempered dark
   (bittersweet) chocolate
   (65% cocoa solids) *(see page 14)*

**For the White Chocolate
Mint Ganache:**

150ml (5fl oz/⅔ cup)
   whipping (pouring) cream
20g (¾oz) fresh mint
280g (9¾oz) white chocolate,
   finely chopped
20g (¾oz) unsalted butter, softened

You will also need:
• *three 6-hole chocolate bar moulds,
   with 110 x 30 x 10mm (4¼ x 1¼ x
   ½ inch) cavities (patterned or plain)*
• *piping (pastry) bag*

**First, make the White Chocolate
Mint Ganache:**

1 Put the cream in a saucepan and bring to the boil. Add the fresh mint, cover with cling film (plastic wrap) and leave to cool and infuse for 2 hours.

2 Strain the infused cream to remove the mint leaves and re-weigh, adding any cream lost during the infusion process. Bring the cream to the boil.

3 Put the chopped chocolate in a mixing bowl. Pour the boiled cream over the chocolate and mix continuously to form an emulsion. Add the butter, mixing until fully incorporated. Leave the ganache to cool for about 15 minutes.

To assemble:

4 Line the bar moulds with the tempered chocolate as instructed on page 16. Leave the chocolate to set for 30 minutes.

5 Put the white chocolate ganache in a piping (pastry) bag and snip the end to make a small hole. Pipe the ganache into the lined bar moulds until they are four-fifths full. Leave to firm for 30 minutes.

6 Cap the tops of the bar mould as instructed on page 16. Leave to set in a cool, dry area for 1–2 hours before de-moulding each bar as instructed on page 16.

These will keep for 1 week stored in an airtight container in a cool, dry area.

FUDGE BAR

*This takes me back to family holidays by the sea.
Every year we would go to a British seaside town. As children my sister Karen and I would always
head straight for the pier to spend our money on slot machines and gorge ourselves on sugary
treats. Fudge was always a favourite! Many people associate fudge with being at the seaside –
apparently the salty air makes people crave sugary snacks.*

Makes 24 bars

500g (1lb 2oz) tempered dark
  (bittersweet) chocolate
  (65% cocoa solids) *(see page 14)*
Edible gold leaf, to decorate

For the fudge:
350ml (12fl oz/1½ cups)
  double (heavy) cream
100g (3½oz/½ cup/1 stick)
  sea salt butter
550g (1lb 3½oz/2¾ cups)
  demerara sugar
200g (7oz/⅔ cup)
  golden (light corn) syrup
1 vanilla pod (bean), split and scraped

You will also need:
• *11 x 37cm (4¼ x 14½ inch) metal
  frame*
• *dipping fork*

Note: This recipe uses double
(heavy) cream rather than evaporated
or condensed milk, so cooking the
mixture slowly for a long time is vital
in order for it to set.

1 Put the 11 x 37cm (4¼ x 14½ inch)
metal frame on a baking tray (sheet)
lined with a non-stick baking mat.

2 Put the cream, butter, sugar, golden
(light corn) syrup, vanilla seeds
and scraped pod (bean) in a large
saucepan and cook, stirring, until the
sugar has dissolved. Cook over a
low heat, stirring frequently, until it
reduces in volume and becomes thick
and pale in colour. Continue to cook
until it reaches 118°C (244°F).

3 Take the saucepan off the heat and
beat the fudge until it has thickened
and lost its shine. Carefully remove
the vanilla pod (bean) and pour the
mixture into the prepared frame.
Leave to set for about 3–4 hours in a
cool, dry area.

4 When completely set, remove the
fudge from the frame and cut into
1.5 x 11cm (¾ x 4¼ inch) sticks.

5 Line a baking tray (sheet) with
silicone (baking) paper.

6 Temper the chocolate. Use
a dipping fork to dip each bar in
tempered chocolate (see page 17)
and carefully place them on the
prepared tray.

7 Decorate with gold leaf to finish.
Leave to set in a cool, dry area for
1–2 hours.

*These will keep for 1 month stored in an
airtight container in a cool, dry area.*

FRUIT & NUT CARAMEL BAR

This confection is all about the different combinations of textures and tastes. The base is crunchy and nutty, and the raisins add a chewy texture as well as acidity to cut through the sweetness of the smooth caramel. I make my own praline paste, which gives a much richer flavour to the bar. Traditionally, it is made with peanuts, but I have used hazelnuts instead as I think they complement the raisins, feuillantine and caramel perfectly.

Makes 14 bars

50g (1¾oz/⅓ cup) raisins
500g (1lb 2oz) tempered milk chocolate
 (see page 15)

For the Feuillantine Base:
125g (4½oz) milk chocolate
60g (2oz) Toscano Nut Brown
 chocolate
80g (3oz) **Praline Paste** *(see page 242)*
110g (4oz) feuillantine wafer
50g (1¾oz/⅓ cup) raisins
50g (1¾oz/½ cup) roasted
 chopped nuts

For the Sea Salt Caramel:
75ml (2½fl oz/⅓ cup) whipping
 (pouring) cream
1 vanilla pod (bean), split and scraped
250g (9oz/1¼ cups) caster
 (superfine) sugar
40g (1½oz) liquid glucose
200g (7oz/generous ¾ cup/1¾ sticks)
 salted butter, cubed

You will also need:
• 18cm (7 inch) square metal frame
• piping (pastry) bag
• 8mm (¼ inch) nozzle (tip)
• dipping fork

First, make the Feuillantine Base:

1 Line a baking tray (sheet) with silicone (baking) paper and place the 18cm (7 inch) square metal frame on top. Melt both chocolates and the Praline Paste in a bain-marie (water bath) set over a saucepan of simmering water. Add the feuillantine wafer, raisins and chopped nuts and mix together. Pour the mixture into the prepared metal frame and spread evenly. Leave to set for 2 hours in a cool, dry area.

Next, make the Sea Salt Caramel:

2 Put the cream and scraped vanilla pod (bean) and seeds in a saucepan and bring to the boil.

3 Put the sugar and liquid glucose in a separate saucepan and cook slowly to form an amber caramel.

4 Gradually add the warm cream to the caramel. Mix well and remove from the heat. Add the butter, piece by piece, then leave to cool and firm for 1 hour uncovered. When cooled, remove the vanilla pod (bean).

To assemble:

5 Line a baking tray (sheet) with silicone (baking) paper. Cut the feuillantine base into 2.5 x 8cm (1 x 3¼ inch) bar shapes. Spoon the caramel into a piping (pastry) bag fitted with an 8mm (¼ inch) nozzle (tip).

6 Pipe 2 lines of caramel on each base and gently push the raisins into the caramel. Place in the fridge to prevent the caramel from falling out of shape.

7 Temper the milk chocolate. Use a small palette knife to re-shape the caramel if necessary. Use a dipping fork to dip each bar in the tempered chocolate (see page 17) and carefully place them on the prepared tray (sheet). Leave to set in a cool, dry area for 1–2 hours.

These will keep for 2 weeks stored in an airtight container in a cool, dry area.

PEANUT NOUGAT BAR

The Snickers, or Marathon as I recall it, has to be one of the most iconic chocolate bars of all time. It was first retailed in the 1930s and has continued to thrive ever since. My mum would often give me one of these as a treat if I had a big day ahead and needed lots of energy. As an adult I have always found them a little too sweet for my taste, so my version is made with dark (bittersweet) chocolate and salted caramel.

Makes 14 bars

50g (1¾oz/⅓ cup) roasted peanuts
500g (1lb 2oz) tempered dark
 (bittersweet) chocolate
 (65% cocoa solids) *(see page 14)*

For the Chocolate Nougat:
75g (2¾oz) dark (bittersweet)
 chocolate (100% cocoa solids),
 finely chopped
38g (1½oz) egg white (about 1–2 eggs)
125g (4½oz/scant ½ cup) honey
250g (9oz/1¼ cups)
 caster (superfine) sugar
45g (1½oz) liquid glucose
95ml (3fl oz/generous ⅓ cup) water
85g (3oz/⅔ cup)
 roasted unsalted peanuts

For the Peanut Caramel:
75ml (2½fl oz/⅓ cup)
 whipping (pouring) cream
1 vanilla pod (bean), split and scraped
250g (9oz/1¼ cups)
 caster (superfine) sugar
40g (1½oz) liquid glucose
200g (7oz/generous ¾ cup/1¾ sticks)
 unsalted butter, cubed
15g (½oz) salted peanut paste

You will also need:
• *18cm (7 inch) square metal frame*
• *piping (pastry) bag*
• *8mm (¼ inch) nozzle (tip)*
• *dipping fork*

First, make the Chocolate Nougat:

1 Line a baking tray (sheet) with silicone (baking) paper and place the 18cm (7 inch) square metal frame on top.

2 Put the chocolate in a bain-marie (water bath) set over a saucepan of simmering water and melt to 45°C (113°F).

3 Begin whisking the egg whites in the bowl of an electric mixer fitted with a whisk attachment on a slow speed.

4 Put the honey in a saucepan and begin to cook over a medium heat. At the same time, put the sugar, glucose and water in a separate saucepan and begin to cook.

5 When the honey reaches 121°C (250°F), gently pour it into the whisking egg whites and continue whisking on a medium speed.

6 When the sugar syrup reaches 145°C (293°F), pour it onto the whisking egg white mixture. Continue to whisk on a medium speed for about 5 minutes until light. Add the warm, melted chocolate and continue to mix until fully combined.

7 Remove from the machine and mix in the peanuts by hand. Spread the mixture evenly into the prepared metal frame.

Next, make the Peanut Caramel:

8 Put the cream and scraped vanilla pod (bean) and seeds in a saucepan and bring to the boil.

9 In a hot saucepan, gradually add the sugar and liquid glucose and cook slowly to form an amber caramel. Gradually add the warm cream. Mix well and remove from the heat.

10 Add the butter, piece by piece, then leave to cool slightly. Add the peanut paste and leave to cool and firm. When cool, remove the vanilla pod (bean).

To assemble:

11 Line a baking tray (sheet) with silicone (baking) paper. Cut the nougat into 2.5 x 8cm (1 x 3¼ inch) bar shapes. Spoon the peanut caramel into a piping (pastry) bag fitted with an 8mm (¼ inch) nozzle (tip). Pipe 2 rows of the caramel on top of each bar, then gently push the peanuts into the caramel. Place in the fridge to prevent the caramel from falling out of shape.

12 Temper the chocolate. Use a small palette knife to re-shape the caramel if necessary. Use a dipping fork to dip each bar in tempered chocolate (see page 17) and carefully place them on the lined tray. Leave to set in a cool, dry area for 1–2 hours.

These will keep for 2 weeks stored in an airtight container in a cool, dry area.

GRANOLA BAR

*Like a lot of children, I was often given granola bars as a healthy alternative to chocolate.
I decided to create a decadent 'grown-up' version, which tastes how I always wanted the
shop-bought ones to taste but never quite did!*

Makes 20–24 bars

40g (1½oz/3 tablespoons) sea salt butter
150g (5½oz/½ cup) honey
110g (4oz/generous ½ cup) brown sugar
50g (1¾oz/½ cup) almond pins
50g (1¾oz/scant ½ cup) chopped hazelnuts
50g (1¾oz/scant ½ cup) chopped walnuts
75g (2¾oz/generous ½ cup) raisins
75g (2¾oz/½ cup) chopped dried apricots
100g (3½oz/¾ cup) oats
40g (1½oz/½ cup) desiccated coconut
50g (1¾oz/scant ½ cup) pumpkin seeds
50g (1¾oz/scant ½ cup) sunflower seeds
500g (1lb 2oz) tempered dark (bittersweet) chocolate
   (70% cocoa solids) *(see page 14)*

You will also need:
• *dipping fork*
• *two 12-hole rectangular silicone moulds,
   with 2.5 x 7.5cm (1 x 3 inch) cavities*

1 Preheat the oven to 180°C (350°F/gas 4). Line a baking
tray (sheet) with silicone (baking) paper.

2 Melt the butter, honey and sugar together in a saucepan.
Put the rest of the ingredients, except the tempered
chocolate, in a large bowl and pour over the melted mixture.
Mix together well.

3 Spoon 40g (1½oz) of the mixture into each hole of the
silicone mould and level off with a small palette knife. Bake
for 20–25 minutes until lightly golden brown. Leave to cool.

4 Once cooled, de-mould each bar. Temper the chocolate.
Use a dipping fork to dip each bar so that it is three-
quarters covered in tempered dark (bittersweet) chocolate
(see page 17) and carefully place them on the prepared tray.
Leave to set in a cool, dry area for 1 hour.

*These will keep for 2 weeks stored in an airtight container in a
cool, dry area.*

3

CURLEY WURLY

If I was given 'ten bob' (money) for every time someone asked me if I made Curley Wurly bars, then I would be a very rich man! After much development work, I have finally come up with a way of making this 1970s classic. It was created by David John Parfitt at the Bournville factory when he was experimenting with leftover toffee. It's a great story to tell to my kitchen staff to discourage them from throwing away any surplus product.

Makes 10 bars

Oil, for greasing
500g (1lb 2oz) tempered dark (bittersweet) chocolate
 (65% cocoa solids) *(see page 14)*

For the Vanilla Toffee:
225g (8oz/generous 1 cup) demerara sugar
175g (6oz/½ cup) golden (light corn) syrup
100g (3½oz/½ cup/1 stick) sea salt butter
30ml (1fl oz) water
30g (1¼oz) liquid glucose
1 vanilla pod (bean), split and scraped

You will also need:
• *marble slab and metal scraper*

1 Lightly grease a marble slab (or greased metal tray) and metal scraper.

2 Put the sugar, syrup, butter, water and glucose in a heavy-based saucepan. Scrape the seeds from the split vanilla pod (bean) into the saucepan and drop in the empty pod (bean) too. Cook over a low heat until all of the sugar dissolves.

3 Increase the heat and bring the mixture to the boil. Continue to cook until the temperature reaches 132°C (269°F). Carefully remove the vanilla pod (bean), then pour onto the prepared marble slab.

4 As the toffee begins to set on the edges, use the prepared scraper to gradually move the mixture from the outside towards the centre. Continue with this process until it is cool enough to handle.

5 Divide the toffee into balls weighing 30g (1¼oz) each. Take one ball of toffee and divide into 3 equal parts. Roll each 10g (¼oz) piece into a strand about 35cm (14 inches) in length. When all 3 are evenly rolled out, press the three ends together.

6 Loosely plait the strands together so that gaps remain between each strand. You can manipulate it once it is complete to make sure it is even. Push the ends together to secure. Repeat this process until all the toffee has been used.

7 Use a hot knife to trim both ends of each toffee plait. Leave in a cool, dry area for at least 2 hours to fully set.

8 Prepare the tempered chocolate. Place the Curley Wurly bars on a wire rack and pour the tempered chocolate over each one. Tap well and use 2 palette knives to place each one on a tray lined with silicone (baking) paper. Leave to set for 1–2 hours.

These will keep for 2 weeks stored in an airtight container in a cool, dry area.

One of the most nostalgic sensations for me, has to be the smell of butter when I walk into a bakery. Like many small towns up and down the country, the bakery in my home town was central to the community. I adore the tradition of visiting a bakery to choose a weekend treat. My mum used to take me when I was a boy, and it will always be a fond memory.

BAKERY *Favourites*

This tradition is getting somewhat lost in Britain, but is still very much a part of the culture in France. I aim to help revive this pleasure for people who visit my shops.

Many towns have their own baked speciality, which can usually be found in the local bakery. A few of my favourite local specials include Eccles cakes, Bakewell tarts, and of course fudge doughnuts – a Fife speciality!

LINING TINS WITH PASTRY

1 Take the rested dough from the fridge and place on a lightly floured work surface. Cut into manageable pieces and work gently on the work surface to soften and make more pliable for rolling.

2 Make the dough into a ball again; it is now ready to begin rolling. Roll the dough out to the desired thickness, lightly flouring the work surface and dough when required to make sure that it does not stick.

3 Cut the dough to the desired size for the tart, this should be about 3–5cm (1¼–2 inches) bigger than the tart ring or tin, depending on the size and depth of the tart. Use the rolling pin to gently pick the rolled dough up and drape it over the top of the tart ring or tin.

4 Gently push the dough into place, ensuring that it sits against the edge and is pushed into the bottom corners.

5 Place the lined ring or tin on a baking tray (sheet) lined with a non-stick baking mat or silicone (baking) paper.

6 Trim the edges gently by running the rolling pin over the top edge of the tin. Use your fingers to ensure the pastry is pressed into the side of the tin and lightly pinch up the edges to form a little crest.

7 Prick the base of the pastry all over with a fork. Place in the fridge to rest for at least 30 minutes.

Note: recipes for doughs are made with specific amounts of flour. When rolling out doughs for lining tarts, use only the minimum amount to prevent it from sticking to the work surface.

2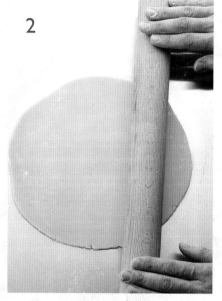

3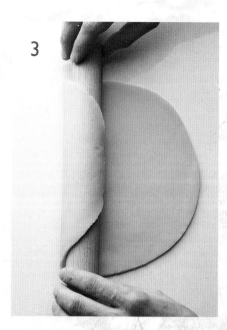

3

3

4

6

2

BLIND BAKING

1 First, you need to make a circle of silicone (baking) paper – fold a sheet in half, now fold it in half again across the other side.

2 Fold one corner to another; you should now have a triangle with the point where all the folds meet to form the centre point of the cartouche. Fold the triangle in half twice again; you should have a long, thin triangle. Hold the triangle's point in the centre of the tart case and cut it to about 2.5cm (1 inch) larger than the tart.

3 Unfold and place the circle of silicone (baking) paper into the lined tart. Ensure the paper fills the tart base and pushes up against the sides. Generously top the paper circle with baking beans so that the tart base is completely covered. Rest for at least 30 minutes.

4 Transfer the tart to a preheated oven and bake until the edges are lightly golden. Remove the tart from the oven, carefully remove the beans from the tart case, then return the tart to the oven to continue cooking until the base of the tart is also lightly golden.

3

4

WORKING WITH YEAST

When cooking with yeast, you learn to work with a living thing. Once an understanding is gained of the process and sensitivities, it will give a foundation for knowledge in making many yeast-based products. The recipe I have used as an example here is the Marignon Dough. However, it can also be used for Savarin and rum baba.

MARIGNON DOUGH

Makes 550g (1lb 4oz)

60ml (2fl oz/¼ cup) milk
20g (¾oz) fresh yeast
230g (8oz/1¾ cups) plain (all-purpose) flour, sifted
20g (¾oz) caster (superfine) sugar
1g (a pinch) salt
150g (5½oz) whole eggs (about 3 eggs)
100g (3½oz/½ cup/1 stick) softened unsalted butter,
  plus a little extra for greasing

1 Crumble the yeast into a small bowl. Put the milk in a saucepan and heat gently to a temperature of around 30–34°C (86–93°F) – be careful not to overheat or you will kill the yeast. Add to the yeast and stir until it is dissolved.

2 Whisk in 30g (1¼oz) of the sifted flour and leave in a warm place for about 20 minutes until doubled in size (this is the sponge ferment).

3 Put the remaining flour, sugar and salt in a bowl and combine well.

4 Add the eggs and the sponge ferment and mix well. Knead the dough until it forms a homogenous mass, becomes elastic and comes away from the side of the bowl. This will take about 10–12 minutes.

5 Add the butter and continue to mix for 2–3 minutes until combined.

6 Pour the mixture into a large bowl and cover with cling film (plastic wrap). Leave the mixture to prove in a warm area until it has doubled in size, about 30 minutes. Knock back the dough and use as instructed in specific recipes.

Use immediately.

ROUGH PUFF PASTRY

Rough puff is a quick and easier way to make puff pastry. Although a little more rustic in appearance, and with slightly less even layers, it is light, flaky and delicious. It was in fact the original variety of puff pastry.

Makes 1.2kg (2lb 6oz)

250g (9oz/1¾ cups) plain (all-purpose) flour, sifted
250g (9oz/1¾ cups) strong flour, sifted
10g (¼oz/2 teaspoons) salt
500g (1lb 2oz/2¼ cups/4½ sticks) unsalted butter, cubed
225ml (8fl oz/scant 1 cup) cold water

1 Sift the flours and salt onto a clean work surface, make a well in the centre and add the cubed butter.

2 Using your fingertips, work the ingredients together until the lumps of butter become smaller and the mixture becomes grainy.

3 Make a well in the centre and pour in the cold water. Use your hands or a pastry scraper to mix until the dough starts to come together.

4 Form the dough into a mass that still contains flakes of butter – but do not knead.

5 Wrap the dough in cling film (plastic wrap) and rest in the fridge for at least 30 minutes.

6 Take the dough out of the fridge, unwrap and roll out to a 50 x 25cm (20 x 10 inch) rectangle on a lightly floured work surface. Use a pastry brush to remove any excess flour during each turn. Make one turn by folding one end of the dough to two-thirds along the length of the dough, then the other end of the dough to meet the fold. Use a rolling pin to roll the dough back out to 50 x 25cm (20 x 10 inches) – this is one turn. Repeat this process, then wrap the dough in cling film (plastic wrap) again and return to the fridge for at least 1 hour.

7 Take the dough out of the fridge and make another 2 turns. Make a small indent in the folded dough to show how many turns have been made. Wrap the dough and rest in the fridge for at least 1 hour. You should now have completed 4 turns and the rough puff pastry is finished and ready to be used.

This pastry can be kept refrigerated for 2 days and frozen for up to 1 month.

FRUITS OF THE FOREST TART

'Fruits of the Forest' was originally an Italian flavour called Frutti di Bosco. During the 1980s, it became a firm favourite in commercial British desserts. Although it sounded very luxurious, even in my boyhood years it never lived up to expectations. It wasn't until my late teens, when I used to get the night bus to Paris and gaze at beautiful fruit tarts in the windows of top pâtisseries, that I realized what 'fruits of the forest' should really represent.

Makes 1 tart (serving 12)

1 quantity of **Pâte Sucrée**
  (see page 228)

1 quantity of **Grand Marnier Syrup**
  (see variation page 238)

1 quantity of **Light Fruit Nappage**
  (see page 239)

½ quantity of **Crème Pâtissière**
  (see page 234)

½ quantity of **Almond Cream**
  (see page 236)

To decorate:

Fresh strawberries, halved, raspberries, blackberries, golden raspberries, pineberries, blueberries, redcurrants

Chocolate Squares and Curls
  (*see pages 248 and 250*)

Edible gold leaf

You will also need:

• 20cm (8 inch) tart ring
• piping (pastry) bags
• 14mm (⅝ inch) nozzle (tip)
• 12mm (½ inch) nozzle (tip)

First, prepare the chocolate decorations:

1 Prepare the Chocolate Squares and Curls as instructed on pages 248 and 250 and leave in a cool, dry area to set for 1–2 hours.

Next, prepare the Pâte Sucrée, Grand Marnier Syrup, Light Fruit Nappage and Creme Pâtissière::

2 Make the Pâte Sucrée as instructed on page 228, then chill the pastry for 2–3 hours.

3 Prepare the Grand Marnier Syrup as instructed on page 238, the **Light Fruit Nappage** as instructed on page 239 and the Crème Pâtissière as instructed on page 234.

Now, prepare the pastry and the Almond Cream:

4 Place the rested dough on a lightly floured surface and roll out to 3mm (⅛ inch) thick. Line the tart case with the pastry (see page 64), then chill for at least 30 minutes.

5 Prepare the Almond Cream as instructed on page 236.

To bake and assemble:

6 Preheat the oven to 180°C (350°F/gas 4).

7 Remove the prepared tart case from the fridge. Put the Almond Cream in a piping (pastry) bag fitted with a 14mm (⅝ inch) nozzle (tip) and pipe a spiral of cream into the tart, filling to just over half the depth of the tart.

8 Bake the tart for 30–35 minutes until golden. Leave to cool before de-moulding from the tart case. Soak the top of the tart with the Grand Marnier Syrup.

9 Spoon the prepared Crème Pâtissière into a piping (pastry) bag fitted with a 12mm (½ inch) nozzle (tip) and pipe the cream in a spiral on top of the tart, leaving a gap of about 2cm (¾ inch) from the edge.

10 Cover the top of the tart with a layer of fruits. Build up the tart with more fruits, then carefully glaze them with the Light Fruit Nappage. Decorate with the prepared chocolate decorations and gold leaf to finish.

Store in the fridge until ready to serve. Best eaten the same day.

CHOCOLATE CHERRY BAKEWELLS

At 15 years old, I was a student at Glenrothes College and beginning my journey in the industry. Dave Bryson was the baker at the college, and was known as one of the finest bakers in Scotland. He was a no-nonsense type of character, which seemed to do me a lot of good at the time! When I was offered the opportunity to compete at the St Andrews Food and Drink Festival, Dave spent endless hours helping me perfect all the techniques of baking. As a result of his efforts, my Bakewell tarts got a gold medal. Although it was a local competition, getting a gold medal meant as much to me then as it did later in my career at international events. These tarts are a tribute to Dave.

Makes 12 tarts

1 quantity of **Almond Pastry**
 (see page 228)
½ quantity of **Cherry Jam**
 (see variation page 241)
1 quantity of **Kirsch Syrup**
 (see variation page 238)
½ quantity of **Confit Cherries**
 (see page 244)
1 quantity of **Chocolate Almond Cream**
 (see variation page 236)
½ quantity of **Fondant** (see page 246)
100g (3½oz) **Chocolate Fondant**
 (see variation page 246)

You will also need:
• *twelve 7cm (2¾ inch) pomponette tart moulds*
• *piping (pastry) bags*
• *12mm (½ inch) nozzle (tip)*
• *paper piping cornet (see page 250)*
• *cocktail sticks*

First, make the Almond Pastry, Cherry Jam, Kirsch Syrup and Confit Cherries:

1 Prepare the pastry as instructed on page 228 and leave to rest in the fridge for 2–3 hours.

2 Prepare the jam and syrup as instructed on pages 241 and 238.

3 Prepare the Confit Cherries. Once cooled, drain 12 cherries and place them on a wire rack to dry for 1 hour.

Next, prepare the Chocolate Almond Cream and bake the tarts:

4 Roll out the chilled pastry to 3mm (⅛ inch) thick on a lightly floured surface and line the tartlet cases (see page 64). Rest for 1 hour in the fridge.

5 Prepare the Chocolate Almond Cream as instructed on page 236.

6 Spoon the jam into a piping (pastry) bag, snip the end to make a small hole and pipe about 8–10g (¼oz) of jam into the base of each tartlet. Spoon the Chocolate Almond Cream into another piping (pastry) bag fitted with a 12mm (½ inch) nozzle (tip) and pipe a bulb into each tartlet until about two-thirds full. Leave to rest for 30 minutes. Preheat the oven to 180°C (350°F/gas 4).

7 Bake for about 20–25 minutes. Remove from the oven and leave to cool fully before de-moulding each tart from the tartlet case.

Prepare both Fondants and finish:

8 Soak each tartlet with the Kirsch Syrup.

9 Prepare both Fondants as instructed on page 246.

10 Spoon the Chocolate Fondant into a paper piping cornet. Glaze each tart with Fondant and pipe a spiral of Chocolate Fondant on top. Use a cocktail stick to create a chocolate lattice by pulling the stick into the centre and out to the edge until the pattern is complete. Finish with a confit cherry in the centre.

Best eaten the same day, but can be stored in an airtight container for up to 2 days.

TARTE AUX POMMES

Every nation seems to have their own version of this hearty apple dish. The traditional English apple pie dates back to the 14th century and first appeared in a cookery book in 1590. Throughout my career I have made many different varieties, but I developed this dish from my two favourite French apple pastries – the topless tarte aux pomme and the classic tarte tatin with caramelized apples – giving a decadent caramel flavour combined with the finesse of the sliced apple topping.

Makes 2 tarts (each serves 6–8)

1 quantity of **Pâte Sucrée** *(see page 228)*
1 quantity of **Apricot Nappage** *(see page 239)*
8 Golden Delicious apples, peeled and cored
Clarified butter *(see page 247)*, for brushing
Icing (powdered) sugar, for dusting

For the Caramelized Apples:
8 Golden Delicious apples
200g (7oz/1 cup) caster (superfine) sugar
60g (2oz/¼ cup/½ stick) unsalted butter
1 vanilla pod (bean), split lengthways
30ml (1fl oz) Calvados

You will also need:
• two 16cm (6¼ inch) tart rings

1 Prepare the Pâte Sucrée as instructed on page 228, then chill for 2–3 hours.

2 While the pastry is resting, prepare the Apricot Nappage as instructed on page 239. Set aside.

3 Next, prepare the Caramelized Apples. Peel and core the apples. Cut each apple into 12 chunks. Heat a heavy-based saucepan, add one-third of the sugar and cook to a light caramel, stirring occasionally. Gradually add the remaining sugar. Cook until an amber caramel forms, then stir in the butter. Toss in the prepared apples and the split vanilla pod (bean), stir and continue to cook over a low heat for 2–3 minutes. Add the Calvados and remove from the heat. Cover with cling film (plastic wrap) and leave the apples to cool in the caramel until ready to use.

Continued on page 76.

3

3

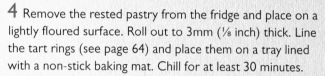

4 Remove the rested pastry from the fridge and place on a lightly floured surface. Roll out to 3mm (⅛ inch) thick. Line the tart rings (see page 64) and place them on a tray lined with a non-stick baking mat. Chill for at least 30 minutes.

5 Prepare the apple slices for the top of the tarts. Cut each apple in half and cut into 1mm thick slices. Preheat the oven to 180°C (350°F/gas 4).

6 Drain the caramelized apples, reserving the excess caramel. Put the excess caramel in a pan and boil to reduce by half, until thickened. Cool the thickened caramel and store in the fridge until ready to use. Remove the rested tarts from the fridge and place the chunks of caramelized apple into the tart case ensuring they are level.

7 Fan out each prepared and sliced apple half and place them in an overlapping spiral on top of the tart, starting from the outside and working towards the centre.

8 Prepare the clarified butter as instructed on page 247 and liberally brush it onto the apples. Dust with icing (powdered) sugar.

9 Bake for 35–40 minutes until golden brown. Leave to cool for 10 minutes before de-moulding from the tart cases. Use a sharp knife to score along the edge of the tart rings as leaked caramel can sometimes stick the pastry to the sides of the tart ring. Melt the Apricot Nappage and use it to glaze the top of each tart to finish. The caramel reduction can be served as an accompaniment to the finished dish.

Best served the same day.

6

7

8

9

REDCURRANT &
LEMON MERINGUE TARTS

This is a very iconic British dish and was one of my grandmother's specialities. She would often bake one on a Sunday for a family get together. The crumbly pastry, sharp acid lemon filling and caramelized meringue swirls really are a perfect combination. My modern take on the lemon meringue includes redcurrant and hazelnut to enhance the elements already found in the classic dish.

Makes 16 tarts

1 quantity of **Redcurrant Jam**
 (see *variation page 241*)
½ quantity of **Grand Marnier Syrup**
 (see *variation page 238*)
1 quantity of **Pâte Sablée** (see *page 229*)
½ quantity of **Lemon Curd** (see *page 237*), made with the addition of 3g (½ teaspoon) pre-soaked gelatine
200g (7oz/2 cups) fresh redcurrants
½ quantity of **Hazelnut Cream**
 (see *variation page 236*)
1 quantity of **Swiss Meringue** (see *page 232*)
Icing (powdered) sugar, for dusting

For the Confit Lemon:
1 lemon, washed
½ quantity of **Simple Syrup** (see *page 238*)

You will also need:
• *16-hole oval silicone mould, with 3 x 5cm (1¼ x 2 inch) cavities*
• *sixteen 7 x 4.5cm (2¾ x 1¾ inch) oval tart cases*
• *piping (pastry) bags*
• *12mm (½ inch) nozzle (tip)*
• *8mm (¼ inch) nozzle (tip)*

First, prepare the Confit Lemon:

1 Use a peeler to peel off small pieces of the lemon skin. Boil a saucepan of water and blanch the lemon peel for about 10 seconds. Strain and rinse under cold water.

2 Prepare the Simple Syrup as instructed on page 238, add the lemon pieces and cook over a low heat for 30 minutes. Strain from the liquid and lay each piece out separately on a tray lined with silicone (baking) paper. Brush each piece with a little of the syrup. Dry the Confit Lemon out at 60°C (140°F) in a dehydrator or oven for up to 4 hours.

Next, prepare the Redcurrant Jam, Grand Marnier Syrup and Pâte Sablée:

3 Prepare the jam and syrup as instructed on pages 241 and 238. Prepare the Pâte Sablée as instructed on page 229 and chill for 2–3 hours.

Now, prepare the Lemon Curd, Hazelnut Cream and bake:

4 Prepare the curd as instructed on page 238, adding the pre-soaked gelatine just prior to adding the butter.

5 Place 5 redcurrants in each hole of the silicone mould. Spoon the Lemon Curd into a piping (pastry) bag, snip off the end and pipe in so each oval is two-thirds full. Transfer to the freezer for at least 2 hours, until fully frozen.

6 Remove the pastry from the fridge and line each oval tart case (see page 64) and then chill for 30 minutes.

7 Preheat the oven to 180°C (350°F/gas 4).

8 Prepare the Hazelnut Cream as instructed on page 236.

9 Remove the tartlet cases from the fridge. Spoon 5g (1 teaspoon) of Redcurrant Jam into the base of each tart. Spoon the Hazelnut Cream into a piping (pastry) bag fitted with a 12mm (½ inch) nozzle (tip) and pipe into each tart until three-quarters full.

10 Bake for 15–18 minutes. Leave to cool before de-moulding.

11 Soak each tart with the Grand Marnier Syrup. Remove the Lemon Curd from the freezer and de-mould from the silicone mould. Place in the centre of each tart.

Finally, prepare the Swiss Meringue:

12 Preheat the oven to 200°C (400°F/gas 6). Prepare the meringue as instructed on page 232, then spoon into a piping (pastry) bag fitted with a 8mm (¼ inch) nozzle (tip). Pipe bulbs of meringue on the tart around the Lemon Curd and continue upwards until the curd is completely covered.

13 Dust with icing (powdered) sugar and bake for 3–4 minutes, until lightly golden. Decorate with a redcurrant and 3 pieces of the Confit Lemon.

Store in the fridge until ready to serve. Best eaten the same day.

JAM TARTS

These have been immortalized in literature by Lewis Carroll in Alice in Wonderland. A trial is held to uncover who has stolen the Queen of Hearts' jam tarts. They really are a fun pastry, but more difficult to get right than people give credit for. When I used to bake with my granny, she would often give me the offcuts of pastry to line small tart cases, which she would then fill with her homemade raspberry jam for us to bake and then devour after our hard work in the kitchen.

Makes 24 tarts

1 quantity of **Pâte Sablée** *(see page 229)*

For the Raspberry Jam:
125g (4½oz/1 cup) raspberries
125g (4½oz) raspberry purée
100g (3½oz/½ cup)
  caster (superfine) sugar
10g (2 teaspoons) pectin
10ml (2 teaspoons) lemon juice

For the Blackcurrant Jam:
125g (4½oz/1¼ cups) blackcurrants
125g (4½oz) blackcurrant purée
100g (3½oz/½ cup) caster
  (superfine) sugar
10g (2 teaspoons) pectin
10ml (2 teaspoons) lemon juice

For the Lemon Curd:
grated zest and juice of 2 lemons
100g (3½oz/½ cup) caster
  (superfine) sugar
50g (1¾oz/3½ tablespoons)
  unsalted butter
75g (2¾oz) whole eggs (about 1–2 eggs)

You will also need:
• *two 12-hole tart tins, with 6 x 1.5cm
  (2½ x ½ inch) cavities*
• *8cm (3¼ inch) fluted cutter*

First, prepare the Pâte Sablée:

1 Prepare the Pâte Sablée as instructed on page 229 and chill for 2–3 hours.

Next, prepare the Raspberry Jam and Blackcurrant Jam:

2 Prepare each flavour of jam separately following this method. Put the fruit, purée and 75g (2¾oz/scant ⅓ cup) of the sugar in a heavy-based saucepan and bring to the boil. Mix the remaining sugar with the pectin, then whisk this into the boiling mixture.

3 Continue to cook over a low heat, stirring continuously, until the mixture reaches 104°C (219°F). Add the lemon juice, whisk in and cook for 2 minutes. Remove from the heat, pour the jam into a shallow tray and leave to cool.

Now, make the Lemon Curd:

4 Heat the lemon juice, zest, sugar and butter in a saucepan. Whisk the eggs in a bowl. When the butter has melted, pour the lemon mixture over the eggs and whisk together. Pour the mixture through a sieve back into the saucepan and cook for 5–10 minutes, stirring continually, until it thickens. Remove from the heat, pour the curd into a shallow tray, cover with cling film (plastic wrap) and leave to cool.

To assemble and bake:

5 Roll out the pastry on a lightly floured surface to 2.5mm (⅛ inch) thick. Use an 8cm (3¼ inch) fluted cutter to cut out 24 discs and use them to line the tart tins (see page 64). Leave to rest for 30 minutes in the fridge.

6 Preheat the oven to 170°C (325°F/gas 3).

7 Remove the tarts from the fridge and fill each tart with about 25g (1oz/2 tablespoons) of jam or curd and bake for 12–15 minutes, until the jam begins to bubble. Leave to cool before de-moulding the tarts

Best served the same day.

CUSTARD TART

I was inspired to put these in the book after a good friend of mine, Neil Borthwick, served me a perfect custard tart at his restaurant. These have been eaten in Britain since Medieval times, although they have evolved somewhat, they have always been pastry with a custard filling. To achieve perfection when making these, the pastry must be golden and the custard must be cooked until just set.

Makes 12 tarts

1 quantity of **Almond Pastry**
  (*see variation page 228*)
1 quantity of **Crème Brûlée**
  (*see page 237*)
1 quantity of **Crystallized Almond Batons** (*see page 243*)
Icing (powdered) sugar, to dust

You will also need:
• *twelve 8cm (3¼ inch) diameter, 2cm (¾ inch) deep tart moulds*

1 First, prepare the Almond Pastry as instructed on page 228. Leave to rest in the fridge for 2–3 hours.

2 Next, make the Crème Brûlée as instructed on page 237.

3 Prepare the Crystallized Almond Batons as instructed on page 243, leave to cool and store in an airtight container until ready to use.

4 Remove the prepared pastry from the fridge, roll out to 3mm (⅛ inch) thick on a lightly floured surface and line the tartlet cases (see page 64). Rest for 30 minutes in the fridge.

5 Preheat the oven to 180°C (350°F/gas 4).

6 Remove the tartlet cases from the fridge and prepare them to blind bake as instructed on page 65. Bake for 12–15 minutes, remove the baking beans, then return the tarts to the oven for a further 6–8 minutes. Turn the oven temperature down to 140°C (275°F/gas 1).

7 Put the Crème Brûlée mixture in a pouring jug and fill each tart until almost full. Bake the tarts for 15–20 minutes, until the Crème Brûlée mixture has just set. Remove from the oven and leave to cool.

8 To finish, place a cluster of Crystallized Almonds in the centre of each tart and dust the edges of each tart with icing (powdered) sugar.

Store in the fridge until ready to serve. Best eaten the same day.

BLACK BUN

While I was growing up it was a tradition for black bun to be eaten as part of the Hogmanay celebrations. Anyone who passes over the threshold after midnight on New Year's Eve, should be welcomed with a dram of whisky and a generous slice of black bun. Originally, the buns were eaten on the Twelfth Night of Christmas, which is also known as the Day of Epiphany. The eating of a festive cake on Twelfth Night was an ancient European custom. In France, still to this day, the Galette des Rois is eaten on the Twelfth Night and is the equivalent of the Scottish black bun.

Makes one bun (serving 12–14)

1 quantity of **Crystallized Almonds** (see page 243)
1 quantity of **Light Fruit Nappage** (see page 239)
1 whole egg, 1 egg yolk and a pinch of salt and sugar, beaten together to make an egg wash
Dried fruits of your choice, to decorate (apricot, prune, fig, cranberries, raisins, sultanas, confit orange)
Edible gold leaf, to decorate

For the Marinated Fruit:
75g (1¾oz/½ cup) raisins
100g (3½oz/¾ cup) sultanas (golden raisins)
40g (1½oz/¼ cup) currants
40g (1½oz) **Confit Orange** (see page 46), roughly chopped
20g (¾oz) dried apricots, roughly chopped
20g (¾oz) dried figs, roughly chopped
20g (¾oz) prunes, roughly chopped
15g (½oz) dried cranberries
125ml (4½fl oz/½ cup) whisky

For the Basque Pastry:
200g (7oz/generous ¾ cup/1¾ sticks) unsalted butter
180g (6oz/scant 1 cup) caster (superfine) sugar
¼ of a vanilla pod (bean), split and scraped
80g (3oz) whole eggs (about 1–2 eggs)
250g (9oz/1¾ cups) plain (all-purpose) flour, sifted
2.5g (½ teaspoon) baking powder
105g (3½oz/1 cup) ground almonds
1.5g (a pinch) salt

For the filling:
100g (3½oz/¾ cup) plain (all-purpose) flour, sifted
1g (a pinch) ground ginger
1g (a pinch) ground nutmeg
1g (a pinch) ground cinnamon
1g (a pinch) bicarbonate of (baking) soda
40g (1½oz/¼ cup) blanched almonds, roughly chopped
50g (1¾oz/¼ cup) muscovado sugar
a small pinch black pepper
25g (1oz) whole eggs (about ½ an egg), beaten

You will also need:
• 16 x 4.5cm (6¼ x 1¾ inch) cake tin

Prepare the Marinated Fruit. This needs to be done at least the night before, but ideally further in advance:

1 Bring a saucepan of water to the boil and add the raisins, sultanas (golden raisins) and currants. Simmer for 2–3 minutes, then strain. Put the soaked fruit in a large bowl and add the rest of the fruits. Pour the whisky over the top. Cover and leave to marinate in the fridge for up to 1 month.

When you are ready to bake, prepare the Basque Pastry:

2 Put the butter in a mixing bowl and beat until soft and smooth. Add the caster (superfine) sugar and vanilla seeds and beat together until smooth. Gradually incorporate the eggs, until they become fully mixed and emulsified.

3 Put the dry ingredients directly on the work surface. Make a well in the centre and use a spatula to spoon the butter mix into the middle of the flour. Use your hands or a pastry scraper to gradually work the flour and butter mixture together to form a smooth, homogenous dough. Shape the dough into a block and wrap it in cling film (plastic wrap). Leave to rest in the fridge for 2–3 hours.

4 When the pastry has rested, remove from the fridge. Cut a one-third portion from the block of pastry and set aside. Roll out the larger piece of pastry on a lightly floured surface to 5mm (¼ inch) thick and use this to line the cake tin (see page 64).

5 Take the smaller piece of pastry and roll out to 5mm (¼ inch) thick, cut into a disc slightly larger then the size of the cake tin – this will be the lid.

The origin of the black bun dates back to the Auld Alliance in the 14th century, when Mary Queen of Scots brought back recipes from France and made them a part of Scottish culture. Queen Mary spent much time in Falkland Palace, Fife, which is near to where I grew up, and I have fond memories of visiting with my family as a young boy.
I am hoping to revive the tradition of the black bun. My version is a tribute to the Auld Alliance. I soaked the fruits in fine Scotch Whisky and used a Basque pastry from South-west France.

6 Line two baking trays (sheets) with non-stick baking mats. Place the cake tin on one tray (sheet) and the rolled pastry on the other, then put them both in the fridge to rest for 30 minutes.

Next, prepare the Crystallized Almonds and Light Fruit Nappage:

7 Make the Crystallized Almonds and Light Fruit Nappage as instructed on pages 243 and 239 and set aside until required.

Now, prepare the filling and bake:

8 Sieve the flour, ginger, nutmeg, cinnamon and bicarbonate of (baking) soda together twice into a bowl and mix well.

9 Combine the marinated fruit and blanched almonds with the muscovado sugar in a separate bowl. Add the sifted dry ingredients to the fruit mixture and fully combine. Add the black pepper, then lastly the beaten egg to bind the mixture together.

10 Preheat the oven to 160°C (325°F/gas 3).

11 Remove the lined cake tin and lid from the fridge. Fill the cake tin almost full with the fruit filling and level the top. Lightly brush egg wash onto the top edge of the pastry case. Use a rolling pin to lift and lay the pastry lid on top of the mixture. Press down gently to seal the lid, trim the edges, then egg wash the top.

11

12 Bake for about 1 hour. Keep checking and when the top of the pastry becomes golden in colour, place some tin foil over it to prevent it from becoming too dark. Remove from the oven and leave to cool fully before de-moulding from the cake tin. Decorate with glazed dried fruits, Crystallized Almonds and gold leaf.

Store for up to 1 week stored in an airtight container in a cool, dry area.

SCOTTISH RASPBERRY BRETON

This dish is a celebration of my favourite summer berry. I use raspberries a lot in my cooking; they are aromatic, colourful and versatile. The best are still grown in Scotland, so this is a very nostalgic flavour for me. I used to go berry picking every summer, and I think like most children who do this, it was always one for my belly, one for the punnet.

....

Makes 2 tarts (each serving 6)

1 quantity **Raspberry Glaze** *(see variation page 239)*

For the Sugar Daisies:
100g (3½oz) sugar paste
1 quantity of **Royal Icing for Piping** *(see variation page 246)*

For the Sable Breton:
250g (9oz/generous 1¾ cups) plain (all-purpose) flour, sieved
8g (¼oz) baking powder
1.5g (a pinch) sea salt
190g (6½oz/¾ cup/1½ sticks) unsalted butter, softened
75g (1¾oz) egg yolks (about 4 eggs)
160g (5¾oz/generous ¾ cup) caster (superfine) sugar

For the Raspberry Mousse:
5g (1 teaspoon) leaf gelatine
250ml (9fl oz/generous 1 cup) whipping (pouring) cream
175g (6oz) raspberry purée
40g (1½oz/scant ¼ cup) caster (superfine) sugar

To decorate:
34 raspberries, halved
Light Fruit Nappage *(see page 239)*
Chocolate Squares and Piped Curls *(see pages 248 and 250)*
Edible gold leaf

You will also need:
• *3 x different-sized daisy cutters*
• *small dome mould*
• *paper piping cornet (see page 250)*
• *no.1 piping tube (tip)*
• *two 10cm (4 inch) tart rings*
• *two 14cm (5½ inch) tart rings*
• *14cm (5½ inch) pastry cutter*
• *daisy-shaped cutters*

First, prepare the Sugar Daisies and chocolate decorations:

1 Prepare the daisies. Roll out the sugar paste very thinly to about 0.5mm thick. Use three different sizes of daisy cutters to cut out flowers. Place the flowers in a small dome mould, so that the petals gently curve upwards. Prepare the Royal Icing as instructed on page 246 and spoon it into a paper piping cornet fitted with a no.1 piping tube (tip). Pipe 7 small bulbs into the centre of each flower, the leave in a cool dry area to set for at least 4 hours.

2 Prepare the Chocolate squares and Curls as instructed on pages 248 and 250 and leave in a cool, dry area to set for 1–2 hours.

Next, prepare the Sable Breton:

3 Sieve the flour, baking powder and salt together twice into a bowl. Put the butter in another bowl and beat until smooth.

4 Put the egg yolks and sugar in a mixing bowl and whisk until light in colour. Add the softened butter and mix together until fully incorporated.

5 Fold in the sieved flour and baking powder and mix together to a dough. Wrap in cling film (plastic wrap) and leave to rest in the fridge for 2–3 hours.

6 Once rested, put the dough between 2 sheets of silicone (baking) paper and roll it to 8mm (⅓ inch) thick, then chill again for 1–2 hours.

Now, prepare the Raspberry Mousse:

7 Use the ingredients to prepare the Raspberry Mousse following the method on page 115.

8 Put two 10cm (4 inch) tart rings on a tray lined with silicone (baking) paper. Use a ladle to spoon the prepared mousse into the tart rings and level the tops with a palette knife. Transfer to the freezer to set for at least 1 hour.

Now, prepare your tart rings and bake:

9 Preheat the oven to 180°C (350°F/gas 4). Line a baking tray (sheet) with a non-stick baking mat and put two 14cm (5½ inch) tart rings on it.

10 Remove the rolled out pastry from the fridge and cut out 2 discs using the 14cm (5½ inch) pastry cutter. Place the two discs into the tart rings on the tray. Bake for about 20–25 minutes until golden brown. Leave to cool before de-moulding from the tart rings.

Next, prepare the Raspberry Glaze:

11 Prepare the glaze as instructed on page 239. Strain into an airtight container and leave to cool to room temperature.

To assemble and finish:

12 Turn the baked pastry discs upside down on a clean tray. Remove the Raspberry Mousse from the freezer, de-mould and put them on a wire rack with a tray underneath. Glaze each mousse with the raspberry glaze, ensuring any excess is tapped off.

13 Use a palette knife to put each mousse onto the centre of the pastry discs. Arrange the raspberry halves in a circle around the raspberry mousse on each tart. Lightly glaze the raspberries and finish by decorating with the prepared daisies, chocolate decorations and gold leaf.

Store in the fridge until ready to serve. Best eaten the same day.

CLASSIC MILLEFEUILLE

Every bakery in the country has a cream slice. Sadly, the beauty and skills of this classic pâtisserie is often forgotten. For a young chef, it is a great way of perfecting essential skills — crispy, caramelized pastry, smooth crème pâtissière and glossy fondant. There is no hiding flaws in this classic dish. It is a favourite of pâtissier Mike Nadell, who has kept up the tradition of teaching the classics to the next generation.

Makes 1 millefeuille (serving 8)

1 quantity of **Rough Puff Pastry** *(see page 67)*
1 quantity of **Crème Pâtissière** *(see page 234)*
Icing (powdered) sugar, for dusting
1 quantity of **Apricot Nappage** *(see page 239)*
1 quantity of **Fondant** *(see page 246)*
1 quantity of **Chocolate Fondant** (see variation page 246)
200g (7oz/2½ cups) toasted flaked almonds, to decorate

You will also need:
• *pastry (piping) bag*
• *12mm (½ inch) nozzle (tip)*
• *paper piping cornet (see page 250)*

1 Prepare the Rough Puff Pastry dough as instructed on page 67 and leave to rest for 2–3 hours.

2 Prepare the Crème Pâtissière as instructed on page 234 and store in the fridge until ready to use.

3 Divide the prepared pastry into 2 pieces. Roll one half out to 3mm (⅛ inch) thick on a lightly floured surface to the size of a 30 x 40cm (12 x 16 inch) rectangle. Place the rectangle of pastry on a tray lined with a non-stick baking mat and transfer to the fridge to rest for 30 minutes. The remaining pastry is extra and can be wrapped in cling film (plastic wrap) and stored in the freezer for up to 1 month. Preheat the oven to 200°C (400°F/gas 6).

4 Take the puff pastry from the fridge, dock (prick) the pastry all over and dust generously with icing (powdered) sugar. Place a sheet of silicone (baking) paper on top and a baking tray (sheet) on top of the paper to weigh it down. Bake for 20–25 minutes until golden and caramelized on top. Remove from the oven and place on a wire rack to cool.

5 Trim the edges of the puff pastry and cut into 3 rectangles, each measuring 10 x 28cm (4 x 11 inches). Beat the prepared Crème Pâtissière until smooth and spoon into a piping (pastry) bag fitted with a 12mm (½ inch) nozzle (tip). Pipe lines along the tops of 2 of the pastry rectangles and stack one on top of the other.

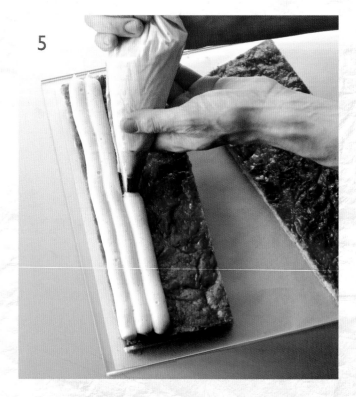

5

6 Melt the Apricot Nappage and brush a thin layer onto the last rectangle of puff pastry.

7 Prepare the Fondant and Chocolate Fondant as instructed on page 246. Spoon some Chocolate Fondant into a paper piping cornet.

8 Use a palette knife to carefully spread a thin layer of Fondant on top of the nappage layer on the puff pastry. Pipe diagonal lines of Chocolate Fondant across the fondant layer. Use a cocktail stick to create a lattice effect by pulling the cocktail stick diagonally across the fondant back and forth. Use a sharp knife to remove any excess fondant from the side of the coated pastry.

9 Place the fondant coated rectangle on top of the two rectangles layered with Crème Pâtissière. Spread a thin layer of Crème Pâtissière lengthways along the sides and coat with the toasted flaked almonds.

Store in the fridge until ready to serve. Best eaten the same day.

ECCLES CAKES

These are named after the small town of Eccles in Lancashire. The first commercial sale of them was in 1793 by James Birch, but they had been made by locals for a long time before that. The texture of the pastry is unique to Eccles cakes so it is important to get it right when making them. It should be very flaky, with a caramelized bubbly texture created by the glaze and sugar dusting.

Makes 20 Eccles cakes

1 quantity of **Rough Puff Pastry** *(see page 67)*
1 egg white
Caster (superfine) sugar, for sprinkling
Icing (powdered) sugar, for dusting

For the Fruit Filling:
50g (1¾oz/3½ tablespoons) unsalted butter
150g (5½oz/¾ cup) soft brown sugar
150g (5½oz/1 cup) sultanas (golden raisins)
50g (1¾oz) Confit Orange *(see page 46)*, roughly chopped
5g (1 teaspoon) freshly grated nutmeg
5g (1 teaspoon) ground cinnamon
Grated zest of 1 lemon
Grated zest of 1 orange
30ml (1fl oz) Grand Marnier

You will also need:
• 10cm (4 inch) pastry cutter

1 Prepare the Rough Puff Pastry as instructed on page 67 and leave to rest for 2–3 hours.

2 To prepare the Fruit Filling, melt the butter in a saucepan and add the sugar. Put the fruit, spices, lemon and orange zest and Grand Marnier in a mixing bowl. Add the butter and sugar mixture and mix until fully combined.

3 When rested, divide the pastry into 2 pieces. Roll each half out to 3mm (⅛ inch) thick on a lightly floured surface and use a 10cm (4 inch) pastry cutter to cut out 20 discs.

4 Weigh the filling into 20g (¾oz) portions and roll into balls. Place a ball of filling onto the centre of each pastry disc.

5 Use a pastry brush to brush egg white onto the edge of the pastry discs. Fold the pastry to the centre to completely encase the filling and push down to seal the fruit inside. Turn each Eccles cake upside down so that the folded side is underneath. Rest in the fridge for 30 minutes.

6 Preheat the oven to 190°C (375°F/gas 5).

7 When rested, gently brush egg white all over the outside of each Eccles cake. Sprinkle with caster (superfine) sugar and lightly dust with icing (powdered) sugar. Push a knife through the pastry three times into the top of each Eccles cake.

8 Bake in the oven for 20–25 minutes, until golden and caramelized.

Best served the same day, but can be stored in an airtight container for up to 3 days.

ÉCLAIRS

Like the cream slice, these can be found in every bakery up and down the country. My mum would buy them as a treat while I was growing up. They were packaged in a box and tied with ribbon. I remember the feeling of anticipation when the box was about to be opened. Even now, I still get that feeling of excitement when I visit pâtisseries of fellow members of Relais Desserts.

....

Makes 30 éclairs (10 of each flavour)

I quantity of **Choux Pastry** (see page 230)
Edible gold, silver and bronze leaf, to decorate

For the Craquelin:
80g (3oz/⅔ cup) plain (all-purpose) flour
10g (¼oz) cocoa powder (or the same amount of freeze-dried
  raspberry powder or pistachio paste for the other flavours)
90g (3¼oz/scant ½ cup) caster (superfine) sugar
75g (2¾oz/⅓ cup/¾ stick) unsalted butter

For the Chocolate Éclairs:
I quantity of **Chocolate** Crème Pâtissière
  (see variation page 234)
I quantity of **Chocolate Fondant**
  (see variation page 246)
Curved Swiped Flicks (see page 248)

For the Raspberry Éclairs:
I quantity of **Raspberry** Crème Pâtissière
  (see variation page 234)
I quantity of **Raspberry Fondant**
  (see variation page 246)
Small Chocolate Squares (see page 248)
Light Fruit Nappage (see page 239), for glazing
5 fresh raspberries, halved
Freeze-dried raspberries, to decorate

For the Pistachio Éclairs:
I quantity of **Pistachio** Crème Pâtissière
  (see variation page 234)
I quantity of **Pistachio Fondant**
  (see variation page 246)
Chopped pistachios, to decorate
Chocolate Discs (see page 248)

You will also need:
• *piping (pastry) bag*
• *15mm (¾ inch) nozzle (tip)*
• *6mm (⅛ inch) nozzle (tip)*

First, prepare the chocolate decorations:

1 Prepare the Curved Swiped Flicks, Small Chocolate Squares and Chocolate Discs as instructed on page 248 and leave in a cool, dry area to set for 1–2 hours.

Next, prepare the three different flavours of Craquelin:

2 To make each one, sift the flour and cocoa powder (or the raspberry powder if you are making the raspberry flavour) together in a mixing bowl. If you are making the pistachio flavour, just sift the flour and move to the next step.

3 Add the sugar and butter to the flour (and pistachio paste if you are making the pistachio flavour) and rub together until the mixture forms a dough. Roll the dough between 2 sheets of silicone (baking) paper to about 1mm thick, then chill for 30 minutes.

Then, prepare the Crème Pâtissière:

4 Prepare each flavour of Crème Pâtissière as instructed on page 234. Leave in the fridge until ready to use.

Now, prepare the Choux Pastry and bake your éclairs:

5 Preheat the oven to 200°C (400°F/gas 6). Prepare the pastry as instructed on page 230.

6 Put the Choux Pastry into a piping (pastry) bag fitted with a 15mm (¾ inch) piping tube. Line 3 baking trays (sheets) with non-stick baking mats and pipe ten 10cm (4 inch) lines on each tray.

7 Cut each flavour of Craquelin into 1.2 x 10cm (½ x 4 inch) rectangles and place 10 of each variety onto the piped Choux Pastry. Bake for 15–18 minutes, then turn the oven temperature down to 180°C (350°F/gas 4) and continue to cook for a further 8 minutes.

8 Remove from the oven and place the éclairs on a wire cooling rack.

7

To fill your éclairs and finish:

9 Use a a 6mm (¼ inch) nozzle (tip) to pierce 3 holes into the base of each éclair.

10 Put the prepared Chocolate Crème Pâtissière into a piping (pastry) bag fitted with a 6mm (¼ inch) tube and pipe into the éclairs topped with the chocolate craquelin, ensuring that they are well filled. Repeat this process with the Raspberry Crème Pâtissière for the éclairs topped with raspberry craquelin and the Pistachio Crème Pâtissière for the éclairs topped with pistachio craquelin.

11 Prepare the 3 different varieties of fondant as instructed on page 246. Dip the éclairs into the appropriate flavoured fondant, removing any excess fondant.

12 Sprinkle the pistachio-flavoured éclairs with chopped pistachio immediately, and then leave all three varieties to set for 5 minutes.

13 For the chocolate éclairs, decorate with chocolate Curved Swiped Flicks and finish with gold leaf.

14 For the raspberry éclairs, glaze 10 raspberry halves with Light Fruit Nappage and place onto each éclair. Decorate with a sprinkle of freeze-dried raspberries, a Chocolate Square and silver leaf.

15 For the pistachio éclairs, decorate with 3 different sizes of Chocolate Disc and finish with bronze leaf.

Store in the fridge until ready to serve. Best eaten the same day.

8

BEIGNETS

There are many different types of beignet, but it is believed that they were originally made with choux pastry. Trade routes from the Middle East brought this type of fried confection to Europe. I remember as a young laddie at Gleneagles Hotel, I would cook hundreds of these in a big fryer in preparation for banquets. The magic of making them is that after they have been cooking for a couple of minutes, they suddenly puff up and triple in size. Staying true to my East Coast heritage, I have filled these with Dundee marmalade as well as crème pâtissière.

Makes 40 beignets

1 quantity of **Marmalade** (see page 242)
1 quantity of **Grand Marnier Crème Pâtissière** (see variation page 234)
1 quantity of **Choux Pastry** (see page 230)

For the Cinnamon Sugar:
500g (1lb 2oz/2½ cups) caster (superfine) sugar
10g (¼oz) ground cinnamon

You will also need:
• *deep fat fryer*
• *piping (pastry) bags*
• *8mm (¼ inch) nozzle (tip)*
• *6mm (⅛ inch) nozzle (tip)*

1 Prepare the Marmalade as instructed on page 242. Prepare the Grand Marnier Crème Pâtissière as instructed on page 234 and store in the fridge until ready to use.

2 To make the Cinnamon Sugar, thoroughly mix the sugar and cinnamon together in a mixing bowl, then tip into a shallow tray.

3 Prepare the Choux Pastry as instructed on page 230. Heat the deep fat fryer to 170°C (325°F) and cut out eight 20 x 4cm (8 x 1½ inch) rectangles of silicone (baking) paper.

4 Spoon the Choux Pastry into a piping (pastry) bag fitted with an 8mm (¼ inch) plain nozzle (tip). Pipe five 2cm (¾ inch) bulbs of pastry onto each rectangle of silicone (baking) paper, leaving gaps in between.

5 Line a tray with kitchen roll (kitchen paper). Take one rectangle with the piped bulbs on it and carefully place it upside down into the fryer. After 20 seconds, the choux buns will separate from the silicone (baking) paper. Use tongs to carefully remove the paper from the fryer. Leave the choux buns to cook for a further 6–8 minutes until golden all over. Remove with a slotted spoon and place them onto the prepared tray to absorb the excess oil. Repeat this process until all 40 buns have been cooked. Leave to cool on the prepared tray.

6 Spoon the Crème Pâtissière into a piping (pastry) bag fitted with a 6mm (⅛ inch) nozzle (tip). Spoon the Marmalade into another piping (pastry) bag and cut a small hole in the tip of the bag. Fill each beignet with a generous bulb of Crème Pâtissière and a small bulb of Marmalade.

7 To finish, roll each beignet in the Cinnamon Sugar.

Best served immediately, but can be stored in the fridge until ready to serve.

BEE STING

*When I worked as head pâtissier at The Savoy in London, Anton Edelmann was the chef de cuisine.
He is from Bavaria, which has a great history of baking. One of the most iconic German pastries
he introduced to the kitchen was the Bee Sting or Beinenstich. It soon became a favourite on the
famous afternoon teas. The origin of these pastries has many different stories, but my favourite
dates back to the 15th century. To repel invaders from neighbouring villages, a group of German
bakers lobbed beehives at the invading parties. After successfully deterring them, the bakers
created the Bee Sting cake to celebrate.*

Makes 16 bee stings

1 quantity of **Grand Marnier Syrup**
  (see variation page 238)
1 quantity of **Honey Mousseline**
  (see variation page 235)

For the Brioche Dough:
32g (1¼oz) fresh yeast
200ml (7fl oz/generous ¾ cup) milk
400g (14oz/3 cups)
  plain (all-purpose) flour, sifted
2g (a pinch) salt
160g (6oz/generous ¾ cup)
  caster (superfine) sugar
80g (3oz) whole eggs (about 2 eggs)
120g (4¼oz/generous ½ cup/1⅛ sticks)
  unsalted butter, softened,
  plus extra for brushing

For the Almond Topping:
50g (1¾oz/3½ tablespoons)
  unsalted butter
150g (5½oz/¾ cup)
  caster (superfine) sugar
100ml (3½fl oz/scant ½ cup)
  whipping (pouring) cream
120g (4oz/scant ½ cup) honey
300g (10½oz/3¾ cups) flaked almonds

You will also need:
• 20cm (8 inch) square cake tin
  or baking tray (sheet)
• piping (pastry) bag
• 15mm (¾ inch) nozzle (tip)

1 First, prepare the Grand Marnier
Syrup as instructed on page 238 and
set aside until needed.

2 Prepare the cake tin by brushing it
with softened butter.

3 Next, make the brioche dough. Put
the yeast in a small bowl, pour in the
milk and whisk together.

4 Sieve together the flour, salt and
sugar and put into the bowl of an
electric mixer fitted with a dough
hook. Add the eggs to the flour
mixture along with the yeast mixture
and beat together. Continue beating
for 10–12 minutes until the mixture is
elastic and comes away from the sides.

5 Add the butter and continue to
beat until the mixture comes away
from the sides again. Cover with
cling film (plastic wrap) and leave
the mixture to prove in a warm area
for about 45 minutes or until it has
doubled in size. Knock back, cover
with cling film (plastic wrap), then
place in the fridge for at least 1 hour.

6 When the dough has firmed, roll
it out to a square shape to fit the tin
and line the tin with the pastry. Dock
(prick) all over and leave to prove in
a warm area for a further 30 minutes,
until it has doubled in size.

7 Preheat the oven to 190°C (375°F/
gas 5).

8 While the dough is proving, prepare
the Almond Topping. Put the butter,
sugar, cream and honey in a saucepan
and bring to the boil. Remove from
the heat and add the flaked almonds.
Use a palette knife to evenly spread
the mixture on top of the proved
doughs. Bake for 30–35 minutes.

9 Now, prepare the Honey
Mousseline as instructed on page 235.

10 Remove the cooked brioche from
the oven and leave to cool before
de-moulding from the tin and slicing in
half through the centre.

11 Soak the inside of the brioche
liberally with Grand Marnier Syrup.
Spoon the prepared mousseline into a
piping (pastry) bag fitted with a 15mm
(¾ inch) nozzle (tip). Pipe lines of
mousseline onto the base of the two
brioche. Carefully place the lid on top
and put in the fridge for 30 minutes to
set. Cut into 5cm (2 inch) squares.

*Store in the fridge until ready to serve.
Best eaten the same day.*

MARIGNONS

When I was an apprentice at Gleneagles Hotel, I would make savarin dough and cook all the different traditional shapes: Savarin, Baba, Pomponette and Marignons. Time seems to have forgotten the Marignon, but it was always my favourite because it allowed for the most filling.

Makes 18 marignons

1 quantity of **Dried Lime Zest**
(see page 247)

1 quantity of **Marignon Dough**
(see page 66)

1 quantity of **Crème Diplomat**
(see page 235)

1½ quantities of **Light Syrup** (see page 238),
made with the addition of 1 sliced lime

100ml (3½fl oz/scant ½ cup) rum

1 whole pineapple

1 quantity of **Apricot Nappage**
(see page 239)

You will also need:
• two 9-hole silicone boat moulds, with
10 x 4.4 x 1.5cm (4 x 1½ x ½ inch)
cavities
• piping (pastry) bags
• 10mm (⅓ inch) nozzle (tip)
• D6 star nozzle (tip)

First, make the Dried Lime Zest and the Marignon Dough:

1 Prepare the Dried Lime Zest and Marignon Dough as instructed on pages 247 and 66.

To bake and assemble:

2 Preheat the oven to 200°C (400°F/ gas 6).

3 Once proved and knocked back, spoon the Marignon Dough into a piping (pastry) bag fitted with a 10mm (⅓ inch) nozzle (tip). Pipe the dough into the marignon moulds until two-thirds full. Leave to prove in a warm area for a further 20 minutes until doubled in size.

4 Bake in the oven for 20–25 minutes, until golden in colour. Remove from the mould and leave to cool on a wire rack.

Now, prepare the Crème Diplomat and Light Syrup:

5 Prepare the Crème Diplomat as instructed on page 235 and store in the fridge until use.

6 Prepare the Light Syrup as instructed on page 239 and cool slightly to 90°C (194°F). Immerse the marignons in the syrup for 2–3 minutes, then flip over to ensure both sides get fully soaked. Use a slotted spoon to remove the marignons from the syrup and place on a shallow tray to cool. Once cooled, drizzle the marignons with the rum.

To finish:

7 Prepare the pineapple pieces by peeling, coring and cutting in quarters vertically. Cut into 2mm (⅛ inch) slices.

8 Cut the marignons along one side on a slight downward angle. Place 3 overlapping slices of pineapple inside each marignon.

9 Melt the Apricot Nappage and carefully glaze the top of each marignon and the pineapple using a pastry brush.

10 Spoon the prepared Crème Diplomat into a piping (pastry) bag fitted with a D6 star nozzle (tip). Pipe small swirls of Crème Diplomat into the inside of the marignon on top of the pineapple slices. Sprinkle with the Dried Lime Zest.

Store in the fridge until ready to serve. Best eaten the same day.

FUDGE DOUGHNUTS

These are a local favourite in my hometown in Scotland, but definitely have a universal appeal. Doughnuts have become very fashionable again in recent years, with hundreds of different flavours, toppings, shapes and sizes. For me, the fudge doughnut will always be the king of the doughnuts.

Makes 25 doughnuts

1 quantity of **Sea Salt Caramel** *(see page 48)*
1 quantity of **Crème Pâtissière**
   (see page 234)
1 quantity of **Caramel Fondant**
   (see variation page 246)
250g (9oz) tempered dark
   (bittersweet) chocolate
   (70% cocoa solids) *(see page 14)*

For the Doughnut Dough:
500g (1lb 2oz/3¾ cups)
   strong flour, sifted
55g (1¾oz/¼ cup)
   caster (superfine) sugar
10g (¼oz) salt
125ml (4½fl oz/½ cup) milk
40g (1½oz) fresh yeast
50g (1¾oz) whole egg (about 1 egg)
100g (3½oz) egg yolks (about 5 eggs)
5g (1 teaspoon) dark rum
100g (3½oz/½ cup/1 stick)
   unsalted butter, cubed and softened

You will also need:
• deep fat fryer
• piping (pastry) bag
• doughnut nozzle (tip)
• paper piping cornet (see page 250)

First, prepare the Sea Salt Caramel and the Creme Pâtissière:

1 Make the caramel as instructed on page 48, then leave to cool.

2 Prepare the Crème Pâtissière as instructed on page 234.

Next, prepare the dough:

3 Put the flour, sugar and salt in a mixing bowl. Put the milk and the yeast in a small bowl and mix together.

4 Put the egg and egg yolks in a mixing bowl and add the milk and yeast mixture. Mix together, then add the rum.

5 Add all the wet ingredients to the dry ingredients and begin to knead by hand, or alternatively use an electric mixer fitted with a dough hook attachment. Continue mixing until the dough is smooth and elastic and comes away from the side of the bowl. Add the butter and continue to mix until the mixture comes away from the side again.

6 Put the dough in a bowl, cover with cling film (plastic wrap) and place in the fridge for 1 hour.

To cook and finish:

7 Remove the prepared dough from the fridge. Cut and weigh the dough into 30g (1¼oz) pieces. Roll each piece into a ball, place on a tray lined with silicone (baking) paper and leave to prove for 45–60 minutes, or until doubled in size.

8 Prepare a tray lined with kitchen roll (kitchen paper). Turn on the fryer and heat the oil to 170°C (338°F). Once the beignets are fully proved, carefully place them into the oil and cook for about 3–4 minutes on each side. Remove from the fryer and drain on the prepared tray to remove excess oil. Leave to cool.

9 Spoon the Crème Pâtissière into a piping (pastry) bag fitted with a doughnut nozzle (tip). Spoon the caramel into a piping bag and snip a small hole in the end. Fill each beignet with a small amount of Sea Salt Caramel and a large bulb of Crème Pâtissière.

10 Prepare the Caramel Fondant as instructed on page 246. Dip the tops of the beignets into the prepared fondant and then leave to set for 5 minutes. Spoon the tempered chocolate into a paper piping cornet and pipe lines on the tops of each doughnut to finish.

Store in the fridge until ready to serve. Best eaten the same day.

9

10

Ever since I made the decision to become a pâtissier, I knew my ambition was to have my own shop. While I was a young trainee, I used to get the night bus to Paris and endlessly search for the best pâtisseries in the city. To this day, the inspiration drawn from the traditions of pâtisserie in France is endless. My respect for the masters of the craft has never ceased, and when I find the time I still adore visiting the boutique pâtisseries of Paris.

The first recipe book I bought for myself was *The Roux Brothers on Pâtisserie*. It instantly became a bible for my craft and I still reference it today. The classic skills of the masters are timeless.

PÂTISSERIE MODERN
Classics

Throughout my career, I have gained an understanding of the history of pâtisserie. The 'Golden Era' and Marie-Antonin Carême are of course two of my favourite topics. I have, however, not forgotten my humble roots as a Scottish laddie, so wanted to embrace this by adding a few of my childhood favourites to this section.

Of course, I adore Carême's grand pâtisserie such as the Charlotte Royale or Russe, but I will always have time for a jaffa cake, a cheesecake or a creamy Black Forest gateau!

ANGLAISE CHOCOLATE MOUSSE

This method works better for smaller batches, so I would recommend it for the beginner.

....

Makes 1.1kg (2lb 5oz)

550ml (19fl oz/scant 2⅓ cups) whipping (pouring) cream
150ml (5fl oz/⅔ cup) milk
60g (2oz) egg yolks *(about 3 eggs)*
30g (1¼oz/2 tablespoons) caster (superfine) sugar
320g (11oz) dark (bittersweet) chocolate
  (66% cocoa solids), chopped

1 Put 150ml (5fl oz/⅔ cup) of the cream in a saucepan and add the milk. Bring to the boil.

2 Meanwhile, whisk the egg yolks and sugar together in a large mixing bowl until the mix becomes light in colour, about 2–3 minutes.

3 When the milk has boiled, pour half of it onto the egg and sugar mixture and mix thoroughly.

4 Pour this mix back into the saucepan and cook over a low heat, stirring continuously, until the mixture is thick enough to coat the back of a spoon, about 82–84°C (180–183°F).

5 Take the saucepan off the heat and pass the mix through a fine sieve (strainer) onto the chopped chocolate in a mixing bowl.

6 Using a spatula, mix until smooth and emulsified, then leave to cool.

7 Put the remaining cream in a mixing bowl and whip until soft peaks form. Alternatively, whisk in an electric mixer fitted with a whisk attachment.

8 Carefully fold the whipped cream into the chocolate.

Use immediately.

SABAYON CHOCOLATE MOUSSE

This method will give a slightly lighter result than the Anglaise Chocolate Mousse (see opposite).

....

Makes 900g (2lb 2oz)

300g (10½oz) dark (bittersweet) chocolate
  (66% cocoa solids), finely chopped
140g (5oz) egg yolks (about 7 eggs)
80g (3oz/⅓ cup) caster (superfine) sugar
40ml (1½fl oz/2½ tablespoons) water
380ml (13fl oz/1½ cups) whipping (pouring) cream

1 Melt the chocolate in a bain-marie (water bath) until it reaches 45°C (113°F).

2 Whisk the egg yolks in an electric mixer fitted with the whisk attachment.

3 Meanwhile, put the sugar and water in a saucepan and bring to the boil. Heat until it reaches 121°C (250°F), then slowly pour the sugar syrup over the egg yolks and continue to whisk to a full sabayon (until the mix reaches the ribbon stage, becoming thick and pale). Continue to whisk the mixture until it is cool.

4 In a separate bowl, whip the cream until it reaches the ribbon stage, then fold the sabayon into the cream.

5 Carefully fold one-third of the mixture into the melted chocolate.

6 Fold in the remaining cream.

Use immediately.

STRAWBERRY BAVAROIS

Originally bavarois was not a dessert, but a drink. It was created in the middle of the 18th century in Paris and named in honour of the Princess of Bavaria, who favoured a sweet tea drink that eventually evolved into this dessert.

Makes 1.1kg (2lb 5oz)

12g (⅓ oz) leaf gelatine
500ml (18fl oz/generous 2 cups) strawberry purée
1 vanilla pod (bean), split and scraped
80g (3oz) egg yolks (about 4 eggs)
80g (3oz/scant ½ cup) caster (superfine) sugar
450ml (15fl oz/scant 2 cups) whipping (pouring) cream

1 Soak the gelatine in a bowl of ice-cold water for a few minutes until soft. Squeeze to remove any excess water.

2 Put the strawberry purée in a saucepan, add the vanilla seeds and scraped pod (bean) and bring to the boil. In a mixing bowl, whisk together the egg yolks and sugar until they are well combined and light in colour.

3 Pour half the boiled liquid onto the egg mixture and mix well.

4 Return the mixture back to the saucepan of strawberry purée and return to the heat. Stir with a spatula.

5 Continue cooking the liquid until it thickens, coats the back of the spatula and reaches a temperature of 82–84°C (180–183°F) on a thermometer.

6 Add the soaked gelatine to the custard and stir until the gelatine has dissolved. Strain through a fine sieve (strainer) into a bowl set in an ice bain-marie (water bath).

7 Whip the cream in a separate bowl to the ribbon stage. When the custard is cold, remove the bowl from the bain-marie (water bath). Be careful not to let it set. Fold the whipped cream into the cold custard.

Use immediately.

Flavour variations: *turn this into a Vanilla Bavarois by replacing the strawberry purée with the same amount of milk. Other flavours can be created by replacing the strawberry purée with another fruit purée, such as raspberry, mango or peach.*

CHERRY MOUSSE

The word 'mousse' dates back to the early 18th century and is a derivative of the old French word mosse, which dates back to 1226. Translated into English, 'mousse' means the froth that appears on the surface of water when it is agitated. The word was later used to describe a dessert that is light and frothy in texture.

Makes 930g (2lb 1oz)

11g (¼oz) leaf gelatine
500ml (18fl oz/generous 2 cups) whipping (pouring) cream
350g (12oz) cherry purée (or other fruit purée)
80g (3oz/scant ½ cup) caster (superfine) sugar

1 Soak the gelatine in a bowl of ice-cold water for a few minutes until soft. Squeeze to remove any excess water. Whip the cream in a bowl to the ribbon stage.

2 Put 150g (5½oz) of the cherry purée in a saucepan and add the sugar. Gently warm, stirring, until the sugar has dissolved completely.

3 Add the soaked gelatine and stir until fully dissolved.

4 Strain through a sieve (strainer) into a mixing bowl. Add the remaining cherry purée.

5 Pour in the whipped cream and fold together until combined.

Use immediately.

Flavour variations: *you can use any flavour of fruit purée to make fruit mousse as long as you use the same weight (350g/12oz); such as apple, nectarine, raspberry, etc. Coconut purée can also be used.*

TROPICAL SNOWBALL

This pâtisserie is based on a marshmallow confection popular in Scotland. I like the concept of the spherical shape with the coconut coating to go with the name 'snowball'. Even in my boyhood years, I found the original confection very sweet and I always wanted there to be a sharp filling in the centre of the marshmallow. When I created my own snowball, I used a passion fruit curd centre to cut through the sweetness of the coconut mousse.

Makes 6 snowballs

Chocolate Triangle Flicks *(see page 248)*, to decorate
½ quantity **Passion Fruit Curd**
  (see variation page 237),
  made with the addition of 3g (⅛oz)
  pre-soaked leaf gelatine
2 passion fruit
½ quantity of **Pain de Gène**
  (see page 231)
I quantity of **Dried Lime Zest**
  (see page 247)
I quantity of **White Chocolate Glaze**
  (see page 240)
I quantity of **Coconut Mousse**
  (see page 113)
I quantity of **Coconut Dacquoise**
  (see variation page 233)
Edible gold leaf, to decorate

For the Poached Mango:
450ml (15fl oz/scant 2 cups) water
375g (13oz/scant 2 cups)
  caster (superfine) sugar
20g (¾oz) freshly grated ginger
Grated zest and juice of I lime
I mango
50ml (2fl oz/scant ¼ cup) dark rum

For the Coconut Decoration:
I coconut, drained and shelled

You will also need:
• *piping (pastry) bags*
• *10mm (⅓ inch) nozzle (tip)*
• *5cm (2 inch) pastry cutter*
• *one 12-hole half-sphere silicone mould,
  with 4cm (1½ inch) cavities*
• *two 6-hole half-sphere silicone moulds,
  with 6cm (2½ inch) cavities*

First, prepare the chocolate decorations and the Poached Mango:

I Prepare the Chocolate Triangle Flicks as instructed on page 248.

2 Make the Poached Mango. Put the water and sugar in a saucepan and bring to the boil. Add the ginger, lime juice and zest and leave to infuse for 20 minutes.

3 Peel, stone and dice the fresh mango into 1cm (½ inch) cubes, then set aside. Strain the infused syrup into another pan, bring back to the boil, then add the mango. Cover with cling film (plastic wrap) and leave to cool in the syrup.

4 When ready to use, strain the mango pieces, reserving 200ml (7fl oz/generous ¾ cup) of the excess syrup. Add the rum to the reserved syrup, cover and store in the fridge until ready to use.

Next, prepare the Passion Fruit Curd:

5 Prepare the curd as instructed on page 237 adding the pre-soaked gelatine just prior to adding the butter. Mix in the seeds from the passion fruit at the end.

6 Pour the curd into a piping (pastry) bag fitted with a 10mm (⅓ inch) nozzle (tip). Put the 12-hole smaller half-sphere mould on a tray and pipe the curd in until each cavity is three-quarters full. Push 3–4 pieces of poached mango into the curd and level off using a small palette knife. Place in the freezer for 2 hours.

Next, prepare the Pain de Gène:

7 Prepare and bake the Pain de Gène as instructed on page 231 and leave to cool.

Now, make the Dried Lime Zest and White Chcolate Glaze:

8 Prepare the Dried Lime Zest as instructed on page 247 and set aside until needed.

9 Prepare the White Chocolate Glaze as instructed on page 240.

Prepare the Coconut Decoration:

10 Preheat the oven to 120°C (240°F/gas ½). Use a peeler to cut strips of fresh coconut. Place on a baking tray (sheet) lined with a non-stick baking mat and bake for 2–3 minutes.

11 When removed from the oven, the coconut should be slightly flexible. Curl the pieces into spirals and return to the oven for a further 15–20 minutes until dried and turning golden along the edges.

Now, prepare the sponge:

12 Use a 5cm (2 inch) pastry cutter to cut the Pain de Gène into 12 discs. Place them on a baking tray (sheet) lined with silicone (baking) paper and soak with the rum syrup.

Next, prepare the Coconut Mousse:

13 Prepare the mousse as instructed on page 113. Put the 6-hole larger half-sphere moulds on a tray and spoon in the Coconut Mousse until each cavity is half full. Reserve any remaining coconut mousse and store in the fridge until needed.

14 Remove the smaller half-sphere mould from the freezer, de-mould and place one curd-filled half-sphere in the centre of the coconut mousse-filled half-spheres and push down gently. Place a disc of Pain de Gène on each and level using a small palette knife. Place in the freezer for at least 2 hours until fully frozen.

Now, prepare the Coconut Dacquoise:

15 Preheat the oven to 170°C (325°F/gas 3). Prepare the Coconut Dacquoise as instructed on page 233. Spoon the mixture into a piping (pastry) bag fitted with an 8mm (⅓ inch) nozzle (tip) and pipe six 5cm (2 inch) spirals on a non-stick baking mat. Bake for 8–10 minutes. Remove from the oven and leave to cool.

To assemble and finish:

16 Melt the White Chocolate Glaze and cool to about 30°C (86°F).

17 Prepare a tray with 6 small metal rings (pastry cutters could also be used). Remove the frozen half-spheres from the freezer and use the reserved coconut mousse to spread a thin layer of mousse onto the top of each half-sphere, place another half-sphere on top and gently push together. Clean any excess mousse from around the join and place onto a ring on the prepared tray to set. Repeat this process until all of the half-spheres are joined to become 6 spheres placed on the rings to set.

18 Put the cooled White Chocolate Glaze in a jug and glaze each sphere by pouring the glaze over them until they are completely covered. Use a hot knife to clean any excess glaze off the base.

19 Place each sphere onto a dacquoise base by lifting with 2 cocktail sticks pushed into the sphere at diagonal angles (this prevents the sphere from rotating as you lift it).

20 Place the coconut decorations up one side and the Chocolate Triangle Flick on the sphere. Dust with Dried Lime Zest and finish with gold leaf.

Store in the fridge until ready to serve. Best eaten the same day.

BLACK FOREST GATEAU

This gateau originates from the Black Forest – the mountainous forest region in Baden-Württemberg, Germany. The image of this traditionally very decadent treat was somewhat damaged during the 1980s with an abundance of manufactured versions. However, I think that it is such a perfect combination of flavours that it deserves to be represented with no compromise on quality of ingredients.

Makes one gateau (serving 8)

½ quantity **Chocolate Genoise**
  (see variation page 230)
1 quantity **Cherry Compote**
  (see page 238)
1 quantity **Kirsch Syrup**
  (see variation page 238)
1 quantity **Anglaise Chocolate Mousse**
  (see page 110)
1 quantity **Crème Chantilly**
  (see page 235)

To finish:
Chocolate Shavings (see page 248)
Chocolate Cherry Stalk (see page 250)
30 griottine cherries
1 x Confit Cherries (see page 244)

You will also need:
• 16cm (6¼ inch) cake tin
• cake board and turntable
• piping (pastry) bag
• 14mm (⅝ inch) nozzle (tip)

First, prepare the Chocolate Genoise:

1 Preheat the oven to 180°C (350°F/ gas 4) and line a 16cm (6¼ inch) cake tin with silicone (baking) paper. Prepare and bake the sponge as instructed on page 230 in the prepared cake tin rather than on a tray. Leave the sponge to cool for at least 1 hour before use.

Next, prepare the Chocolate Shavings and Cherry Stalk, Cherry Compote and Kirsch Syrup:

2 Make Chocolate Shavings and the Chocolate Cherry Stalk as instructed on pages 248 and 250. Store on a tray in a cool, dry area until needed.

3 Make the Cherry Compote as instructed on page 238. Pour into a shallow tray, leave to cool, then put in an airtight container and transfer to the fridge until required.

4 Make the Kirsch Syrup as instructed on page 238. Set aside until needed.

Prepare the Anglasise Chocolate Mousse and begin to assemble:

5 Make the mousse as instructed on page 110.

6 Cut the sponge horizontally with a serrated knife into 4 flat slices. Place the base slice on a cake board, which has been positioned on top of a turntable. Use a pastry brush to soak the sponge well with the Kirsch Syrup, then spread a thin layer of compote on top.

7 Spread an even layer of chocolate mousse over the compote about 1.5cm (¾ inch) high. Place the next layer of sponge on top and transfer to the fridge to set for 20 minutes.

Prepare the Crème Chantilly and finish:

8 Make the Crème Chantilly as instructed on page 235 and place in a piping (pastry) bag fitted with a 14mm (⅝ inch) nozzle (tip). Strain about 30 griottine cherries from their juice.

9 Remove the gateau from the fridge and soak the top sponge with Kirsch Syrup. Pipe a spiral of Chantilly, leaving a 1.5cm (¾ inch) gap between each ring. Fill the gap between the cream with the strained griottine cherries.

10 Place the next layer of sponge on top of the Chantilly and soak well with Kirsch Syrup. Spread a thin layer of compote on top of the sponge, followed by an even layer of chocolate mousse about 1.5cm (¾ inch) high. Place the final layer of sponge on top and soak well with Kirsch Syrup.

11 Use a scraper to coat the entire gateau with a thin layer of chocolate mousse. Transfer to the fridge to set for a further 20 minutes.

12 Remove from the fridge and generously coat with a layer of Chantilly. Cover with Chocolate Shavings and place a Confit Cherry with a Chocolate Stalk in the centre.

Store in the fridge until ready to serve. Best eaten the same day.

PEACH & STRAWBERRY CHARLOTTE RUSSE

This entremet was created by the great chef, Marie-Antonin Carême during the early 1800s. Initially, it was named the Charlotte Parisienne but latterly became the Charlotte Russe. During that time, everything Russian was considered extremely fashionable, and after Carême had spent time as the executive chef to the Tsar of Russia he decided to rename his iconic entremet. It clearly is a dessert that will never go out of fashion.

Makes I russe (serving 6–8)

I quantity of **Strawberry Compote**
  (see page 238)
100g (3½oz) strawberries, chopped
I quantity of **Strawberry Glaze**
  (see variation page 239)
I quantity of **Peach Curd** *(see page 237)*
I quantity of **Strawberry Bavarois**
  (see page 112)

For the Biscuits à la Cuillère:
120g (4oz) egg yolks
  (about 6 eggs), beaten
190g (6½oz/scant I cup)
  caster (superfine) sugar
180g (6oz) egg whites (about 6 eggs)
190g (6½oz/1⅓ cups)
  plain (all-purpose) flour, sifted
icing (powdered) sugar, for dusting

For the Poached Peaches in Vanilla Syrup:
150g (5½oz/¾ cup)
  caster (superfine) sugar
500ml (18fl oz/2 cups
  plus 2 tablespoons) water
I vanilla pod (bean), split and scraped
2 peels of lemon zest
2 peaches, stoned and cut into
  8 even segments
50ml (2fl oz/scant ¼ cup)
  Grand Marnier

To finish:
Chocolate Squares and Curls
  (see pages 248 and 250)
Peach slices and hulled strawberries
I quantity of **Light Fruit Nappage**
  (see page 239)
Edible gold leaf

You will also need:
• *piping (pastry) bag*
• *12mm (½ inch) nozzle (tip)*
• *12cm (4½ inch) entremet ring*
• *14cm (5½ inch) entremet ring*
• *60cm (24 inch) pink satin ribbon*

First, prepare the chocolate decorations and Biscuits à la Cuillière:

1 Prepare the Chocolate Squares and Curls as instructed on pages 248 and 250.

2 Make the Biscuits à la Cuillière. Preheat the oven to 190°C (375°F/ gas 5) and line two 30 x 40cm (12 x 16 inch) baking trays (sheets) with silicone (baking) paper (you could also use a non-stick baking mat of the same size). Put the egg yolks and half the sugar in a bowl and whisk until it reaches the ribbon stage. Whisk the egg whites in a clean mixing bowl, gradually adding the remaining sugar and increasing the speed. Whisk to a soft peak meringue. Transfer the egg yolk mixture to a clean mixing bowl and fold in the meringue. Fold in the sifted flour.

3 Place half the mixture into a piping (pastry) bag fitted with a 12mm (½ inch) nozzle (tip). Pipe 7cm (2¾ inch) long fingers (you need about 20) onto the prepared tray and dust them with icing (powdered) sugar. Use a palette knife to spread the remaining mixture onto the second baking tray (sheet). Bake in the oven for 12–15 minutes until golden brown. Leave to cool.

Poach the peaches and prepare the Strawberry Compote and Glaze:

4 Put the sugar, water, lemon peel and vanilla seeds and pod (bean)

in a saucepan and bring to the boil. Prepare the peaches and place them in the syrup. Cover with a disc of silicone (baking) paper and cook for 6–8 minutes, until the peaches are soft. Leave the peaches to cool in the syrup, then drain the excess liquid, retaining 200 ml (7fl oz/generous ¾ cup) of the syrup. Add the Grand Marnier to the reserved syrup.

5 Prepare the Strawberry Compote as instructed on page 238, adding the roughly chopped strawberries to the cooled compote. Make the Strawberry Glaze as instructed on page 239 and set aside until needed.

Begin the assembly and make the Peach Curd:

6 Cut the sheet of cooled sponge into 2 discs: one 12cm (4½ inches) and one 14cm (5½ inches).

7 Make the Peach Curd as instructed on page 237.

8 Line a tray (sheet) with silicone (baking) paper and place the 12cm (4½ inch) entremet ring on it. Place the poached peaches in the entremet ring arranged in a spiral.

9 Pour 120g (4oz) of the Peach Curd on top of the poached peaches. Level the top and place in the freezer for at least 2 hours to set.

Prepare the Strawberry Bavarois:

10 Make a bavarois as instructed on page 112.

11 Place the 14cm (5½ inch) entremet ring onto a baking tray (sheet) lined with silicone (baking) paper. Place the 14cm (5½ inch) disc of sponge on the base and soak lightly with the Grand Marnier syrup. Spread a generous layer of Strawberry Compote on the sponge.

12 Fill the mould one-quarter full with the bavarois and use a small palette knife to push the bavarois up the sides. Transfer to the fridge to set for 15 minutes.

To finish:

13 Place the 12cm (4½ inch) sponge disc on top of the layer of bavarois in the 14cm (5½ inch) ring and soak generously with Grand Marnier syrup. De-mould the frozen peach curd and place on top of the sponge. Top up the mould completely with the remaining bavarois. Level the top, then transfer to the fridge to set for 2–3 hours.

14 Gently melt the Strawberry Glaze and coat the top of the entremet with an even layer. Leave to set in the fridge for 15 minutes.

15 Remove from the fridge, place on a serving dish and remove from the mould. Place the Biscuits à la Cuillière around the entremet and tie a ribbon around the base to secure.

16 Cut the peaches and strawberries and glaze them with Light Fruit Nappage. Place the fruits down the centre of the entremet and finish with a Chocolate Square, Chocolate Curls and gold leaf.

Store in the fridge until ready to serve. Best eaten the same day.

13

13

CHARLOTTE ROYALE

The original Charlotte cake was a hot dessert made with bread and baked apple. It is thought it was created by an English chef in the late 1700s in honour of Queen Charlotte, wife of King George III. It wasn't until Marie-Antonin Carême came to Brighton, England to cook for George IV that it evolved to become the cold set dessert we know today.

Makes 1 royale (serving 8)

Chocolate Joined-up Curves
(see page 250), to decorate
1 quantity of **Raspberry Jam**
(see page 241)
1 quantity of **Kirsch Syrup**
(see variation page 238)
2 quantities of **Swiss Roll Sponge**
(see page 231)
1 quantity of **Raspberry Bavarois**
(see variation page 112)
1 quantity of **Vanilla Bavarois**
(see variation page 112)
1 quantity of **Apricot Nappage**
(see page 239)
150g (5½oz) raspberries
(setting aside 1, halved and glazed with nappage, for decoration)
1 quantity of **Crème Chantilly**
(see page 235)
Edible gold leaf, to decorate

You will also need:
• 14cm (5½ inch) entremet ring
• 16cm (6¼ inch) entremet ring
• 18cm (7 inch) diameter metal half-sphere mould
• piping (pastry) bag
• D6 star nozzle (tip)

First, prepare the chocolate decorations, Raspberry Jam and Kirsch Syrup:

1 Prepare the Chocolate Joined-up Curves as instructed on page 250. Prepare the jam and syrup as instructed on pages 241 and 238 and set aside until needed.

Next, prepare the Swiss Roll Sponge:

2 Prepare and bake the Swiss Roll Sponge as instructed on page 231. When cooled, turn one of the sponge sheets upside down onto a piece of silicone (baking) paper. Cut in half widthways and trim the edges. Spread a thin layer of jam on the sponge, ensuring it is evenly covered. Roll lengthways into a tight spiral and repeat with the other half. Wrap in silicone (baking) paper and place in the freezer for at least 2 hours.

5

8

9

3 Cut 2 discs out of the second sponge – one 14cm (5½ inch) and the other 16cm (6¼ inch) in diameter. Set aside until ready to use.

Now, prepare the Vanilla Bavarois:

4 Prepare the bavarois following the instructions on page 112.

5 Line the 18cm (7 inch) half-sphere mould with cling film (plastic wrap). Remove the frozen Swiss roll from the freezer and cut it into 1cm (½ inch) slices and place them in the dome mould, starting in the centre and working outwards. Gently push them together to ensure there are no gaps and continue until the entire dome is covered.

6 Place a 14cm (5½ inch) entremet ring on a tray, then place the half-sphere mould on the ring to stop it from wobbling. Pour in the Vanilla Bavarois until just over one-third full and put it in the fridge to set for 30 minutes.

Next, prepare the Raspberry Bavarois:

7 Prepare the bavarois as instructed on page 112.

8 Generously soak the prepared sponge discs with Kirsch Syrup. Use a small palette knife to spread jam onto the discs so that they are evenly covered.

9 Remove the dome from the fridge and place the 14cm (5½ inch) sponge disc, jam side down, onto the layer of Vanilla Bavarois.

10 Pour the Raspberry Bavarois into the dome mould, leaving a gap of about 1.5cm (¾ inch) at the top – enough for the fresh raspberries and the final piece of sponge to fit in. Put the dome in the fridge to set for a further 10 minutes.

11 When semi-set, remove from the fridge and gently push raspberries into the bavarois.

12 Place the larger sponge disc, jam side down, on top of the raspberries. Return to the fridge for 2 hours to fully set.

To finish:

13 Melt the Apricot Nappage and remove the dome from the fridge. To de-mould, turn upside down onto a serving plate and gently lift the mould away and the layer of cling film (plastic wrap). Brush all over with nappage.

14 Prepare the Crème Chantilly following the instructions on page 235 and spoon into a piping (pastry) bag fitted with a D6 star nozzle (tip). Pipe rosettes around the base of the dome. Decorate with the reserved raspberry halves glazed with nappage, Chocolate Joined-up Curves and gold leaf to finish.

Store in the fridge until ready to serve. Best eaten the same day.

10

11

12

TRIPLE CHOCOLATE MOUSSE

Some of my most valuable early cooking experience was working with Scott Lyall at The Rescobie, near my home town in Fife. It was my first time in a professional kitchen. They were great days; not only was I doing a job that I loved, I was also fortunate enough to learn that Scott, like myself, was a massive Dundee United football supporter. This meant that we could nip out every Saturday to see the 'World Famous'! Scott taught me many cooking skills, but also taught me precision and patience. This pâtisserie requires both, and is also very traditional. The desserts served at The Rescobie were inspired by French classics. This was the beginning of my journey of discovering French haute cuisine.

Makes 25 individual mousses

25 x **Two-tone Chocolate Copeaux**
 (see page 250), to decorate
I quantity of **Chocolate Pâte Sucrée**
 (see variation page 228)
200g (3½oz) finely grated chocolate,
 to decorate

For the Dark (Bittersweet) Chocolate Mousse:

110g (3¾oz) dark (bittersweet)
 chocolate (70% cocoa solids)
60g (2oz) egg yolk (about 3 eggs)
75g (2¾oz/⅓ cup) caster (superfine)
 sugar
20ml (¾fl oz) water
300ml (½ pint/1¼ cups) whipping
 (pouring) cream

For the Milk Chocolate Mousse:

2.5g (⅛oz) leaf gelatine
150g (5½oz) milk chocolate
60g (2oz) egg yolk (about 3 eggs)
75g (2¾oz/⅓ cup) caster (superfine)
 sugar
20ml (¾fl oz) water
300ml (½ pint/1¼ cups) whipping
 (pouring) cream

For the White Chocolate Mousse:

3g (⅛oz) leaf gelatine
205g (7oz) white chocolate
80g (3oz) egg yolk (about 4 eggs)
40g (1½oz/scant ¼ cup) caster
 (superfine) sugar
10ml (2 teaspoons) water
320ml (11oz/1⅓ cups) whipping
 (pouring)cream

For the Cocoa Nib Streusel:

70g (2¾oz/½ cup) icing (powdered)
 sugar
70g (2¾oz/⅓ cup/⅔ stick)
 unsalted butter
100g (3½oz/¾ cup) plain
 (all-purpose) flour
50g (1¾oz) chopped cocoa nibs

You will also need:
• *twenty-five 5cm (2 inch) mousse rings*
• *twenty-five 18 x 5cm (7 x 2 inch) pieces of acetate*
• *piping (pastry) bag*
• *12mm (½ inch) nozzle (tip)*
• *5cm (2 inch) pastry cutter*

First, make the chocolate decorations and Chocolate Pâte Sucrée:

I Prepare the Two-tone Chocolate Copeaux as instructed on page 250. Prepare the Chocolate Pâte Sucrée as instructed on page 228, then rest in the fridge for 2–3 hours.

While the pastry is resting, prepare the layers of mousse:

2 Line a tray with silicone (baking) paper and place twenty-five 5cm (2 inch) mousse rings on it. Line each ring with a strip of acetate.

3 Make the Dark (Bittersweet) Chocolate Mousse. Melt the chocolate in a bain-marie (water bath) until it reaches 45°C (113°F). Whisk the egg

yolks in an electric mixer fitted with the whisk attachment.

4 Meanwhile, put the sugar and water in a saucepan and bring to the boil. Heat until it reaches 121°C (250°F), then slowly pour the sugar syrup over the egg yolks and continue to whisk to a full sabayon (until the mix reaches the ribbon stage, becoming thick and pale). Continue to whisk the mixture until it is cool.

5 In a separate bowl, whip the cream until it reaches the ribbon stage, then fold the sabayon into the cream. Carefully fold one-third of the mixture into the melted chocolate. Fold in the remaining sabayon mixture.

6 Spoon the prepared mousse into a piping (pastry) bag fitted with a 12mm (½ inch) nozzle (tip) and pipe the mousse into each mould to come one-third of the way up the side (about 20g/¾oz). Transfer to the fridge to set for 20 minutes.

7 Prepare the Milk Chocolate Mousse next using the same method as for the dark, but soak the gelatine in a bowl of ice-cold water for a few minutes until soft, then squeeze to remove any excess water. Add the soaked gelatine to the whisking sabayon straight after pouring the syrup onto the egg yolks. Spoon the prepared mousse into a piping (pastry) bag fitted with a 12mm (½ inch) nozzle (tip) and pipe into each mould until it comes two-thirds of the way

up the side (another 20g/¾oz). Place back in the fridge to set for 30 minutes.

8 Lastly, prepare the White Chocolate Mousse using the same method as for the Milk Chocolate Mousse. Fill the moulds to the top, then put back in the fridge to set for at least 1 hour.

Now, bake the pastry and prepare the Cocoa Nib Streusel:

9 Remove the rested pastry from the fridge. Roll it out to 3mm (⅛ inch) thick on a lightly floured surface and use a 5cm (2 inch) cutter to cut out 25 discs. Place them on a baking tray (sheet) lined with a non-stick baking mat and return to the fridge to rest for 30 minutes.

10 Next, make the streusel. Preheat the oven to 180°C (350°F/Gas 4). Put the sugar, butter and flour in a mixing bowl and mix gently until a light crumble is formed. Add the cocoa nibs and mix in. Make into small pieces of crumble lightly pushed together. Place them on a baking tray (sheet) lined with a non-stick baking mat and bake for 6–8 minutes until golden.

11 Keep the oven at the same temperature and bake the pastry discs for 10–12 minutes.

To finish:

12 Place the chocolate pastry discs on a tray lined with silicone (baking) paper. Remove the set mousses from the fridge and gently de-mould, placing each one on top of a pastry disc. Dust with the finely grated chocolate and remove the layer of acetate on the outside of each mousse.

13 Decorate with a Chocolate Square, a piece of Cocoa Nib Streusel and a Two-tone Chocolate Copeaux.

Store in the fridge until ready to serve. Best eaten the same day.

BLACKCURRANT CHEESECAKE

The evolution of pâtisserie in recent years has continued to move towards achieving lighter texture in creams and mousses and also maintaining fresher and cleaner flavours. Cheesecake has remained the same for a long time. I have created a version made with an almond streusel base and a fromage blanc mousse made with sabayon to create a very light texture.

Makes 2 cheesecakes (serving 6–8)

Chocolate Curls *(see page 250)*
1 quantity of **Kir Royale Jelly**
(see variation page 237)
200g (7oz/2 cups) blackcurrants, plus
  extra to decorate
1 quantity of **Crème Chantilly**
(see page 235)
Edible gold leaf, to decorate

For the Almond Streusel:
60g (2oz/⅓ cup) icing (powdered) sugar
60g (2oz/¼ cup/½ stick)
  cold unsalted butter, cubed
60g (2oz/generous ½ cup)
  ground almonds
60g (2oz/½ cup) plain (all-purpose) flour

For the Fromage Blanc Mousse:
180ml (6fl oz/⅔ cup)
  whipping (pouring) cream
380g (13oz) fromage blanc
  (or cream cheese)
12ml (⅓fl oz) lemon juice
Grated zest of 1 lemon
12g (⅓oz) leaf gelatine
60g (2oz) egg yolk (about 3 eggs)
50g (1¾oz) whole egg (about 1 egg)
115g (4oz/generous ½ cup)
  caster (superfine) sugar
36ml (1¼fl oz/generous
  2 tablespoons) water

You will also need:
• *two 16cm (6¼ inch) entremet rings*
• *two 12cm (4½ inch) silicone discs*
• *piping (pastry) bag*
• *St Honore nozzle (tip)*

First, prepare the chocolate decorations and streusel base:

1 Prepare the Chocolate Curls as instructed on page 250. Preheat the oven to 180°C (350°F/gas 4). Line a baking tray (sheet) with a non-stick baking mat and place two lightly greased 16cm (6¼ inch) entremet rings on top.

2 Put the sugar, butter, ground almonds and flour in a mixing bowl and mix gently until a light crumble is formed.

3 Spoon the mixture into the prepared entremet rings (about 120g/4¼oz in each) and press it down so that it compacts slightly and is evenly spread. Bake for 15–20 minutes until golden, then leave to cool.

Next, prepare the Kir Royale Jelly:

4 Make the jelly as instructed on page 237. Place the silicone moulds on a tray and cover the base with a layer of blackcurrants. Pour the jelly mixture in to the top of the moulds, then transfer to the freezer to set for 2–3 hours. There will be a small quantity of jelly left over, set aside until assembling the final dish.

Then, prepare the Fromage Blanc Mousse:

5 Put the cream in a mixing bowl and whip until soft peaks form. Put the fromage blanc, lemon juice and lemon zest in a separate mixing bowl and beat until smooth. Mix in the semi-whipped cream.

6 Soak the gelatine in ice-cold water for a few minutes until soft. Squeeze the gelatine to remove excess water.

7 Whisk the egg yolk and whole egg together to make a sabayon (the mixture will reach ribbon stage and becomes light in colour). At the same time, put the sugar and water in a saucepan and cook to 121°C (250°F). Add the soaked gelatine to the syrup, pour into the sabayon and continue to whisk until the sabayon cools. Fold the sabayon into the cream and fromage blanc.

8 Ladle 250g (9oz) of the mousse into the entremet rings on top of the streusel and level with a palette knife. Place in the fridge for 2 hours to set.

To finish:

9 Prepare the Crème Chantilly following the instructions on page 235.

10 Remove the set cheesecake from the fridge and the jelly from the freezer. De-mould the cheesecakes from the entremet rings and place on serving plates. De-mould the jelly and carefully place on the centre of each cheesecake. Place in the fridge for 1 hour.

11 Melt a small quantity of the reserved jelly. Use a pastry brush to lightly coat the top of the set jelly to give a shiny finish. Spoon the Chantilly into a piping (pastry) bag fitted with a St Honore nozzle (tip) and pipe quenelles around the top edge of the cheesecakes. Decorate with blackcurrants, Chocolate Curls and gold leaf.

Store in the fridge until ready to serve. Best eaten the same day.

MOKA

The word 'mocha' comes from the Yemen sea port, which between the 15th and 18th centuries was one of the busiest ports importing and exporting coffee beans.
This gateau was created in 1857 by a Parisian pâtissier in the district of L'Odeon. Coffee cake is often a teatime favourite. This modern entremet is based on the French classic, which is a lavish coffee gateau, classically made with layers of soaked genoise, coffee buttercream and walnuts.

Makes 2 moka gateau (serving 10–12)

Chocolate Slivers, Squares and Joined-up Curls *(see pages 248 and 250)*
1 quantity of **Crème Brûlée** *(see page 237)*
½ quantity of **Hazelnut and Almond Dacquoise** *(see page 233)*
½ quantity of **Genoise** *(see page 230)*
1 quantity of **Milk Chocolate Glaze** *(see page 240)*
1 quantity of **Coffee Macarons** *(see variation page 233)*
Edible gold leaf, to decorate

For the Espresso Syrup:
150ml (5fl oz/⅔ cup) strong espresso coffee
25g (1oz) caster (superfine) sugar
60ml (2fl oz/¼ cup) brandy

For the Coffee and Gianduja Mousse (anglaise method):
110ml (4fl oz/scant ½ cup) milk
470ml (15fl oz/scant 2 cups) whipping (pouring) cream
10g (¼oz/2 teaspoons) fresh ground coffee
2g (⅛oz) leaf gelatine
40g (1½oz) egg yolks (about 2 eggs)
25g (1oz) caster (superfine) sugar
300g (10½oz) gianduja, finely chopped
100g (3½oz) dark (bittersweet) chocolate (70% cocoa solids), finely chopped

You will also need:
• *22 x 28cm (8½ x 11 inch) silicone baking mat with sides*
• *piping (pastry) bag*
• *12mm (½ inch) nozzle (tip)*
• *two 16cm (6¼ inch) entremet rings*
• *14cm (5¼ inch) entermet ring*

First, prepare the chocolate decorations and Crème Brûlée:

1 Prepare the Chocolate Slivers, Squares and Joined-up Curls as instructed on pages 248 and 250.

2 Preheat the oven to 140°C (275°F/gas 1) and place the 22 x 28 (8½ x 11 inch) silicone baking mat with sides on a baking tray (sheet). Prepare the Crème Brûlée as instructed on page 237 and pour it into the prepared baking mat. Bake for 20–25 minutes until just set. Leave to cool, then place in the freezer for at least 2 hours.

Now, make the Dacquoise and Genoise:

3 Preheat the oven to 170°C (325°F/gas 3) and line a tray with a non-stick baking mat. Prepare the Dacquoise as instructed on page 233. Spoon the mixture into a piping (pastry) bag fitted with a 12mm (½ inch) nozzle (tip) and pipe two 15cm (6 inch) spirals onto the prepared tray. Bake for 18–20 minutes until lightly golden.

4 Increase the oven temperature to 190°C (375°F/gas 5) and prepare the Genoise as instructed on page 230. Bake for 12–15 minutes until golden brown and the sponge springs back when pressed gently.

Next, make the Espresso Syrup and the Milk Chocolate Glaze:

5 To make the syrup, prepare the espresso coffee, add the sugar and mix until fully dissolved. Leave to cool fully

before adding the brandy and store in the fridge until ready to use.

6 Prepare the Milk Chocolate Glaze as instructed on page 240.

7 Place the two 16cm (6¼ inch) entremet rings on a tray lined with silicone (baking) paper and place a Dacquoise disc into the base of each ring, trimming if necessary.

8 Take the Crème Brûlée from the freezer and de-mould from the baking mat. Cut out two 14cm (5¼ inch) discs, then place them back in the freezer. Cut out two 14cm (5¼ inch) discs from the Genoise and set aside until needed.

Prepare the Coffee and Gianduja Mousse:

9 Put the milk and 110ml (3½fl oz/scant ½ cup) of the cream in a saucepan and bring to the boil. Add the coffee, cover with cling film (plastic wrap), then leave to infuse for 30 minutes.

10 Soak the gelatine in a bowl of ice-cold water for a few minutes until soft. Squeeze the gelatine to remove any excess water.

11 Strain the coffee cream infusion, return to the saucepan and bring back to the boil. Continue to make the mousse following the instructions on page 110, then add the soaked gelatine to the custard before pouring over the chocolate and mix until fully combined. Leave to cool slightly, then fold in the cream. Use immediately.

12 Place a generous spoonful of the coffee mousse on top of the Dacquoise in the base of the entremet rings. Use a small palette knife to push the mousse up the sides.

13 Place a Genoise sponge disc on top of the mousse in each entremet ring and press gently so that it is level. Soak generously with the Espresso Syrup. Place a Crème Brûlée disc on top of each sponge. Top up the mould with the remaining mousse and level off with a palette knife. Transfer to the freezer to set for 3–4 hours.

Make the Coffee Macarons and finish:

14 Preheat the oven to 150°C (300°F/gas 2). Prepare the macaron mixture as instructed on page 233 but pipe each macaron 2cm (¾ inch) in size. Leave to dry for 20 minutes, then bake for 14–16 minutes.

15 Melt the Milk Chocolate Glaze and cool to room temperature. De-mould the frozen moka entremets and place on a wire rack. Place the glaze into a jug, cool to 32°C (90°F), then pour gently over the entremets ensuring they are covered evenly. Allow to set for 2–3 minutes, then transfer to a serving dish. Place the macarons around the sides of the entremet. Leave to defrost for at least 2–3 hours in the fridge.

16 When ready to serve, decorate with a macaron, the prepared chocolate decorations and gold leaf.

Store in the fridge until ready to serve. Best eaten the same day.

CHOCOLATE MILLEFEUILLE

The inspiration behind this dish is Pierre Hermé. He has always been very influential to me, and I was thrilled when he agreed to write the foreword to my last book Pâtisserie. I used a similar chocolate millefeuille as part of a dessert, which I prepared for 'The Culinary Olympics Germany 2004'. The Scottish team won gold, an achievement that I am still very proud of today.

Makes 12 millefeuille

1 x sheet of 2.5 x 8cm (1 x 3¼ inch) **Chocolate Rectangles** (see page 248)
12 **Chocolate Waves** (see page 248)
1 quantity of **Anglaise Chocolate Mousse** (see page 110)
1 quantity of **White Chocolate and Grand Marnier Crème Diplomat** (see variation page 235)
1 quantity of **Grand Marnier Syrup** (see variation page 238)
½ quantity of **Hazelnut Dacquoise** (see variation page 233)
½ quantity of **Alhambra Sponge** (see page 231)
Edible gold leaf, to decorate

For the Praline Feuillantine:
75g (2¾oz) milk chocolate, finely chopped
15g (½oz) cocoa butter, finely chopped
60g (2oz) **Praline Paste** (see page 242)
65g (2¼oz) feuillantine wafer, crushed

You will also need:
• piping (pastry) bags
• 8mm (⅓ inch) nozzle (tip)

1 First, make the Chocolate Rectangles and Chocolate Waves as instructed on page 248.

2 Prepare the Dark (Bittersweet) Chocolate Mousse and the Crème Diplomat as instructed on pages 000 and 235. Prepare the Grand Marnier Syrup as instructed on page 238.

3 Preheat the oven to 170°C (325°F/gas 3). Prepare the Hazelnut Dacquoise as instructed on page 233 and bake for 18–20 minutes until golden.

4 When the dacqoiuse is done, increase the oven temperature to 190°C (375°F/gas 5). Prepare the Alhambra Sponge as instructed on page 231 and bake for 8–10 minutes until the sponge springs back when gently pressed.

5 Line a tray with silicone (baking) paper. When both sponges have cooled, cut each sponge into twelve 2.5 x 8cm (1 x 3¼ inch) rectangles and place on the prepared tray.

6 Make the Praline Feuillantine by placing the chocolate and cocoa butter in a mixing bowl and melting it over a bain-marie (water bath). Mix in the Praline Paste. When fully combined, add the feuillantine wafer and mix in well. Spread the mixture on top of each dacquoise rectangle, then place in the fridge for 10 minutes to set.

7 Spoon a small quantity of Dark (Bittersweet) Chocolate Mousse into a piping (pastry) bag and snip the end to make a small hole. Remove the dacquiose and feuillantine rectangles from the fridge. Pipe a thin line of mousse along the top of the set Praline Feuillantine and place a Chocolate Rectangle on top.

8 Pipe another thin line of mousse along the top of the Chocolate Rectangle. Place the Alhambra Sponge rectangles on top and push down gently. Soak the sponge with Grand Marnier Syrup. Pipe a small line of chocolate mousse on top of the soaked sponge and place a second Chocolate Rectangle on top.

9 Spoon the Crème Diplomat into a piping (pastry) bag fitted with an 8mm (⅓ inch) nozzle (tip). Pipe 2 rows of 7 bulbs on top of each millefeuille. Place a Chocolate Rectangle on top and push down very slightly. Place in the fridge to set for at least 20 minutes.

10 Remove the millefeuille from the fridge. Use a warm spoon to quenelle the Dark (Bittersweet) Chocolate Mousse on top of each millefeuille. Finish with the Chocolate Wave and gold leaf.

Store in the fridge until ready to serve. Best eaten the same day.

CHESTNUT ROLL

Roll cake is essentially a Japanese version of a Swiss Roll (in Britain) or Roulade (in France). It was created in the French Alps during the 19th century. When it was brought to England it was christened a Swiss Roll, despite being a French creation, and has many other different names all over the world. I have visited Japan many times and have always been incredibly impressed by the quality of their pâtisserie. Roll cake has become a speciality in Japan, and chestnut is a very popular flavour to use. The Mont Blanc is another iconic pâtisserie. It celebrates the tallest mountain in the Alps so it feels fitting to combine two great pâtisserie associated with that part of world.

Makes 1 roll (serving 10)

Chocolate Copeaux, Squares and Piped Curls *(see page 250 and 248)*
Edible gold leaf, to decorate
1 quantity of **Swiss Roll Sponge**
  (see page 231)
1 quantity of **Rum Ganache**
  (see variation page 19)
1 quantity of **Crème Chantilly**
  (see page 235)
200g (7oz) shop-bought confit
  chestnuts, chopped,
  plus extra to decorate
Cocoa powder, for dusting

For the Chestnut Mousse:
5g (⅛oz) leaf gelatine
120g (4oz) unsweetened
  chestnut purée
85g (3oz) **Simple Syrup** *(see page 238)*
20ml (¾fl oz) dark rum
200ml (7fl oz/generous ¾ cup)
  double (heavy) cream, semi-whipped

You will also need:
• *piping (pastry) bags*
• *Mont Blanc nozzle (tip)*
• *D8 star nozzle (tip)*

First, make the chocolate decorations and Chestnut Mousse:

1 Prepare the Chocolate Copeaux, Squares and Piped Curls as instructed on pages 250 and 248.

2 Soak the gelatine in a bowl of ice-cold water for a few minutes until soft. Squeeze the gelatine to remove excess water. Place the chestnut purée in a saucepan with the Simple Syrup and bring to the boil. Take off the heat and add the gelatine. Mix well and pass through a fine sieve (strainer), then leave to cool to room temperature.

3 Mix in the dark rum, then fold in the cream. Place in the fridge to set for at least 2 hours.

Now, prepare the Swiss Roll Sponge and Rum Ganache:

4 Preheat the oven to 190°C (375°F/gas 5) and line a tray with a non-stick baking mat. Prepare the Swiss Roll Sponge as instructed on page 231. Use a step-palette knife to spread the mixture evenly into the prepared tray. Bake for about 12–15 minutes, until it begins to colour and the sponge springs back when gently pressed. Cover with a sheet of silicone (baking) paper and leave to cool.

5 Prepare the Rum Ganache as instructed on page 19 and leave to cool and thicken slightly for 8–10 minutes.

To assemble and finish:

6 Prepare the Crème Chantilly as instructed on page 235.

7 When cooled, turn the sponge sheet upside down onto a piece of silicone (baking) paper and trim about 1cm (½ inch) from each edge. Spread a thin layer of ganache evenly onto the sponge and leave to firm slightly for 5 minutes. Use a palette knife to spread an even layer (about 5mm/⅛ inch thick) of Crème Chantilly on top of the ganache on the sponge.

8 Place the chopped chestnuts along the edge of one length of the sponge. Starting on the side of the sponge with the chestnuts, roll the sponge into a tight spiral. Place the roll cake in the fridge to set for at least 30 minutes.

9 Spoon the Chestnut Mousse into a piping (pastry) bag fitted with a Mont Blanc nozzle (tip). Remove the roll cake from the fridge, trim the ends, then place it on a serving dish. Pipe the mousse across the roll cake, moving along the length until it is completely covered.

10 Spoon the remaining Chantilly into a piping (pastry) bag fitted with a D8 star nozzle (tip). Dust the top of the roll cake lightly with cocoa powder. Pipe a wiggle of Chantilly on the centre and decorate with glazed chestnut halves, chocolate decorations and gold leaf.

Store in the fridge until ready to serve. Best eaten the same day.

STRAWBERRY SHORTCAKE

Strawberries and cream is the ultimate British summertime treat. This dessert really is about quality of ingredients. It has maintained seasonality due to the summer being the only time of year that the flavour of the strawberries will do it justice. Rather than a bowl of whipped cream to dip whole strawberries in, I created a refined dish by sandwiching strawberries, jam and crème diplomat between two discs of crumbly pâte sablée.

Makes 8 shortcakes

8 Chocolate Hoops *(see page 250)*
I quantity of **Pâte Sablée** *(see page 229)*
I quantity of **Strawberry Jam**
 (see variation page 241)
I quantity of **Crème Diplomat**
 (see page 235)
I quantity of **Apricot Nappage**
 (see page 239)
I quantity of **Water Icing** *(see page 247)*
400g (14oz) strawberries
I quantity of **Light Fruit Nappage**
 (see page 239)

You will also need:
• *7cm (2¾ inch) fluted pastry cutter*
• *piping (pastry) bag*
• *10mm (⅓ inch) nozzle (tip)*
• *F8 star nozzle (tip)*

1 Prepare the Chocolate Hoops as instructed on page 250. Prepare the Pâte Sablée as instructed on page 229 and rest in the fridge for 2–3 hours.

2 Prepare the Strawberry Jam and the Crème Diplomat as instructed on pages 241 and 235.

3 Remove the pastry from the fridge and roll it out to 3mm (⅛ inch) thick on a lightly floured surface. Use a 7cm (2¾ inch) fluted cutter to cut out 16 discs and place them on a baking tray (sheet) lined with silicone (baking) paper. Leave to rest for 30 minutes.

4 Preheat the oven to 180°C (350°F/ gas 4). Remove the pastry discs from the fridge and bake for 10–12 minutes until golden brown. Leave to cool.

5 Increase the oven temperature to 200°C (400°F/gas 6). Prepare the Apricot Nappage and Water Icing as instructed on pages 239 and 247. Place half the cooked pastry discs on a wire rack and set aside the remaining half. Melt the Apricot Nappage and use a pastry brush to glaze the top of each disc on the wire rack.

6 Use a small palette knife to spread an even layer of Water Icing on top of each glazed disc. Place the wire rack on a baking tray (sheet) and place in the oven for 1–2 minutes. The icing will become slightly translucent and the excess icing will drip off the biscuits. Use a sharp knife to remove any drips and ensure that the sides are tidy in appearance.

7 Remove the stalks from the strawberries and trim the bases so they are all the same height. Cut each strawberry in half.

8 Spoon the Strawberry Jam into a piping (pastry) bag fitted with a 10mm (⅓ inch) nozzle (tip) and pipe a bulb of jam onto the centre of each un-iced pastry disc. Place the strawberries in a circle around the jam.

9 Spoon the prepared Crème Diplomat into a piping (pastry) bag fitted with a F8 star nozzle (tip) and pipe a tall rosette of cream in the centre of the strawberries. Melt the Light Fruit Nappage and lightly brush onto the strawberries. Place the iced lids onto each shortcake base and gently push down. Decorate with a glazed strawberry half, a Chocolate Hoop and gold leaf.

Store in the fridge until ready to serve. Best eaten the same day.

APRICOT CROUSTADE

This was one of the first pâtisserie that I sold in my boutique. The inspiration comes from my time with Pierre Koffmann at La Tante Claire, where he was famed for making his own filo pastry; a tradition that comes from Gascony, France, where he is from. Classically, a croustade is made with apples. My version is to celebrate summer, so I have used fresh seasonal fruits.
The flavour combination is delicious, but equally the colours of the apricots, cherries and pistachios are very vibrant. To have colourful pâtisserie on display in a boutique is very important for catching the eye of the customers.

Makes 8

1 quantity of **Filo Pastry** (see page 229)
Clarified butter (see page 247)
Flour, for dusting
150g (5½oz/¾ cup) **Vanilla Sugar**
  (see page 247)
1 quantity of **Cherry Jam**
  (see variation page 241)
1 quantity of **Pistachio and Kirsch**
  Frangipane (see variation page 236)
10–12 apricots
12 cherries
1 quantity of **Apricot Nappage**
  (see page 239)
50g (1¾oz) chopped pistachios

You will also need:
• *eight 7cm (2¾ inch) pomponette*
  moulds
• *piping (pastry) bag*
• *10mm (⅓ inch) nozzle (tip)*

1 Prepare the Filo Pastry as instructed on page 229 and leave to rest. Prepare the Clarified Butter as instructed on page 247 and use it to lightly grease the tart tins.

2 Line the table with a tablecloth and lightly dust with flour. Put the rested Filo Pastry in the centre of the tablecloth. Place your hands under the dough and gently begin to pull it out from underneath, going around the dough and pulling from every corner. Allow the dough to rest at intervals to let it relax, this will make it easier to pull. Continue to pull until it has reached a square measuring about 1 metre (40 inches).

3 Trim the thick edges and leave the dough to dry slightly for 5–10 minutes (how long will depend on the temperature and humidity in the room). Brush the melted Clarified Butter over the pastry, then sprinkle with the Vanilla Sugar. Cut into 7cm (2¾ inch) squares and line each mould with 3 layers in each. Leave the pastry cases to dry for 2–3 hours or ideally overnight.

4 Prepare the Cherry Jam and Pistachio and Kirsch Frangipane as instructed on pages 241 and 236.

5 When the tart cases are fully dried, stone the apricots and cherries and carefully cut them into quarters. Preheat the oven to 180°C (350°F/gas 4).

6 Spoon the frangipane into a piping (pastry) bag fitted with a 10mm (⅓ inch) nozzle (tip) and pipe a bulb about two-thirds filling each tart case. Spoon a heaped teaspoon of jam on top of each tart. Place 5–6 apricot quarters and 6 cherry quarters on top of each tart.

7 Brush the fruit with Clarified Butter and sprinkle with Vanilla Sugar. Bake for 25–30 minutes until the pastry is crisp and golden. Leave to cool before de-moulding. Brush with Apricot Nappage and sprinkle with chopped pistachios.

Best served the same day.

JAFFA CAKE TARTS

I have already featured two different versions of a jaffa cake in both my previous books. It was always one of my favourites growing up as it is such a great flavour combination. I use marmalade instead of orange jelly inside them, it gives a more intense flavour and reminds me of where I come from, where marmalade is very popular. I have already developed a bouchée and a large entremet using this flavour combination, so thought a jaffa tart would be a good addition. This take was inspired by my good friend Bruce Sangster.

Makes 12 tarts

12 **Chocolate Sticks** *(see page 250)*
1 quantity of **Marmalade**
  (see page 242)
1 quantity of **Grand Marnier Syrup**
  (see variation page 238)
1 quantity of **Chocolate Pâte Sucrée**
  (see variation page 228)
1 quantity of **Anglaise Chocolate**
  Mousse *(see page 110)*
1 quantity of **Orange Almond Cream**
  (see variation page 236)
1 quantity of **Dark (Bittersweet)**
  Chocolate Glaze *(see page 240)*
20g (¾ oz) **Dried Orange Zest**
  (see page 247)
Edible gold leaf, to decorate

For the Caramelized Oranges:
125g (4½oz/scant ⅔ cup)
  caster (superfine) sugar
50ml (2fl oz/scant ¼ cup) orange juice
  (squeezed from the leftover flesh of
  the oranges)
4 oranges, segmented

You will also need:
• *12-hole 6cm (2½ inch) mince pie tin*
• *twelve 6cm (2½ inch) tart moulds*
• *9cm (3½ inch) pastry cutter*

First, prepare the chocolate decorations, Marmalade and Grand Marnier Syrup:

1 Make the Chocolate Sticks as instructed on page 250. Then make the Marmalade and Grand Marnier Syrup as instructed on pages 242 and 238.

Next, prepare the Caramelized Oranges:

2 Put the sugar in a saucepan and make a dry amber caramel. Remove from the heat and carefully add the orange juice. Add the orange segments. Leave to marinate for about 30 minutes, then drain off any excess syrup. Set aside.

Now, prepare the Chocolate Pâte Sucrée.

3 Make the pastry as instructed on page 228 and leave to rest in the fridge for 2–3 hours.

Next, make the Anglaise Chocolate Mousse:

4 Make the mousse as instructed on page 110.

5 Line the mince pie tins with mousse and place 2–3 segments of Caramelized Orange into each. Top up with mousse and flatten with a small step-palette knife. Place in the freezer to set for at least 2 hours.

6 Roll out the rested pastry to 3mm (⅛ inch) thick on a lightly floured surface. Cut out 12 discs using a 9cm (3½ inch) cutter and carefully line the tartlet cases (see page 64). Rest for 1 hour in the fridge.

Now, make the Orange Almond Cream and finish assembling:

7 Make the cream as instructed on page 236.

8 Remove the tarts from the fridge and pipe 8–10g (¼oz) of Marmalade into the base of each one. Pipe a bulb of Orange Almond Cream on top and rest in the fridge for 30 minutes.

9 Prepare the Dark (Bittersweet) Chocolate Glaze as instructed on page 240. Leave to cool to about 30°C (86°F).

10 Preheat the oven to 180°C (350°F/gas 4). Bake the tarts for about 15 minutes. Leave them to cool, then de-mould from the tartlet case. If necessary, level the tops of the tarts using a serrated knife. Soak each tart with the prepared Grand Marnier Syrup.

11 De-mould the mousse from the mince pie moulds and place on a wire rack. Put the cooled glaze in a small jug and pour the glaze over each dome, ensuring each one is completely coated. Place them on top of each tartlet. Leave to defrost in the fridge for 20 minutes, then decorate with Dried Orange Zest, a Chocolate Stick and gold leaf to finish.

Store in the fridge until ready to serve. Best eaten the same day.

PONT NEUF

This great French classic was originally created in order to use up scraps of pastry, excess choux pastry and crème pâtisserie. Although it looks simple to make, like many classics, it is very technical so may take some practise to perfect. This pâtisserie dates back to the 'Golden Era' in French pâtisserie, and by the 1860s was being made all over France. It is named after the Pont Neuf Bridge in Paris. It is a very old tradition across much of Europe to place a cross onto a baked item as it was believed to ward off evil spirits. The Pont Neuf traditionally is red and white with a cross in the centre, to represent a mitre, the traditional bishop's hat.

Makes 10 pont neuf

1 quantity of **Rough Puff Pastry**
 (see page 67)
1 quantity of **Redcurrant Jelly**
 (see variation page 241), for glazing
½ quantity of **Choux Pastry** (see page 230)
½ quantity of **Crème Pâtissière**
 (see page 234)
25g (1oz) crème fraiche
25ml (1fl oz) rum
1 beaten egg, for brushing
Icing (powdered) sugar, for dusting

For the Apple Compote:
400g (14oz) apples
30g (1¼oz) unsalted butter
50g (1¾oz/¼ cup) caster (superfine) sugar
5ml (1 teaspoon) lemon juice
½ vanilla pod (bean), split and scraped

You will also need:
• 9cm (3½ inch) pastry cutter
• ten 7cm (2¾ inch) pomponette moulds
• piping (pastry) bags
• 12mm (½ inch) nozzles (tips)

1 Prepare the Rough Puff Pastry as instructed on page 67 and rest for 2–3 hours. Prepare the Redcurrant Jelly as instructed on page 241.

2 Make the Apple Compote. Wash, peel and core the apples. Roughly chop them and put in a saucepan with the butter, sugar, lemon juice and the vanilla seeds. Cook for 2–3 minutes, stirring occasionally. Place a lid on the saucepan and simmer over a low heat, stirring occasionally for about 10 minutes until the apples are soft.

3 Prepare the Choux Pastry as instructed on page 230 and store in the fridge until ready to use.

4 Prepare the Crème Pâtissière as instructed on page 234. Cool, and store in the fridge until ready to use.

5 Roll the Rough Puff Pastry out to 2.5mm (⅛ inch) thick on a lightly floured surface and dock (prick) all over. Rest for 30 minutes.

6 Cut a 9cm (3½ inch) square of the rolled and rested Rough Puff Pastry and place it in the fridge until ready to use (this is for the cross decoration). Use a 9cm (3½ inch) pastry cutter to cut out 10 discs from the remaining rolled out puff pastry. Line each mould (see page 64) and trim the edges. Return to the fridge to rest for a further 20 minutes.

7 Preheat the oven to 160°C (325°F/gas 3).

8 When the pastry cases are rested, spoon the apple compote into a piping (pastry) bag fitted with a 12mm (½ inch) nozzle (tip) and pipe the compote into the tart until one-third full.

9 Beat together 150g (5½oz) of the prepared Choux Pastry and 150g (5½oz) of the Crème Pâtissière. Add the crème fraiche and rum and mix well. Spoon into a piping (pastry) bag fitted with a 12mm (½ inch) nozzle (tip) and pipe on top of the compote in the tarts to four-fifths full.

10 Remove the square of puff pastry from the fridge and cut into strips 3mm (⅛ inch) wide. Place the strips in a cross shape on top of each tart and trim the excess pastry. Lightly egg wash the pastry cross and bake for 30–35 minutes until the tops are golden brown. If the tops colour before the tarts are fully cooked, place a sheet of tin foil over them to prevent further colouration while they continue to cook.

11 Leave to cool fully before de-moulding the Pont Neuf from the tart cases. Dust 2 opposite corners liberally with icing (powdered) sugar and use a dry brush to remove the sugar that has fallen on the other two corners. Boil the prepared Redcurrant Jelly and use a small brush to coat the 2 undusted corners of the Pont Neuf with the jelly.

Best served the same day.

This section embodies two very different
nostalgic experiences for me.

While growing up, the sound of the ice cream van always signified
the beginning of summer. I lived by the sea so even if the weather
wasn't hot, a scoop of milk ice cream with a cone and flake, while
sitting watching the sea with my sister Karen was just magic.

ICE CREAM &
Gateau

For me, this part of the book also represents a very different type
of nostalgia – decadent ice cream gateau served at banquets and in
grand hotels. It has gone out of fashion to serve these type of dishes
now, but I think they are timeless, skilled and delicious.

It makes me think of the 'Golden Era' and the way in which pâtissiers
tested their limits and evolved their skills to such a degree
that we still rely on their knowledge today.

ICE CREAM ANGLAISE

Crème anglaise is the base for all traditionally made ice cream. Once this method is mastered, the flavour combinations you can create are limitless.

Makes 700ml (1½ pints/3 cups)

For Vanilla Ice Cream Anglaise:
400ml (14fl oz/1¾ cups) milk
100ml (3½fl oz/scant ½ cup)
  whipping (pouring) cream
1 vanilla pod (bean), split lengthways
120g (4oz) egg yolks (about 6 eggs)
100g (3½oz/½ cup)
  caster (superfine) sugar

For Chocolate Ice Cream Anglaise:
500ml (18fl oz/ generous 2 cups) milk
100ml (3½fl oz/scant ½ cup)
  whipping (pouring) cream
120g (4oz) egg yolks (about 6 eggs)
85g (3oz/scant ½ cup)
  caster (superfine) sugar
50g (1¾oz/scant ½ cup) cocoa powder
75g (2¾oz) dark (bittersweet) chocolate
  (63% cocoa solids), chopped

For Strawberry Ice Cream Anglaise:
250ml (8½fl oz/1 cup) milk
250ml (8½fl oz/1 cup) whipping cream
120g (4oz) egg yolks (about 6 eggs)
100g (3½oz/½ cup)
  caster (superfine) sugar
300g (10½oz) strawberry purée
10ml (2 teaspoons) lemon juice

For Mint Ice Cream Anglaise:
400ml (14fl oz/1¾ cups) milk
100ml (3½fl oz/scant ½ cup)
  whipping (pouring) cream
20g (¾oz) fresh mint
120g (4oz) egg yolks (about 6 eggs)
100g (3½oz/½ cup)
  caster (superfine) sugar

Note: *An ice bain-marie (water bath) is used to rapidly cool a custard or cream. It can be made by putting ice into a bowl or tray and placing a smaller container in the centre, filled with the custard or cream that needs to be cooled.*

1 Prepare an ice bain-marie (water bath). Put the milk and cream in a saucepan. Scrape the vanilla seeds into the saucepan and drop in the split pod (bean) too. Bring to a simmer.

2 Meanwhile, beat together the egg yolks and sugar until the mixture is light in colour.

3 Pour one-third of the hot liquid – make sure it is not boiling – onto the egg yolks and sugar. Whisk until the milk is fully incorporated.

4 Return the mixture to the saucepan and place over a low heat. Stir continuously with a spatula until the mixture thickens, coats the back of the spoon and reaches a temperature of 82–84°C (180–183°F).

5 Take the custard off the heat and pass through a fine sieve (strainer) into a bowl in the ice bain-marie (water bath) to cool rapidly. Place the vanilla pod (bean) back into the anglaise to continue infusing as it cools.

Store in an airtight container in the fridge and use within 2 days.

For the Chocolate Anglaise: whisk the cocoa powder with the egg yolks and sugar. When the anglaise is cooked, mix with the chocolate, before straining into the bowl in the ice bain-marie.

For the Strawberry Anglaise: add the strawberry purée and lemon juice once the anglaise has cooled. Mix well.

For the Mint Anglaise: boil the milk and cream, add the mint, cover and leave in the fridge to infuse for 2 hours. Strain, reweigh and continue as above.

CHURNING ICE CREAM

1 Once the ice cream anglaise has matured in the fridge for at least 4 hours, place into the canister of an ice cream machine. The length of time it takes to fully churn will vary depending on the individual ice cream machine used. When ready, the ice cream will appear light in colour and texture, and will hold its shape when scooped. Return to the freezer until ready to use. Alternatively, pour the matured anglaise into a pacojet canister and freeze overnight. Churn when required.

Store in an airtight container in the freezer. Best served the same day but can be stored for up to 2 weeks.

MILK ICE CREAM

Makes about 1kg (2¼lb)

800ml (28fl oz/scant 3⅓ cups) milk
75g (2¾oz/generous ⅓ cup) caster (superfine) sugar
½ vanilla pod (bean), split and scraped
100ml (3½fl oz/⅓ cup) condensed milk
25g (1oz) liquid glucose

1 Place the milk, sugar and vanilla seeds and scraped pod (bean) into a saucepan and cook over a low heat until the weight of the mixture reduces to 500g (1lb 2oz).

2 Add the condensed milk and glucose to the reduced mixture and continue to cook over a low heat until fully dissolved.

3 Bring to the boil, then remove from the heat. Pass through a fine sieve (strainer). then leave to cool.

4 Churn the mixture into ice cream.

Store in an airtight container in the freezer. Best served the same day but can be stored for up to 2 weeks.

FRUIT SORBET

Sorbets are very simple to make. Traditionally they are just made from fruit purée mixed with a sugar syrup, then churned. Unusual flavours can be created by infusing herbs and spices into the mixture, or for a bit of extra decadence, alcoholic beverages can be added such as liqueurs, champagne or whisky.

....

Makes about 850g (1lb 13oz)

120ml (4¼fl oz) **Simple Syrup** *(see page 238)*
750g (1lb 10oz) fruit purée

1 Make the Simple Syrup as instructed on page 238.

2 Whisk together the raspberry purée with the syrup.

3 Churn the mixture in an ice cream machine.

Store in an airtight container in the freezer. Best served the same day but can be stored for up to 2 weeks.

2

RASPBERRY RIPPLE

During the end of the 19th Century, ice cream became very popular in Scotland. This was due to an influx of Italian immigrants setting up ice cream parlours, particularly in Glasgow. Many of the original parlours remain to this day, often in very elaborate Art Deco buildings. Many years ago, a Clyde FC football fan called McCallum was in his local ice cream parlour enjoying a portion of vanilla ice cream. He then requested some raspberry sauce to squeeze over the ice cream to create the colours of his favourite football team. He asked the ice cream maker to add it to the menu as a way to advertise Clyde FC. It became a rather popular dish and was christened a 'McCallum'. Classically, it was two balls of vanilla ice cream, with raspberry sauce drizzled over and a wafer in the centre. Over time, it evolved to become 'Raspberry Ripple', now an international favourite. Not many people know the humble origins, but in Scotland, you can still ask for a 'McCallum' in the old Italian ice cream parlours of Glasgow.

....

Makes about 800g (1lb 12oz)

600g (1lb 6oz) churned **Vanilla Ice Cream Anglaise**
 (see page 152)
200g (7oz) **Raspberry Sorbet** *(see opposite)*

You will also need:
• *piping (pastry) bag*
• *10mm (⅓ inch) nozzle (tip)*

1 Prepare and churn the ice cream as instructed on pages 152–3 and the sorbet as instructed opposite. Place the churned ice cream into a bowl.

2 Spoon the churned Raspberry Sorbet into a piping (pastry) bag fitted with a 10mm (⅓ inch) nozzle (tip). Pipe the sorbet into the ice cream.

3 Use a spatula to swirl the sorbet through the ice cream.

Store in an airtight container in the freezer. Best served the same day but can be stored for up to 2 weeks.

1

2

3

3

NEAPOLITAN BAKED ALASKA

China was the first culture to develop a hot ice cream dessert, which dates back to over a thousand years ago. It wasn't until the 1860s that a Parisian chef adapted this ancient concept by covering ice cream in meringue and baking it briefly in a hot oven. The French dish was christened Omelette Norvegienne, as Norway was considered 'The Land Of Snow'. I have always known the dish as 'Baked Alaska', which is the American name for it due to the white meringue bombe shape reflecting the image of the igloos that the Alaskan Inuits lived in. The Neapolitan filling is an ice cream combination created by an Italian confectioner called Tortoni at the beginning of the 19th century. He named it after the city of Naples. I often served Baked Alaska at banquets at The Savoy Hotel – it always looked very fitting in the grand surroundings of the hotel.

Makes 1 Alaska (serving 8)

1 quantity of **Chocolate Ice Cream Anglaise** *(see page 152)*

1 quantity of **Vanilla Ice Cream Anglaise** *(see page 152)*

1 quantity of **Strawberry Ice Cream Anglaise** *(see page 152)*

1 quantity of **Grand Marnier Syrup** *(see variation page 239)*

1 quantity of **Swiss Roll Sponge** *(see page 231)*

1 quantity of **Italian Meringue** *(see page 232)*

You will also need:
- *16cm (6¼ inch) half-sphere dome mould*
- *14cm (5½ inch) mousse ring*
- *piping (pastry) bag*
- *D6 star nozzle (tip)*
- *blowtorch*

1 Prepare each ice cream as instructed on page 152. Leave in the fridge for 4 hours to thicken.

2 Prepare the Grand Marnier Syrup and the Swiss Roll Sponge following the instructions on pages 239 and 231.

3 Line the dome mould with cling film (plastic wrap). Place a mousse ring on a tray and the dome mould onto the ring so that it doesn't wobble.

4 Cut a 14cm (5½ inch) disc of sponge and set it to one side until ready to use. This will be the base.

5 To line the mould, cut a 14cm (5½ inch) disc of the prepared sponge and place it in the centre of the dome mould. Cut two 22.5 x 5cm (8½ x 2 inch) rectangles of sponge. Place both rectangles in the dome so that the sides are fully lined with sponge, then trim any excess. Lightly soak the sponge with the prepared Grand Marnier Syrup.

6 Churn the Strawberry Ice Cream Anglaise, then spoon enough of it into the lined dome mould to fill the bottom third. Level with a small palette knife and place in the freezer to set for at least 30 minutes.

7 Repeat this process with the Vanilla Ice Cream Anglaise, filling the mould another third full and leave to set for at least 30 minutes.

8 Lastly, repeat with the Chocolate Ice Cream Anglaise. Fill the mould almost to the top, but leave a 1cm (½ inch) gap.

9 Lightly soak the prepared base disc of sponge with Grand Marnier Syrup and position it on top of the chocolate layer. It should be level, so that when the dome is later de-moulded it has a flat base. Place the full dome in the freezer for at least 2–3 hours until fully frozen.

10 Prepare the Italian Meringue following the instructions on page 232.

11 Remove the dome from the freezer and de-mould onto a serving plate. Remove the cling film (plastic wrap). Use a small palette knife to coat the dome with the prepared meringue and spread in an upward motion to create a lined pattern, fully coating the dome as you go.

12 Spoon the remaining meringue into a piping (pastry) bag fitted with a D6 star nozzle (tip). Pipe rosettes along the base and decorate the top with a swirl of meringue. Blowtorch all over until it begins to turn golden. Alternatively, bake in an oven preheated to 220°C (425°F/gas 7) for 2–3 minutes until golden.

Serve immediately.

PRALINE VIENNETTA

I based this ice cream gateau on the popular retro dessert, Viennetta, as I love the texture created by the thin sheets of chocolate layered through the ice cream. Although Viennetta has only been around since the 1980s, the ice cream gateau has a long history dating back to the 17th century, and in the 1920s it became a very fashionable dish to serve during extravagant banquets in grand hotels. As an apprentice working under Ian Ironside, I was introduced to the art of iced desserts. Ian was a master of his craft and passed his passion on with great enthusiasm in training the next generation.

Makes 1 Viennetta (serving 8–10)

Chocolate Squares and Piped Curls
  (see pages 248 and 250)
1 quantity of **Chocolate Ice Cream Anglaise** *(see page 152)*
300g (10½oz) tempered dark (bittersweet) chocolate (70% cocoa solids) *(see page 14)*
½ quantity of **Caramelized Hazelnuts** *(see variation page 243)*
½ quantity of **Hazelnut and Almond Dacquoise** *(see page 233)*
1 quantity of **Crème Chantilly** *(see page 235)*
Cocoa powder, for dusting
Edible gold leaf, to decorate

For the Praline Ice Cream:
1 quantity of **Vanilla Ice Cream Anglaise** *(see page 152)*, but omitting the vanilla
150g (5½oz) **Praline Paste** *(see page 242)*

You will also need:
• *21 x 10.5 x 6cm (8¼ x 4 x 2½ inch) cake tin*
• *piping (pastry) bags*
• *12mm (½ inch) nozzle (tip)*
• *St Honore nozzle (tip)*

1 Prepare the Chocolate Squares and Piped Curls chocolate decorations as instructed on pages 248 and 250. Leave to set in a cool, dry area for 1–2 hours.

2 Make the Chocolate Ice Cream Anglaise as instructed on page 152 and leave it in the fridge to thicken for 4 hours.

3 To make the Praline Ice Cream, use the ingredients to make a Vanilla Ice Cream Anglaise as instructed on page 152, then stir the praline paste through the prepared base mixture. Mix it in well, then leave to thicken in the fridge for 4 hours.

4 Put the cake tin on a tray in the freezer until needed.

5 Temper the chocolate and prepare the chocolate sheets. Following the instructions on page 248, make eight 17 x 8 cm (6½ x 3¼ inch) rectangles, then leave to set in a cool dry area.

6 Prepare the Caramelized Hazelnuts as instructed on page 243 and leave to cool. Reserve 6 Caramelized Hazelnuts for decoration and then once cool, finely chop the remaining nuts. Store in an airtight container.

7 Churn the thickened Chocolate Ice Cream Anglaise in an ice cream maker. Remove the prepared tin from the freezer and use a palette knife to line the sides and base with chocolate ice cream. Return to the freezer for 30 minutes until the ice cream firms up.

8 Churn the Praline Ice Cream and fold the chopped nuts through.

9 Remove the lined tin from the freezer. Spoon the Praline Ice Cream into a piping (pastry) bag fitted with a 12mm (½ inch) nozzle (tip). Pipe a thin layer into the tin and place the first chocolate rectangle on top. Repeat this process again 7 times until the tin is full. Return to the freezer for at least 2 hours to firm.

10 Preheat the oven to 170°C (325°F/gas 3). Prepare the Hazelnut and Almond Dacquoise as instructed on page 233. Once cool, cut into a 21 x 11cm (8¼ x 4¼ inch) rectangle.

11 Prepare the Crème Chantilly and spoon it into a piping (pastry) bag fitted with a St Honore nozzle (tip).

12 To serve, place the dacquoise on a serving dish. De-mould the viennetta by dipping the base and the sides in warm water, then carefully sliding it out of the tin. Immediately place it on the prepared dacquoise. Pipe a wiggle of Crème Chantilly along the centre of the viennetta. Dust lightly with cocoa powder and decorate with Caramelized Hazelnuts, Chocolate Squares, Piped Curls and gold leaf.

Serve immediately.

ICE CREAM SANDWICH

This dish will always remind me of my childhood family holidays to 'The Transport and General Workers Centre' in Eastbourne. As a docker, my father adored visiting there as not only could he catch up with colleagues from all over the country, he could also be sure to get his full English breakfast, a decent pint and his daily bet. My mother loved the centre for the nightly dinner dance and, of course, the sunshine – Eastbourne has long been known as the sunniest town in Britain. The ice cream sandwich was both of my parents favourite. The classic is made with wafer, mallow, chocolate and ice cream – a clever combination. I have used macarons to maintain the diversity of textures, combined with truly nostalgic ice cream flavours – Rum and Raisin and Mint Choc Chip.

Makes 18 of each flavour

1 quantity of **Dark (Bittersweet) Chocolate Macarons** *(see page 233)*
1 quantity of **Milk Chocolate Macarons** *(see variation page 233)*
Cocoa nibs, for sprinkling
Feuillantine wafer, crushed, for sprinkling
300g (10½oz) tempered dark (bittersweet) chocolate (66% cocoa solids) *(see page 14)*
300g (10½oz) tempered milk chocolate *(see page 15)*

For the Rum and Raisin Ice Cream:
150g (5½oz) Rum-soaked Raisins *(see variation page 244)*
1 quantity of **Vanilla Ice Cream Anglaise** *(see page 152)*, but omitting the vanilla
60ml (2fl oz/¼ cup) dark rum

For the Mint Choc Chip Ice Cream:
1 quantity of **Mint Ice Cream Anglaise** *(see page 152)*
150g (5½oz) dark (bittersweet) chocolate chips (these can be either be finely chopped (70% cocoa solids) chocolate or piped with tempered chocolate)

You will also need:
• *thirty-six 6cm (2½ inch) metal rings*
• *piping (pastry) bags*
• *10mm (⅓ inch) nozzle (tip)*

1 First, prepare the Rum-soaked Raisins as instructed on page 244.

2 Next, make the Rum and Raisin Ice Cream base by making the Vanilla Ice Cream Anglaise as instructed on page 152 without adding the vanilla pod (bean). When the base has cooled, add the rum and leave the mixture in the fridge for 4 hours to thicken.

3 Then, make the Mint Chop Chip Ice Cream by making the Mint Ice Cream Anglaise as instructed on page 152 and leave the mixture in the fridge for 4 hours to thicken.

4 Line 2 trays with silicone (baking) paper, place eighteen 6cm (2½ inch) metal rings on each tray and put in the freezer until ready to use.

5 When the two anglaise have thickened in the fridge, churn the rum mixture in an ice cream maker, add the Rum-soaked Raisins, then mix until the raisins are evenly dispersed. Remove one of the trays from the freezer and fill each ring with the Rum and Raisin Ice Cream, using a small step-palette knife to level the top of each. Return to the freezer for at least 2–3 hours.

6 Churn the mint mixture in an ice cream maker, add the chocolate chips and mix until evenly dispersed. Remove the unused tray from the freezer and fill each ring with the Mint Choc Chip Ice Cream, using a small step-palette knife to level the tops.

Return the tray to the freezer for at least 2–3 hours.

7 Preheat the oven to 150°C (300°F/gas 2) and line a baking tray (sheet) with a non-stick baking mat. Spoon the two different macaron mixtures into a piping (pastry) bag each fitted with a 10mm (⅓ inch) nozzle (tip). Pipe an even number of 5cm (2 inch) bulbs (they will spread slightly as they cook) on the baking tray (sheet) – you will need a total of 36 of each flavour to make 18 sandwiched macarons. Sprinkle half the dark chocolate macarons with cocoa nibs and half the milk chocolate macarons with feuillantine wafer to make the macaron lids. Leave the macarons to dry out for 30 minutes, then bake for 20–25 minutes.

8 Temper both chocolates. When the macarons are fully cooled, dip the base of each Milk Chocolate Macaron into tempered milk chocolate and dip the base of each Dark (Bittersweet) Chocolate Macaron into tempered dark (bittersweet) chocolate. Leave to set in a cool, dry area for 1 hour.

9 Before serving, de-mould the ice cream discs. Sandwich the Rum and Raisin Ice Cream discs between the Milk Chocolate Macarons. Sandwich the Mint Choc Chip Ice Cream discs between the Dark (Bittersweet) Chocolate Macarons.

Serve immediately.

BOUNTY ICE CREAM BAR

'A taste of paradise.' The bounty bar itself dates back to 1951 in Britain. Growing up it was one of my favourites, and I still love the simplicity of the flavour combination. My mum would buy it for me and my sister to share, as there were two bars in a pack. As the elder sibling, I would always eat mine fast to try to pinch some of my sister's. I did a take on this confection in my first book, Couture Chocolate, *but I think this iced version is even better. I add freshly grated coconut to the ice cream to make it extra special.*

Makes 16 bars

1 quantity of **Strawberry Ice Cream Anglaise** *(see page 152)*, but replace the strawberry purée with the same amount of coconut purée
½ a fresh coconut, grated
500g (1lb 2oz) **tempered dark (bittersweet) chocolate (65% cocoa solids)** *(see page 14)*
500g (1lb 2oz) **tempered milk chocolate** *(see page 15)*

You will also need:
• *two 8.4 x 2.6 x 2cm (3¼ x 1 x ¾ inch) bar moulds*
• *piping (pastry) bag*
• *12mm (½ inch) nozzle (tip)*

1 Prepare the coconut ice cream by making the Strawberry Ice Cream Anglaise as instructed on page 152, but replace the strawberry purée with coconut purée. Place the anglaise in the fridge to thicken for 4 hours.

2 Temper both chocolates. Line one of the bar moulds in tempered dark (bittersweet) chocolate and the other in milk chocolate as instructed on page 16. Leave to set in a cool, dry area for 1 hour.

3 When the anglaise has thickened, churn it in an ice cream maker. Mix in the grated coconut. Spoon the prepared ice cream into a piping (pastry) bag fitted with a 12mm (½ inch) nozzle (tip). Pipe the ice cream into each bar mould until four-fifths full. Use a small step-palette knife to level the ice cream. Return to the freezer to set for at least 30 minutes.

4 Temper both chocolates. When the ice cream is fully frozen, cap the moulds with tempered dark (bittersweet) and milk chocolate. This technique has to be done quickly as the chocolate sets very fast on the frozen bar moulds. Return to the freezer to set for at least 2 hours.

5 To serve, de-mould and place on serving dishes.

Serve immediately.

RHUBARB MIVVI

While I was growing up during the 1970s and 80s, the creativity of the ice cream industry was at its peak. I have fond memories of the sound of the ice cream van arriving and expectantly queuing for my strawberry mivvi lolly. I have used rhubarb instead of strawberry to flavour my version of this classic ice lolly. As a child I would sometimes be given a stick of rhubarb dipped in sugar so the flavour always takes me back to those days.

Makes 12 mivvi

1 quantity of **Milk Ice Cream**
(see page 153)
1 quantity of **Fruit Sorbet** (see page 154),
made with rhubarb purée
1 quantity of **Pain de Gène**
(see page 231)
400g (14oz) fresh rhubarb
1 quantity of **Crème Diplomat**
(see page 235)
1 quantity of **Light Syrup**
(see page 239)
Edible gold leaf, to decorate

You will also need:
• *twelve 5cm (2 inch) dome moulds*
• *twelve 7cm (2¾ inch) dome moulds*
• *twelve 5cm (2 inch) metal rings*
• *piping (pastry) bag*
• *7mm (¼ inch) plain nozzle (tip)*

First, make the Milk Ice Cream:

1 Put the 5cm (2 inch) dome moulds on a tray and place in the freezer. Line a tray with silicone (baking) paper and place in the freezer.

2 Prepare the Milk Ice Cream as instructed on page 153. When the Milk Ice Cream has cooled, churn in an ice cream maker. Remove the prepared tray from the freezer and spoon the milk ice cream into each dome. Use a small palette knife to push the ice cream into the sides of the dome mould and level the tops of each. Place in the freezer to set for 2 hours.

3 Place the 7cm (2¾ inch) dome moulds onto a tray in the freezer.

4 When the ice cream domes are fully frozen, de-mould them and put them on the prepared tray from the freezer, then return to the freezer.

Next, make the Rhubarb Sorbet:

5 Make the Rhubarb Sorbet as instructed on page 154 and churn in an ice cream maker. Remove one of the 7cm (2¾ inch) dome moulds from the freezer, hold it with a tea towel to prevent warming it, and use a palette knife to line it with about 50g (1¾oz) Rhubarb Sorbet. Place a dome of ice cream into the sorbet and use more sorbet to level the dome, so that the ice cream is completely encased in sorbet. Return it to the tray and place in the freezer.

6 Repeat this process until each dome is filled. Leave the domes in the freezer for at least 1–2 hours or until ready to serve.

Now, make the rhubarb tuile hoops and prepare the Pain de Gène:

7 Prepare the tuile hoops. Grease twelve 5cm (2 inch) metal rings and place them on a baking tray (sheet). Use a peeler to peel strips from 200g (7oz) of the fresh rhubarb. Cut each strip into 17cm (6½ inch) pieces and place each one around the prepared metal ring so that the ends overlap

slightly. Place in a dehydrator at 60°C (140°F) for 4 hours. Alternatively, you can use an oven preheated to its lowest setting – this may take less time to dry. Store in an airtight container until ready to use.

8 Prepare the Pain de Gène as instructed on page 231. Leave to cool, then cut into 7cm (2¾ inch) discs.

Finally, make the Crème Diplomat, assemble and serve:

9 Prepare the Crème Diplomat as instructed on page 235 and store in the fridge until ready to use.

10 Cut a stick of the remaining rhubarb diagonally into 1.5cm (¾ inch) pieces. Poach for 10 seconds in the Light Syrup, then leave to cool and strain, reserving the syrup.

11 To serve, soak each sponge disc with the reserved syrup and place on the base of each frozen dome. De-mould each dome and place on individual serving dishes. Spoon the prepared Crème Diplomat into a piping (pastry) bag fitted with a 7mm (¼ inch) plain nozzle (tip). Pipe bulbs of Crème Diplomat around each dome. Decorate with rhubarb tuile hoops, a piece of poached rhubarb and some gold leaf.

Serve immediately.

JELLY & ICE CREAM

While I was growing up this was a favourite dessert at children's parties, and still is to this day. It is such a nostalgic combination. My young daughter, Amy Rose, has already developed a fascination for different flavours and textures. It is in many ways an unusual combination of textures, but for some reason it really does work! This dish is a grown-up version, using the most sophisticated ingredients – Champagne, vanilla and strawberries.

Makes 8 glasses

1 quantity of **Vanilla Ice Cream Anglaise**
  (see page 152)
1 quantity of **Panna Cotta** *(see page 238)*
1 quantity of **Champagne Jelly**
  (see page 237)
200g (7oz) strawberries, hulled
8 **Joined-up Chocolate Curves**
  (see page 250)
Edible silver leaf, to decorate

For the Strawberry Tuile Baskets:
40g (1½oz) caster (superfine) sugar
10g (¼oz) pectin
120g (4oz) strawberry purée

For the strawberry jelly:
200g (7oz) strawberry purée
20g (¾oz) sugar
40ml (1½fl oz) water
2.5g (½ teaspoon) leaf gelatine

You will also need:
• 5cm (2 inch) pastry cutter
• sixteen 6cm (2½ inch) fluted tart cases
• 8 Martini glasses

First, make the Vanilla Ice Cream Anglaise:

1 Make the Vanilla Ice Cream Anglaise as instructed on page 152. Leave in the fridge to thicken for 4 hours, then churn in an ice cream maker. Store the ice cream in a container and place in the freezer until ready to use.

Now, make the Strawberry Tuile Baskets:

2 Line a 30 x 40cm (12 x 16 inch) tray with a non-stick baking mat. Mix the sugar and pectin together in a small bowl. Put the strawberry purée in a saucepan and bring to the boil. Take off the heat and whisk in the sugar and pectin. Return to the heat and bring back to the boil, stirring continuously. Cook for 1 minute, then take off the heat.

3 Use a step-palette knife to spread out thinly on the prepared tray. Place in an oven preheated to its lowest setting for about 30 minutes.

4 When the tuile has dried enough to hold its shape, but still remains flexible, use a 5cm (2 inch) pastry cutter to cut out 8 discs. If the tuile is too dry to be flexible, leave it out at room temperature for 30 minutes and it will become flexible again.

5 Put each disc in a fluted tart case and put another tart case into it. Push gently so that the tuile fills the fluted shape. Place in a dehydrator at 60°C (140°F) for 4 hours. Alternatively, you can use an oven preheated to its lowest setting – this may take less time to dry. Store in an airtight container until ready to use.

Now, make the Strawberry Jelly:

6 Set the Martini glasses at an angle on a tray. Prepare the strawberry jelly following the method for Flavoured Jelly on page 237, substituting the Champagne for strawberry purée. Carefully spoon 20g (¾oz) of jelly into the base of each glass, then transfer to the fridge to set for 30 minutes.

7 Make the Panna Cotta as instructed on page 238. When the Strawberry Jelly has fully set, remove the glasses from the fridge and place upright on a tray. Spoon the Panna Cotta into each glass until it is level with the tip of the strawberry jelly and return to the fridge to set for 30 minutes.

8 Pour a thin layer of Champagne Jelly into the martini glasses.

To finish:

9 Cut the strawberries into sixths and place on top of the Champagne Jelly. Return the glasses to the fridge to allow the jelly to set. When the first layer of Champagne Jelly is fully set, pour in another layer until the strawberries are covered. Place the glasses in the fridge to set for at least 1 hour.

10 To serve, remove the prepared Martini glasses from the fridge and place a tuile basket onto the centre of each. Use an ice cream scoop to place a ball of ice cream into the basket of each dessert. Finish with a Joined-up Chocolate Curve and silver leaf.

Serve immediately.

PRUNE & ARMAGNAC ICE CREAM

*This has to be my favourite ice cream, and I am sure Pierre Koffmann would agree.
He always had this on the menu at La Tante Claire. He taught me that the key to this dish is
marinating the prunes for a long time, and serving a generous helping with lashings of Armagnac
– the more the merrier! The generosity of Pierre's food is not only due to his personality, but also
a reflection of where he comes from; Tarbes in the heartland of South West France.
I adore the Basque region – the rawness of the landscape reminds me of Scotland,
and its food and culture has helped shape my career.*

Makes 8 portions

I quantity of **Marinated Prunes**
 (see page 244)
I quantity of **Vanilla Ice Cream Anglaise**
 (see page 152)
60ml (2¼fl oz/¼ cup) Armagnac

For the Chocolate Tuile:
*Makes two 30 x 40cm (12 x 16 inch)
 baking trays (sheets)
40g (1½oz/⅓ cup)
 plain (all-purpose) flour
7g (¼oz) cocoa powder
150g (5½oz/¾ cup)
 caster (superfine) sugar
Ig (a pinch) pectin
60ml (2fl oz/¼ cup) full-fat milk
50g (1¾oz/3½ tablespoons)
 unsalted butter

The day before, prepare the Marinated Prunes:

I Prepare the Marinated Prunes as instructed on page 244 and leave to marinate for at least 24 hours.

The next day, make the Chocolate Tuile:

2 Preheat the oven to 180°C (350°F/gas 4).

3 Sift the flour and cocoa powder together in a bowl. Mix 30g (1¼oz) of the sugar and the pectin together in another bowl.

4 Put the milk, butter and the remaining sugar in a saucepan and bring to the boil. Add the pectin and sugar mixture and cook for 2 minutes, stirring continuously. Take off the heat and add the dry ingredients. Mix until smooth.

5 Spread the mixture out thinly on a baking tray (sheet) lined with a non-stick baking mat. Place another non-stick baking mat on top, then bake for 8–10 minutes. Leave to cool, then carefully remove the baking mat. Store in an airtight container until ready to use.

Next, prepare the Vanilla Ice Cream Anglaise:

6 Prepare the the Vanilla Ice Cream Anglaise as instructed on page 152. When the anglaise has cooled, add the Armagnac and mix well. Return to the fridge to thicken for 4 hours.

To assemble and serve:

7 Strain 200g (7oz) of the Marinated Prunes, reserving the excess syrup. Put the excess syrup in a saucepan and boil to reduce by half, until thickened. Cool the thickened syrup and store in the fridge until ready to use. Roughly chop the strained prunes.

8 When the prepared anglaise has thickened, churn in an ice cream maker, then mix in the chopped prunes. Store the ice cream in a container and place in the freezer until ready to use.

9 To serve, use an ice cream scoop to ball the ice cream into serving glasses. Decorate with the prepared chocolate tuile and pour the syrup over each serving.

Serve immediately.

For many people, cakes and biscuits embrace home cooking and
evoke memories of time spent with family baking together.

For me, it was my granny who taught me how to bake.
She has always been my inspiration and one of the main reasons
I became a chef. I would spend Sunday with her helping to prepare
high tea for the afternoon.

AFTERNOON *Treats*

Empire biscuits, Viennese whirls and lemon cake
were a few of my favourites.

Even with all the decadence and luxury within my industry, you can't
beat a freshly baked homemade cake for a tasty afternoon treat.

CHOCOLATE & PRALINE MARBLE CAKE

Everyone loves chocolate cake. My taste buds have somewhat evolved since the days of scoffing gooey chocolate fudge cake and getting as much on my face as in my belly, so I have created a chocolate marble cake with praline and a crunchy dacquiose topping.

Makes 3 cakes (each serving 4)

140g (5oz/⅔ cup/1¼ sticks) unsalted butter, plus extra for greasing
150g (5½oz) whole eggs (about 3 eggs)
140g (5oz/scant ¾ cup) caster (superfine) sugar
15g (½oz) invert sugar
190g (6½oz/scant 1½ cups) plain (all-purpose) flour
1.5g (a pinch) baking powder
25ml (1fl oz) whipping (pouring) cream
90g (3¼oz) **Praline Paste** (see page 242)
10g (¼oz) cocoa powder
60g (2oz/scant ½ cup) hazelnuts, chopped and lightly roasted

For the Dacquoise Topping:

20g (¾oz) icing (powdered) sugar
20g (¾oz) cornflour (cornstarch)
10g (¼oz) cocoa powder
80g (3oz/¾ cup) ground almonds
100g (3½oz) egg whites (about 3–4 eggs)
70g (2¾oz/⅓ cup) caster (superfine) sugar

You will also need:
• *three 14 x 7 x 5cm (6¼ x 2¾ x 2 inch) cake tins*
• *piping (pastry) bags*
• *12mm (½ inch) nozzle (tip)*

First, prepare the cake mixture:

1 Grease the cake tins with a small amount of softened butter, line each one with silicone (baking) paper and put them on a baking tray (sheet). Preheat the oven to 170°C (325°F/ gas 3).

2 Melt the butter in a saucepan and leave to cool.

3 Put the egg, sugar and invert sugar in a clean sterilized bowl and whisk over a bain-marie (water bath) until it reaches 30°C (86°F) and the sugar has dissolved.

4 Sieve together the flour and baking powder twice into a bowl, then fold it into the egg mix.

5 Mix the cream and Praline Paste together in a separate bowl until fully combined, then add to the cake mixture. Lastly, mix in the melted butter.

6 Put one-third (about 220g/8oz) of the mixture in a separate bowl and mix the sieved cocoa powder into this smaller amount of cake mixture.

7 Spoon the praline cake mixture into the prepared tins so that it is evenly divided. Spoon the chocolate mixture into a piping (pastry) bag and snip the end to make a small hole. Pipe one-third of the mixture in a line in the centre of each cake, then use a small knife to create a marble effect by swirling the mixtures together.

8 Sprinkle a third of the hazelnuts on to the top of each cake.

Next, prepare the Dacquoise Topping:

9 Sieve together the icing (powdered) sugar, cornflour (cornstarch) and cocoa powder and mix with the ground almonds in a bowl.

10 Whisk the egg white in a clean bowl and gradually add the caster (superfine) sugar until soft peaks form. Fold the dry ingredients into the meringue.

11 Spoon the mixture into a piping (pastry) bag fitted with a 12mm (½ inch) nozzle (tip) and pipe 10 bulbs onto the top of each cake. Lightly dust with icing (powdered) sugar.

12 Bake for about 20–25 minutes. To check if the cake is cooked through, insert a small, sharp knife into the centre and if it comes out clean, the cake is ready. Leave to cool before de-moulding from the cake tins.

Store in an airtight container and consume within 3 days.

LEMON DRIZZLE CAKE

This is a sophisticated lemon cake. The best recipe for lemon cake comes from Raymond Blanc. He used to serve it with afternoon tea in the gardens of Le Manoir Aux Quat'Saisons. The key to a good lemon drizzle cake is to soak it really well and to seal it inside a crisp glaze.

Makes 3 cakes (each serving 6)

1 quantity of **Apricot Nappage**
(see page 239)
1 quantity of **Water Icing** (see page 247)

80g (3oz/⅓ cup/¾ stick) unsalted
  butter, plus extra for greasing
220g (8oz/1⅔ cups)
  plain (all-purpose) flour
4g (⅛oz/1 teaspoon) baking powder
1g (a pinch) salt
200g (7oz) whole eggs (about 4 eggs)
280g (9¾oz/scant 1½ cups)
  caster (superfine) sugar
Grated zest of 4 lemons
120ml (4fl oz/½ cup)
  whipping (pouring) cream
20ml (¾fl oz) dark rum

For the Confit Lemon:
1 lemon, thinly sliced
1 quantity of **Simple Syrup** (see page 238)

For the Lemon Syrup:
200ml (7fl oz/generous ¾ cup)
  lemon juice
80ml (3fl oz/⅓ cup) water
100g (3½oz/½ cup) caster
  (superfine) sugar

You will also need:
• *three 23 x 3.5 x 6cm*
  (9 x 1¼ x 2½ inch) loaf tins
• *glazing rack*

1 First, make the Confit Lemon. Place the lemon slices in a saucepan filled with boiling water. Blanch for 1–2 minutes, then drain. Bring the Simple Syrup to a boil in another saucepan. Add the lemon slices, reduce to a low heat and cook for about 45 minutes, checking regularly to ensure the pan does not boil dry. Cover and leave to cool overnight in the syrup. The next day, drain off excess syrup and place the slices on a rack to dry for 1–2 hours.

2 Make the Lemon Syrup by boiling all the ingredients together in a saucepan to make a syrup.

3 Preheat the oven to 170°C (325°F/gas 3). Grease the loaf tins and line with silicone (baking) paper.

4 Melt the butter in a saucepan and leave to cool. Sieve together the flour, baking powder and salt twice into a bowl.

5 Put the eggs, sugar and lemon zest in a mixing bowl and beat together. Gradually add the cream and rum. Slowly add the butter, then fold in the dry ingredients. Spoon 300g (10½oz) cake batter into each prepared tin.

6 Bake for 25–30 minutes. To check if the cake is cooked, insert a small, sharp knife into the centre and if it comes out clean, the cake is ready. Remove from the oven and place the cakes on a wire rack to cool slightly in their tins.

7 Increase the oven temperature to 200°C (400°F/gas 6). De-mould the cakes and place them on a wire rack. Brush the cakes with the Lemon Syrup while still warm, then glaze with Apricot Nappage.

8 Prepare the Water Icing and brush onto the cakes. Return to the oven to bake for 2–3 minutes. Leave the cakes to cool, then decorate with Confit Lemon pieces.

Store in an airtight container and consume within 2–3 days.

PECAN & BANANA CAKE

While at The Savoy Hotel, loaf cakes were always a major part of the world famous afternoon tea, and this recipe was one of my favourites. Banana cake embodies comfort food, but I have added pecan nuts and a streusel topping to add texture.

Makes 8 small cakes

60g (2oz/¼ cup/½ stick)
   unsalted butter, softened,
   plus extra for greasing
200g (7oz/1½ cups)
   plain (all-purpose) flour
5g (1 teaspoon)
   bicarbonate of (baking) soda
100g (3½oz/½ cup) caster
   (superfine) sugar
3g (⅛oz/½ teaspoon) salt
112g (4oz) whole eggs (about 2–3 eggs)
50g (1¾oz/3 tablespoons) honey
50g (1¾oz/½ cup) pecans,
   roughly chopped
400g (14oz) peeled banana,
   roughly chopped

For the Pecan Streusel topping:
50g (1¾oz/3½ tablespoons)
   cold unsalted butter, cubed
50g (1¾oz/generous ⅓ cup)
   plain (all-purpose) flour, sifted
50g (1¾oz/¼ cup)
   caster (superfine) sugar
50g (1¾oz/½ cup) ground pecan nuts
80g (3oz/¾ cup) pecan nuts,
   roughly chopped

You will also need:
• eight 4 x 4 x 7cm
   (1½ x 1½ x 2¾ inch) loaf tins

1 Preheat the oven to 170°C (325°F/ gas 3). Grease the loaf tins and line with silicone (baking) paper.

2 Sieve together the flour and bicarbonate of (baking) soda twice into a bowl.

3 Put the softened butter, sugar and salt together in a bowl and beat until light and creamy in texture.

4 Gradually add the eggs and continue mixing until fully incorporated. Add the honey, pecans and banana, then gently fold in the sieved flour and bicarbonate of (baking) soda.

5 Divide the mixture between the prepared tins (about 120g/4¼oz in each tin) and level the tops using a small palette knife.

6 Prepare the streusel topping. Put the butter, flour, sugar and ground pecans in a mixing bowl and rub together until a crumble texture forms. Stir through the chopped pecans.

7 Spoon the streusel generously on top of each cake, ensuring it is completely covered.

8 Bake for 20 minutes. To check if the cake is cooked through, insert a small, sharp knife into the centre and if it comes out clean, the cake is ready. Leave to cool, then de-mould.

Store in an airtight container and consume within 2–3 days

OTHELLOS, DESDEMONAS & IAGOS

As a young laddie, I attended the 'City and Guilds Advanced Pastry' course at Glasgow College. My teacher was Willie Pike, who has always been a true inspiration and still is. His method of teaching was unique and captivating and he has always gone out of his way to support aspiring chefs. Othellos are a forgotten classic, inspired by Shakespeare's famous play. These days it is rare to find Othello cakes but they are a perfect combination of sponge, custard and fondant. Othellos are the chocolate flavour, Desdemonas are vanilla and Iagos are coffee. Willie introduced these to me while at college to help train me in the art of fondant work and fine chocolate decorations.

Makes 24 (8 of each flavour)

½ quantity of **Chocolate Crème Pâtissière** (*see variation page 234*)
½ quantity of **Crème Pâtissière** (*see page 234*)
½ quantity of **Coffee Crème Pâtissière** (*see variation page 234*)
1 quantity of **Apricot Nappage** (*see page 239*)
1 quantity of **Chocolate Fondant** (*see variation page 246*)
1 quantity of **Vanilla Fondant** (*see page 246*)
1 quantity of **Coffee Fondant** (*see variation page 246*)
24 **Chocolate Piped Small Single Curves** (*see page 250*)
Edible gold, silver and bronze leaf

For the sponge:
90g (3¼oz/⅔ cup) plain (all-purpose) flour, sifted
120g (4oz) egg whites (about 4 eggs)
45g (1½oz/¼ cup) caster (superfine) sugar
60g (2oz) egg yolks (about 3 eggs)

You will also need:
• *piping (pastry) bags*
• *12mm (½ inch) nozzle (tip)*
• *Parisienne scoop*

First, make the sponge:

1 Preheat the oven to 190°C (375°F/gas 5) and line 2 baking trays (sheets) with a non-stick baking mat. Sieve the flour.

2 Put the egg whites and one-third of the sugar in a mixing bowl. Whisk together, then gradually add the remaining sugar until the meringue forms soft peaks.

3 Lightly beat the egg yolks in a separate bowl, then gradually add them to the whisking meringue. Once fully incorporated, fold in the flour.

4 Spoon the mixture into a piping (pastry) bag fitted with a 12mm (½ inch) nozzle (tip). Pipe 3cm (1¼ inch) bulbs onto the prepared tray (you need 48 in total) and bake for 12–15 minutes until lightly golden.

Next, prepare the Crème Pâtissière flavours:

5 Prepare the 3 flavours of Crème Pâtissière as instructed on page 234.

6 When the sponges have cooled, trim the peaks of half of them – these will be the bases. Use a Parisienne scoop to scoop out the centre of all of them.

7 To prepare the Othellos, spoon the Chocolate Crème Pâtissière into a piping (pastry) bag, snip the end to make a small hole and fill 16 of the prepared sponges (8 bases and 8 tops), then sandwich them together.

8 Melt the Apricot Nappage and brush a layer onto each Othello.

Now, prepare the Fondants:

9 Prepare the Chocolate Fondant as instructed on page 246. Put the chocolate-filled Othellos on a fine wire rack and pour Chocolate Fondant over each one so it is completely covered. Leave to set for 2–3 minutes. Spoon a small quantity of Chocolate Fondant into a paper cornet and pipe a fine spiral onto each Othello. Place them on a serving dish and finish with Chocolate Piped Small Single Curves and gold leaf.

10 Repeat this process with the vanilla flavours and silver leaf to make Desdemonas and coffee flavours and bronze leaf to make Iagos.

Best stored in the fridge and eaten the same day.

VISITANDINES

These were the original financier. They were first made during the 1700s by convent nuns called the 'Sisters of the Visitation', commonly known in France as the Visitandines. Egg yolk was used for paintings at the time so the egg whites were a by-product. The resourceful nuns used the egg whites up as part of this delicious recipe. During the late 1800s, the pâtissier Lasne in Paris adapted the Visitandine recipe for the stockbrokers and named his new recipe the Financier. Instead of the eggs whites being a by-product, the yolks would now be left over after making the Visitandine recipe. Therefore, I have included a buttercream topping to finish the cakes and utilize the egg yolks.

Makes 24 visitandines

1 quantity of **Rum Syrup**
  (see variation page 238)
1 quantity of **Apricot Nappage**
  (see page 239)
100g (3½oz/⅔ cup) sesame seeds
1 quantity of **Sesame Buttercream**
  (see page 236)
24 **Chocolate Flat Wavy Sticks**
  (see page 248)

For the Visitandines:
185g (6½oz/¾ cup/1½ sticks)
  unsalted butter
35g (1¼oz/¼ cup)
  plain (all-purpose) flour
125g (4½oz/1¼ cups) ground almonds
130g (4¼oz) egg whites (about 4 eggs)
125g (4½oz/generous ¾ cup)
  icing (powdered) sugar
12g (½oz) shop-bought sesame paste

You will also need:
• *two 12-hole silicone boat (barquette)*
  moulds, with 7.2 x 3cm (2¾ x 1¼ inch)
  cavities
• *piping (pastry) bags*
• *10mm (⅓ inch) nozzle (tip)*
• *small petal nozzle (tip)*

1 First, make the Visitandine mixture. Put the butter in a saucepan and bring to the boil. Cook over a gentle heat until you have a beurre noisette (see page 247), then take off the heat and leave to cool.

2 Sieve the flour into a mixing bowl. Add the ground almonds and mix well.

3 Put the egg whites and icing (powdered) sugar together in a mixing bowl. Mix gently until fully combined (do not aerate).

4 Fold the dry ingredients into the egg white mixture, then mix in the cooled beurre noisette and the Sesame Paste. Mix until fully combined, then rest for 1 hour before baking.

5 Prepare the Rum Syrup and Apricot Nappage following the instructions on pages 238 and 239.

6 Preheat the oven to 170°C (325°F/gas 3). Spoon the rested Visitandine mixture into a piping (pastry) bag fitted with a 10mm (⅓ inch) piping nozzle (tip) and pipe into each cavity in the mould until three-quarters full. Decorate with sesame seeds and bake for 12–15 minutes until a light golden colour. Leave to cool, then remove from the moulds.

7 Prepare the Sesame Buttercream as instructed on page 236.

8 Soak each Visitandine with Rum Syrup. Melt the Apricot Nappage and use it to glaze the top of each Vistandine.

9 Spoon the Sesame Buttercream into a piping (pastry) bag fitted with a small petal nozzle (tip) and pipe onto the top of each cake. Finish with a Chocolate Flat Wavy Stick.

Best served the same day.

ROUT BISCUITS

In old English a 'rout' was the word for a large gathering or evening party. This biscuit dates back to the 17th century, when they would have been served at such events. Traditionally they are piped through flower-shaped moulds, but as my version is based on a Jammie Dodger it is a disc with jam in the centre.

Makes 40 biscuits

½ quantity of **Hazelnut and Almond Pastry** *(see page 228)*
1 quantity of **Apricot Jelly**
(see variation page 241)
1 quantity of **Redcurrant Jelly**
(see variation page 241)

For the Hazelnut Paste:
130g (4½oz/1⅓ cups) ground hazelnuts
130g (4½oz/1⅓ cups)
  icing (powdered) sugar
26g (1oz) egg white (about 1 egg)
26ml (1fl oz) water

For the glaze:
10g (¼oz) gum Arabic *(see Note)*
60ml (2¼fl oz/¼ cup) warm water

You will also need:
• *4cm (1½ inch) fluted cutter*
• *piping (pastry) bag*
• *C8 star nozzle (tip)*

Note: Gum Arabic is a natural glaze made from tree sap. It is ideal for use on biscuits to add shine.

1 Prepare the Hazelnut and Almond Pastry as instructed on page 228, then leave to rest in the fridge for 2–3 hours.

2 Prepare the Apricot and Redcurrant Jellies following the instructions on page 241.

3 When the pastry has rested, roll it out to 2.5mm (⅛ inch) thick on a lightly floured surface. Use the 4cm (1½ inch) fluted cutter to cut out 40 discs and place each one on a baking tray (sheet) lined with a non-stick baking mat. Return to the fridge to rest for 30 minutes.

4 Make the Hazelnut Paste. Sieve together the ground hazelnuts and icing (powdered) sugar in a bowl, then add the egg white and water and beat to a paste.

5 Preheat the oven to 170°C (325°F/gas 3).

6 Spoon the mixture into a piping (pastry) bag fitted with a C8 star nozzle (tip).

7 Remove the prepared pastry discs from the fridge and pipe a circle of Hazelnut Paste around the edge of each disc. Bake for 12–15 minutes until crisp and golden, then remove from the oven and turn the temperature up to 190°C (375°F/gas 5).

8 Prepare the glaze by mixing the gum arabic with the warm water – don't worry if it looks lumpy initially as the lumps will dissolve in the water.

Use a small paintbrush to coat each biscuit in a thin layer of the glaze, then return the biscuits to the oven for 1–2 minutes. Leave to cool.

9 Melt the Apricot Jelly and spoon a small quantity into the centre of half the cooked and cooled biscuits. Repeat this process with the Redcurrant Jelly and fill the remaining biscuits. Leave to cool.

Store in an airtight container and consume within 2–3 days.

EMPIRE BISCUITS

They were originally called Linzer biscuits, after the famous Linzer Torte. Over time the name changed to Empire Biscuits as they are popular throughout the Commonwealth. My granny was the best at making these Scottish favourites – she would fill them with buttercream and jam to serve as an afternoon treat. My Empire biscuits are based on my granny's recipe.

Makes 12 biscuits

12 Sugar Daisies *(see page 90)*, to decorate
1 quantity of **Lemon Marmalade**
  (see variation page 242)
½ quantity of **Apricot Nappage**
  (see page 239)
1 quantity of **Lemon Zest Water Icing**
  (see variation page 247)
1 quantity of **Lemon Buttercream**
  (see variation page 236)

For the Lemon Biscuit:
150g (5½oz/⅔ cup/1¼ sticks)
  unsalted butter, softened
115g (4oz/scant 1 cup) icing
  (powdered) sugar, sifted
3g (½ teaspoon) grated lemon zest
½ vanilla pod (bean), split lengthways
65g (2oz/⅔ cup) ground almonds,
  sieved
40g (1½oz) whole egg (about 1 egg)
250g (9oz/1¾ cups) plain (all-purpose)
  flour, sifted, plus extra for flouring

For the Confit Lemon:
Peel of 1 lemon, sliced into fine slivers
½ quantity of **Simple Syrup**
  (see page 238)

You will also need:
• *6.5cm (2½ inch) fluted cutter*
• *piping (pastry) bags*
• *10mm (⅓ inch) nozzle (tip)*

First, make the Sugar Daisies:

1 Prepare the Sugar Daisies as instructed on page 90 and leave in a cool, dry area to set for at least 4 hours.

Now, prepare the biscuits:

2 Roughly chop the butter. Place in a mixing bowl and beat until smooth. Add the sugar, lemon zest and the seeds scraped from the split vanilla pod (bean). Beat together until light in texture and colour. Add the ground almonds and mix well.

3 Beat the eggs and gradually add them to the mixture. Add the flour and mix together ensuring the mixture comes together into a smooth and homogeneous mass. Put the dough on a floured tray, wrap in cling film (plastic wrap) and rest in the fridge for at least 1 hour.

Next, make the Confit Lemon:

4 Place the slivers of lemon peel in a pan filled with boiling water. Blanch for 10 seconds. Strain and rinse with cold water. Boil the Simple Syrup in another pan and add the lemon slivers. Simmer over a low heat for 20 minutes. Leave to cool, strain excess syrup and shape into small nests on a silicone-lined tray. Leave to dry for 1–2 hours.

Now, prepare the Lemon Marmalade and Apricot Nappage:

5 Prepare the Lemon Marmalade and Apricot Nappage as instructed on pages 242 and 239.

To bake and finish:

6 When the biscuit mixture has rested, roll out to 2.5mm (⅛ inch) thick on a lightly floured surface. Use a 6.5cm (2½ inch) fluted cutter to cut out 24 discs and put them on a baking tray (sheet) lined with a non-stick baking mat. Rest in the fridge for at least 30 minutes. Preheat the oven to 180°C (350°F/gas 4).

7 Bake the biscuits for 12–15 minutes until golden.

8 Prepare the Lemon Zest Water Icing and melt the Apricot Nappage. Ice half the lemon biscuits as instructed on page 174. These will be the tops.

9 Prepare the Lemon Buttercream as instructed on page 236. Spoon the mixture into a piping (pastry) bag fitted with a 10mm (⅓ inch) nozzle (tip) and pipe a ring of buttercream around the edge of the un-iced biscuits (these are the bases).

10 Spoon the Lemon Marmalade into a piping (pastry) bag. Snip the end to make a hole and pipe a bulb of marmalade into the centre of the buttercream ring. Place an iced biscuit on top and gently push down to stick together.

11 To decorate, place a Confit Lemon nest and a Sugar Daisy onto the centre of each biscuit.

Best served the same day, but can be stored in an airtight container for up to 2 days.

VIENNESE WHIRLS

Despite the name, these are actually a British creation. Originally made with florettes of vanilla dough and filled with raspberry jam and buttercream, I have evolved what some consider a dated 'biscuit tin' snack into a contemporary product, laced with plenty of chocolate.

Makes 12 biscuits

1 quantity of **Sea Salt Caramel**
(see page 48)
1 quantity of **Beurre de Sel Ganache**
(see variation page 19)

For the Spiral Sable Biscuits:
400g (14oz/3 cups)
   plain (all-purpose)flour
30g (1¼oz/¼ cup) cocoa powder
380g (13oz/1⅔ cups/scant 3½ sticks)
   room temperature unsalted butter
200g (7oz/1½ cups)
   icing (powdered) sugar, sifted
2g (a pinch) sea salt
100g (3½oz) egg whites (about 3–4 eggs)

You will also need:
• *piping (pastry) bags*
• *8mm (⅓ inch) nozzles (tips)*

1 First, prepare the Sea Salt Caramel as instructed on page 48 and leave to cool.

2 Prepare the ganache as instructed on page 19 and leave to semi-set at room temperature for 1 hour.

3 Preheat the oven to 180°C (350°F/ gas 4) and line a baking tray (sheet) with a non-stick baking mat.

4 Prepare the biscuit mixture. Sieve the flour and cocoa powder together twice into a bowl.

5 Cream the butter and icing (powdered) sugar together in a separate bowl. Add the salt and continue to cream until light in colour.

6 Gradually add the egg white. When the egg is fully mixed in, add the flour and cocoa powder, then mix until combined.

7 Spoon the mixture into a piping (pastry) bag fitted with an 8mm (⅓ inch) nozzle (tip). Pipe 24 spirals onto the prepared tray – each spiral should be about 6cm (2½ inches) in diameter.

8 Bake for 15–18 minutes until slightly firm to touch. Leave to cool.

9 When the biscuits have cooled, turn half of them upside down (these will be the bases). Place the ganache into a piping (pastry) bag fitted with an 8mm (⅓ inch) nozzle (tip) and pipe a spiral on each base. Leave a space in the centre by beginning the spiral half way out of the centre of the biscuit.

10 Spoon the Sea Salt Caramel into a piping (pastry) bag and snip the end to make a small hole. Pipe a bulb of caramel inside the ganache spiral.

11 Top with the other biscuits and gently push down to stick together.

Store in an airtight container and consume within 2–3 days.

CHOCOLATE CHIP COOKIES

Growing up, my sister and I would be given chocolate cookies with a glass of milk while my parents had an afternoon cup of tea. The best cookies are crispy around the edge and slightly chewy in the middle. You can be quite adventurous with the flavours you use, but I have stuck with two classic flavour combinations.

Makes 20 cookies

175g (6oz/1⅓ cups) plain (all-purpose) flour, plus extra for dusting
2g (½ teaspoon) bicarbonate of (baking) soda
2g (½ teaspoon) salt
110g (4oz/½ cup/1 stick) unsalted butter, softened
85g (3oz/scant ½ cup) caster (superfine) sugar
85g (3oz/scant ½ cup) soft brown sugar
¼ vanilla pod (bean), split lengthways
50g (1¾oz) whole eggs (about 1 egg)
100g (3½oz) dark (bittersweet) chocolate, roughly chopped
75g (2¾oz/½ cup) hazelnuts, lightly roasted and roughly chopped
250g (9oz) tempered dark (bittersweet) chocolate (66% cocoa solids)
(see page 14)

1 Preheat the oven to 190°C (375°F/ gas 5).

2 Sieve the flour, bicarbonate of (baking) soda and salt together twice into a bowl.

3 Beat the butter, sugar, brown sugar and vanilla seeds together in a separate bowl until creamy. Beat the eggs in a separate bowl, then gradually add to the mixture.

4 Gradually mix in the flour mixture, then stir in the chopped chocolate and chopped nuts.

5 Roll the dough into a sausage shape on a lightly floured surface, about 5cm (2 inches) in diameter and 30cm (12 inches) in length. Wrap in cling film (plastic wrap) and transfer to the fridge for at least 1 hour.

6 When you are ready to bake the cookies, simply cut the log into 1.5cm (¾ inch) thick slices and lay them on a baking tray (sheet), widely spaced apart. Bake for 15–18 minutes until golden brown. Leave to cool.

7 Temper the chocolate and spoon it into a paper piping cornet. Pipe lines of chocolate onto the cookies, then leave to set for 20 minutes.

Store in an airtight container and consume within 1 week.

FLAVOUR VARIATION

WHITE CHOCOLATE, MACADAMIA & CRANBERRY

Replace the dark (bittersweet) chocolate with 75g (2¾oz) of white chocolate and the hazelnuts with 50g (1¾oz) macadamia nuts and add 50g (1¾oz/⅓ cup) of dried cranberries. Make following the instructions above. Pipe with tempered white chocolate instead of dark (bittersweet) chocolate. Makes 20 cookies

CHOCOLATE HOBNOBS

These are essentially a sweet version of an oatcake. Oatcakes are a Scottish tradition believed to predate the Roman Empire and are oatmeal and water cooked on a griddle. Hobnob biscuits began to be produced commercially in 1985. The term 'hobnob' was first used by Shakespeare in Twelfth Night. *I would always choose them first out of the biscuit tin as I love the way the chocolate melts when they are dipped in a cup of tea.*

Makes 24 biscuits

150g (5½oz/generous 1 cup)
   plain (all-purpose) flour
4g (1 teaspoon)
   bicarbonate of (baking) soda
120g (4½oz/scant 1 cup) rolled oats
150g (5½oz/¾ cup)
   caster (superfine) sugar
150g (5½oz/⅔ cup/1¼ sticks)
   unsalted butter
15g (1 tablespoon) golden syrup
   (light corn syrup)
500g (1lb 2oz) tempered dark
   (bittersweet) chocolate
   (65% cocoa solids) *(see page 14)*

You will also need:
• *patterned plastic sheet*

1 Preheat the oven to 180°C (350°F/ gas 4) and line two baking trays (sheets) with silicone (baking) paper or a non-stick baking mat.

2 Sieve together the flour and bicarbonate of (baking) soda twice into a bowl. Add the oats and sugar and mix well until evenly combined.

3 Melt the butter in a saucepan over a low heat. Add the golden syrup (light corn syrup) and mix together. Pour this into the dry mixture and mix well.

4 Divide the mix into 24 balls and place them on the prepared baking trays (sheets). Gently push down on each ball to flatten them slightly. Bake for 18–20 minutes until golden brown. Remove from the oven and place on a wire rack to cool.

5 Temper the chocolate, then dip the top of each biscuit in the tempered chocolate. Place, chocolate side down, on the patterned plastic sheet, push down gently and leave to set for 1–2 hours. Carefully remove from the hobnobs from the plastic.

Store in an airtight container and consume within 1 week.

DUTCH MACARONS

French macarons are hugely popular all over the world, but it is very unusual to find the Dutch version, despite being equally tasty. I learnt to make these while working for Pierre Koffmann at La Tante Claire. I would make and pipe them in the evening after service, then leave them to dry out overnight before cutting the centres and cooking them for petits fours the next day.

Makes 20 macarons

175g (6oz/1¼ cups)
  icing (powdered) sugar, sifted
125g (4½oz/1¼ cups) ground almonds,
  sifted
75g (2¾oz) egg white (about 2–3 eggs)
50g (1¾oz/¼ cup)
  caster (superfine) sugar
20ml (¾fl oz) water
1 quantity of **Almond Praline Ganache**
(see variation page 19)

You will also need:
• *piping (pastry) bags*
• *10mm (⅓ inch) nozzle (tip)*
• *8mm (⅓ inch) nozzle (tip)*

1 Put 125g (4½oz/1 cup) of the icing (powdered) sugar, the ground almonds and egg white in a bowl and beat together.

2 Make a syrup with the caster (superfine) sugar and water, cook to 116°C (240°F), then pour the syrup into the beating mixture. Beat for 5 minutes, then mix in the remaining icing (powdered) sugar.

3 Spoon the mixture into a piping (pastry) bag fitted with a 10mm (⅓ inch) plain nozzle (tip). Line a tray with a non-stick baking mat and pipe forty 2 x 3cm (¾ x 1¼ inch) ovals onto the tray. Leave in a cool, dry area for about 12 hours (ideally overnight) to fully dry out the macarons.

4 When the macarons are dry and have formed a skin, preheat the oven to 180°C (350°F/gas 4).

5 Prepare the Almond Praline Ganache as instructed on page 19 and leave to semi-set at room temperature for 1 hour.

6 Use a sharp knife to cut a slit in the centre of each macaron, then bake for 15–18 minutes until they have puffed up and turned golden. Leave to cool fully.

7 Spoon the prepared ganache into a piping (pastry) bag fitted with a 8mm (⅓ inch) nozzle (tip). Turn half the macarons upside down on the tray. Pipe a bulb of ganache onto each upside down macaron, then sandwich with the other halves and gently push together. Leave to set for 20 minutes in a cool, dry area.

Store in an airtight container and consume within 2–3 days.

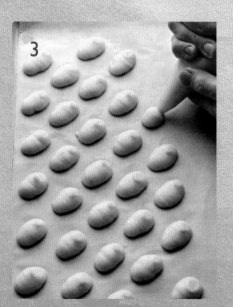

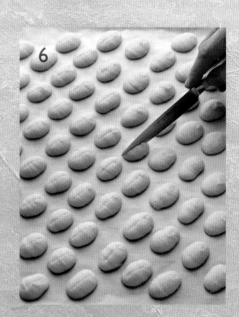

ARLETTE BISCUITS

Though these biscuits are simple to make, it takes a little bit of practice to perfect them. When they are made right, if you hold them up to the light, you should be able to see the spiral running through it. While working in the restaurants of Pierre Koffmann and Marco Pierre White, I used to make a summer dessert of Arlette biscuits layered with crème diplomat and fresh berries. The layers of buttery, caramelized pastry is very addictive, so they usually get eaten very fast!

Makes about 50 biscuits

1 quantity of **Rough Puff Pastry**
  (see page 67)
500g (1lb 2oz/4 cups)
  icing (powdered) sugar
10g (¼oz) ground ginger
20g (¾oz) egg yolk (about 1 egg)
10ml (2 teaspoons) milk
25g (1oz/⅓ cup) flaked almonds,
  lightly toasted

1 Prepare the Rough Puff Pastry as instructed on page 67 and leave to rest in the fridge for 2–3 hours.

2 Sift together the icing (powdered) sugar and the ginger powder in a bowl.

3 When the Rough Puff Pastry has rested, cut away one-third of the dough from the rest (about 400g/14oz) – the remainder of the pastry can be wrapped in cling film (plastic wrap) and kept in the freezer for up to 1 month for other uses. Roll the pastry out to about 3mm (⅛ inch) thick on a lightly floured surface.

4 Beat together the egg yolk and milk. Lightly brush the egg mixture all over the sheet of pastry. Sprinkle the flaked almonds evenly onto the pastry and dust generously with the ginger icing (powdered) sugar. Roll into a tight spiral, wrap in cling film (plastic wrap) and return to the fridge to firm for 1 hour.

5 Line two baking trays (sheets) with non-stick baking mats. Remove the prepared dough from the fridge and use a sharp knife to slice into 5mm (¼ inch) pieces. Dust the work surface with ginger icing (powdered) sugar and use a rolling pin to shape each cut slice into a very thin disc of pastry about 1mm thick. Place each disc on the prepared baking tray (sheet) and leave to rest in the fridge for 30 minutes.

6 Preheat the oven to 200°C (400°F/gas 6). Bake the biscuits for 6–8 minutes, then use a palette knife to turn each one upside down. If the pastry has puffed up, you can gently press them down with a palette knife. Return to the oven to bake for a further 4–5 minutes until the pastry has caramelized. Leave to cool, then store immediately in an airtight container.

Store in an airtight container and consume within 1–2 days.

This section is all about fun.

Some of these recipes are quick and easy to make, but are very
striking, such as the pignons and rocher noix de coco; while others
are throwbacks to being a child in a sweet shop, such as cherry
drops, fruit pastilles and marshmallow.

Frivolities

While working in restaurants, I would always enjoy creating petits
fours as it allowed for a little bit of extra creativity in the kitchen.

They are such an important part of a Michelin-starred establishment
because they are served at the very end of a meal to impress the
guests and give a lasting impression.

CHERRY DROPS

These cherry drops are inspired by boiled sweets, which were a favourite of mine when I was a young laddie. Sadly, they are no longer a favourite as I now find even the smell artificial. I created these as a way of naturally capturing the intense cherry flavour that I loved as a child.

Makes 36 pieces

Chocolate Shavings and Chocolate
  Cherry Stalks *(see pages 248 and 250)*
½ quantity of **Cherry Mousse**
  (see page 113)
1 quantity of **Cherry Jam**
  (see variation page 241)
1 quantity of **Kirsch Syrup**
  (see variation page 238)
1 quantity of **Cherry Glaze**
  (see variation page 239)

For the Almond Financier:
225g (8oz/1 cup/2 sticks)
  unsalted butter
225g (8oz) egg whites (about 7–8 eggs)
255g (9oz/1¼ cups)
  caster (superfine) sugar
150g (5½oz/1½ cups) ground almonds
75g (2¾oz/½ cup)
  plain (all-purpose) flour, sifted

You will also need:
• *piping (pastry) bags*
• *two 18-hole (3cm/1¼ inch) half sphere*
  fleximat moulds
• *12mm (½ inch) nozzle (tip)*
• *two 18-hole (4cm/1½ inch) savarin*
  fleximat moulds
• *dipping fork*

1 First, prepare the Chocolate Cherry Stalks and Chocolate Shavings as instructed on pages 248 and 250 and leave in a cool, dry area to set for 1–2 hours.

2 Make the Cherry Mousse as instructed on page 113. Spoon into a piping (pastry) bag and snip the end to make a small hole. Put the half-sphere moulds on a tray and pipe the mousse into each cavity. Level with a palette knife and place in the freezer to set for at least 2 hours until fully frozen.

3 To make the Almond Financiers, first prepare beurre noisette using the butter as instructed on page 247 and leave to cool but not set. In a separate bowl, beat together the egg white and sugar and add the ground almonds. Mix in the sifted flour. Lastly, add the cooled beurre noisette and mix until fully combined. Place the mixture in an airtight container and leave in the fridge to rest for 1 hour.

4 Prepare the Cherry Jam, Kirsch Syrup and Cherry Glaze as instructed on pages 241, 238 and 239. Preheat the oven to 170°C (325°F/gas 3).

5 When the financier mixture has rested in the fridge, spoon into a piping (pastry) bag fitted with a 12mm (½ inch) nozzle (tip). Place the savarin moulds on a baking tray (sheet) and pipe the financier mixture into each cavity until three-quarters full. Bake for 12–15 minutes until a light golden colour. Leave to cool before de-moulding.

6 Put the financiers on a tray lined with silicone (baking) paper and soak each one generously with Kirsch Syrup.

7 Spoon the prepared Cherry Jam into a piping (pastry) bag and snip the end to make a small hole. Pipe a small bulb into the cavity in the centre of each financier.

8 Melt and cool the prepared Cherry Glaze, then leave it to thicken slightly. Remove the Cherry Mousse half-spheres from the freezer and de-mould them. Use a dipping fork to dip each dome in the glaze so that they are completely covered, then place them in the centre of each financier. Use a cocktail stick to place Chocolate Shavings around the edge of each glazed dome and finish by placing a Chocolate Cherry Stalk in the centre of each dome.

Store in the fridge until ready to serve. Best eaten the same day.

ALLUMETTES
ALMOND PRALINE AND CHOCOLATE

The word allumette means 'matchstick' in French. They were created in Brittany, France, during the 19th century by a Swiss pâtissier called Planta. There are many different versions of this pastry, but the one with glacé royal is the most technical to make. These are often used as petits fours and I made them many times in the Michelin-starred restaurants where I trained. They are usually served unfilled, but I could not help adding another dimension to them by layering them with a rich crème mousseline.

**Makes 60 allumettes
(30 of each flavour)**

1 quantity of **Rough Puff Pastry**
  (see page 67)
plain (all-purpose) flour, for dusting
2 quantities of **Royal Icing** (see page 246)

For the Almond Praline Flavour:
1 quantity of **Praline Mousseline**
  (see variation page 235)
30 pieces of flaked almonds,
  lightly toasted

For the Chocolate Flavour:
1 quantity of **Chocolate Mousseline**
  (see variation page 235)
20g (¾oz) cocoa nibs

You will also need:
• *piping (pastry) bag*
• *flat piping nozzle (tip)*

1 Prepare the Rough Puff Pastry as instructed on page 67 and leave to rest for 2–3 hours in the fridge.

2 When the pastry has rested, divide the dough in half – one half is surplus to this recipe so can be wrapped in cling film (plastic wrap) and stored in the freezer for up to 1 month. Divide the remaining half into 2 pieces and roll out to 2.5mm (⅛ inch) thick on a lightly floured surface. Place them in the fridge to rest for at least 30 minutes before transferring to the freezer for 30 minutes.

3 Prepare the Royal Icing as instructed on page 246.

4 Remove the pastry from the freezer and use a step-palette knife to spread a thin layer of Royal Icing on top of the puff pastry. Return to the freezer for 1 hour.

5 Prepare both mousselines following the instructions on page 235 and set aside until ready to use.

6 Preheat the oven to 170°C (325°F/ gas 3). Take the pastry out of the freezer and cut each sheet into thirty 2 x 7cm (¾ x 2¾ inch) rectangles. Place them on a tray lined with a non-stick baking mat. Place an almond flake in the centre of half the rectangles, and place three cocoa nibs in the centre of the other half of the rectangles.

7 Bake for 10–12 minutes. Once the pastry has turned golden brown, reduce the oven temperature to 150°C (300°F/gas 2) and cook for a further 5–6 minutes to dry out the pastry.

8 Leave the baked allumettes to cool, then cut each one in half along the centre to create a base and a lid. Spoon the Praline Mousseline into a piping (pastry) bag fitted with a flat nozzle (tip). Pipe waves of mousseline along the base of each almond allumette, then gently place the lid on top. Repeat this process with the Chocolate Mousseline and the chocolate allumettes.

Store in the fridge until ready to serve. Best eaten on the same day.

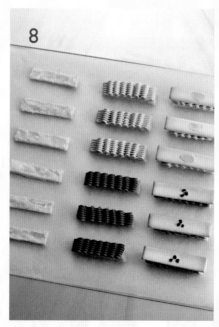

CIGARILLOS, TUILES

I spent many years working in Michelin-starred restaurants, and each one featured some sort of tuile on the menu. While I worked for Marco Pierre White at the Oak Room, he would always have a selection of tuiles proudly displayed at the top of his petits fours stand.

CIGARILLOS

Makes 50 of each flavour

For the Vanilla & Pistachio Cigarillo:
75g (2¾oz/¾ cup) ground almonds
75g (2¾oz/⅔ cup)
   icing (powdered) sugar, sifted
75g (2¾oz/⅓ cup) caster (superfine) sugar
100g (3½oz/⅔ cup)
   plain (all-purpose)flour, sifted
75g (2¾oz/⅓ cup/¾ stick)
   unsalted butter, melted
75g (2¾oz) egg white (about 3 eggs)
75ml (2¾fl oz/⅓ cup)
   double (heavy) cream
½ vanilla pod (bean), split lengthways

For the Chocolate Cigarillo:
75g (2¾oz/¾ cup) ground almonds
75g (2¾oz/⅔ cup)
   icing (powdered) sugar, sifted
75g (2¾oz/⅓ cup)
   caster (superfine) sugar
90g (3¼oz/⅔ cup)
   plain (all-purpose) flour, sifted
15g (½oz) cocoa powder, sifted
75g (2¾oz/⅓ cup/¾ stick)
   unsalted butter, melted
75g (2¾oz) egg white (about 3 eggs)
75ml (2½fl oz/⅓ cup)
   double (heavy) cream

To finish:
300g (10½oz) tempered dark
   (bittersweet) chocolate
   (66% cocoa solids) *(see page 14)*
50g (1¾oz/⅓ cup) chopped pistachios
50g (1¾oz/generous ⅓ cup) chopped
   cocoa nibs

You will also need:
• *a circular stencil, made by cutting a*
   6cm (2½ inch) disc from flexible plastic

To make the Vanilla and Pistachio Cigarillos:

1 Make the vanilla cigarillo: mix together all the dry ingredients. Add the wet ingredients and the vanilla seeds, then mix with the dry ingredients until fully combined. Store in the fridge until ready to use.

2 Preheat the oven to 180°C (350°F/ gas 4). Line a baking tray (sheet) with a non-stick baking mat. Place the circular stencil on the tray and use a small step-palette knife to spread a thin layer of the chilled mixture across the stencil. Lift the stencil to leave a disc of mixture. Repeat the process until the tray is full.

3 Bake for 5–6 minutes until just golden brown. Remove from the oven and immediately roll each circle into a cigar shape.

4 When the cigarillos are completely cooled, dip each end of the Cigarillos in tempered chocolate, then immediately dip into a bowl containing the chopped pistachios. Place on a tray lined with silicone (baking) paper and leave in a cool, dry area to set for 30 minutes, then store in an airtight container.

5 For the chocolate cigarillos, repeat this process but omit the vanilla and add the cocoa powder to the dry ingredients. When dipping the ends, replace the chopped pistachios with cocoa nibs.

Store in an airtight container and consume within 1–2 days.

NUT TUILES

Makes 50 of each flavour

For the Hazelnut Tuile:
50g (1¾oz/½ cup) ground hazelnuts
190g (6½oz/scant 1 cup)
   caster (superfine) sugar
25g (1oz) plain (all-purpose) flour, sifted
25ml (1fl oz) hazelnut oil
150g (5½oz) egg white (about 5 eggs)
150g (5½oz/generous 1 cup)
   chopped hazelnuts

For the Almond Tuile:
250g (9oz/1¼ cups)
   caster (superfine) sugar
75g (2¾oz/½ cup)
   plain (all-purpose) flour, sifted
75g (2¾oz/⅓ cup/¾ stick)
   unsalted butter, melted
160g (5¾oz) egg whites
   (about 5–6 eggs)
¼ vanilla pod (bean), split lengthways
250g (9oz/3 cups) flaked almonds

For the Coconut Tuile:
250g (9oz/3⅓ cups) desiccated coconut
140g (5oz/¾ cup)
   caster (superfine) sugar
15g (½oz) plain (all-purpose) flour, sifted
150ml (5fl oz/⅔ cup)
   double (heavy) cream
15ml (1 tablespoon) milk
40g (1½oz) egg whites (about 1–2 eggs)

You will also need:
• *a circular stencil, made by cutting a*
   6cm (2½ inch) disc from flexible plastic

& CROQUANT WAFERS

*The detail and effort that went into making each tuile was remarkable.
Marco never did anything in half measures; if he was going to do something,
he would make sure it was outstanding, which to this day I still find inspiring.*

CROQUANT WAFERS

To make the Hazelnut Tuiles:

1 Mix together all the dry ingredients. Add the wet ingredients, then mix with the dry ingredients until fully combined. Lastly, mix in the chopped hazelnuts. Store in the fridge until ready to use.

2 Preheat the oven to 180°C (350°F/ Gas 4). Line a baking tray (sheet) with a non-stick baking mat.

3 Place the circular stencil on the tray and use a small step-palette knife to spread a thin layer of the chilled mixture across the stencil. Lift the stencil to leave a disc of mixture. Repeat the process until the tray is full.

4 Bake for 5–6 minutes until just golden. Remove from the oven and immediately use a palette knife to lift each tuile and lay over a thin rolling pin. Push the tuile around the rolling pin to get a curved shape. Leave to cool, then place in an airtight container.

5 For the Almond Tuile, follow the same method but add the vanilla seeds with the wet ingredients.

6 For the Coconut Tuile, follow the same method as for the Hazelnut Tuile.

Store in an airtight container and consume within 1–2 days.

Makes 50 of each flavour

For the Chocolate Croquant Wafers:
100g (3½oz/scant ½ cup)
  caster (superfine) sugar
25g (1oz/1½ tablespoons)
  unsalted butter
30g (1¼oz) liquid glucose
12ml (1 tablespoon) milk
10g (¼ oz/2 teaspoons)
  cocoa powder, sifted
20g (¾oz/1 tablespoon) cocoa nibs
20g (¾oz/1 tablespoon) almond nibs

**For the Sesame and
Orange Croquant Wafers:**
125g (4½oz/generous ½ cup)
  caster (superfine) sugar
60g (2oz/¼ cup/½ stick)
  unsalted butter
50ml (2fl oz/scant ¼ cup) orange juice
Grated zest of ½ an orange
40g (1½ oz/⅓ cup)
  plain (all-purpose) flour, sifted
30g (1¼oz/¼ cup)
  toasted white sesame seeds
30g (1¼oz/¼ cup) black sesame seeds

To make the Chocolate Croquant Wafers:

1 Put the sugar and all the wet ingredients in a saucepan and bring to the boil. Add the dry ingredients and mix in the cocoa nibs and almond nibs. Store in the fridge until ready to use.

2 Preheat the oven to 190°C (375°F/ gas 5). Line a baking tray (sheet) with a non-stick baking mat.

3 Roll the Chocolate Croquant mixture into balls of about 3g (⅛oz) and place on the prepared tray. When cooking, they will spread out to discs of about 6cm (2½ inches) so leave plenty of space between each ball. Gently push each ball so it slightly flattens then bake in the oven for 5–6 minutes.

4 Remove from the oven, leave to sit for 30 seconds, then use a palette knife to lift each wafer and lay over a thin rolling pin. Push the wafer around the rolling pin to get a curved shape. Leave to cool and place in an airtight container.

5 For the Sesame and Orange Croquant Wafers, follow the same method but use a spoon to place the mixture onto the prepared baking tray (sheet).

Store in an airtight container and consume within 1–2 days.

PIGNONS

Pignon de pin is French for pine nut. These are yet another great but simple French petits four. I was first shown this recipe by Daniel Martelat who I worked for while still at college. He is from Symphorien d'Ozon, just outside Lyon. It is a region renowned for its history of cuisine so he loved to show me traditional recipes from there. Pignons were one of my favourites – Daniel taught me how to get the perfect shape and caramelization on them.

Makes 38 pignons

200g (7oz/2 cups) ground almonds
100g (3½oz/scant 1 cup)
  icing (powdered) sugar
1 vanilla pod (bean), split lengthways
50g (1¾oz) egg whites (about 2 eggs)
30g (1¼oz) **Confit Orange**
  (see page 46), finely chopped
120g (4½oz/1 cup) pine nuts
10g (¼oz) gum Arabic powder
60ml (2¼fl oz/¼ cup) warm water

1 Sift the ground almonds and icing (powdered) sugar together. Scrape the seeds from the vanilla pod (bean) into the bowl and add the egg whites. Beat together until it forms a paste and the vanilla seeds are evenly dispersed.

2 Add the chopped Confit Orange and mix into the paste so it is dispersed throughout the mixture.

3 Roll into a sausage shape and cut into pieces weighing 10g (¼oz) each.

4 Preheat the oven to 160°C (325°F/gas 3) and line a baking tray (sheet) with a non-stick baking mat.

5 Place the pine nuts in a shallow dish or tray. Roll each piece of mixture into a ball and then into a small cylinder shape. Roll in the tray of pine nuts, pushing slightly to ensure they stick to the cylinder. Place them on the prepared baking tray (sheet) and curve the 2 ends to shape into crescents.

6 Bake for 12–15 minutes until golden. When they are cooked, remove from the oven and turn the temperature up to 190°C (375°F/gas 5).

7 Prepare a glaze by mixing the gum Arabic powder with the warm water in a small bowl – don't worry if it looks lumpy initially as the lumps will dissolve in the water. Use a small brush to coat each pignon with the glaze, then return them to the oven for 2–3 minutes.

Store in an airtight container and consume within 2–3 days.

ROCHER NOIX DE COCO

This is a classic after-dinner petit four, which can be found in many top restaurants in France. I learned to perfect the shape during my time at Marc Meneau's three Michelin-starred L'Espérance in Burgundy. This is where I went after winning the 'William Heptinstall Scholarship' – it was an amazing experience for me and I really believe that all young chefs should spend time training in France.

Makes 20 rocher noix de coco

150g (5½oz/2 cups) desiccated coconut
90g (3¼oz/scant ¾ cup) icing
  (powdered) sugar, sifted
70g (2¾oz) egg white (about 2–3 eggs)
300g (10½oz) tempered dark
  (bittersweet) chocolate
  (70% cocoa solids) *(see page 14)*

1 Preheat the oven to 180°C (350°F/ gas 4). Line 2 baking trays (sheets) with silicone (baking) paper.

2 Whisk together the coconut, sugar and egg white over a bain-marie (water bath) until the mixture reaches 45°C (113°F).

3 Divide the mixture into 20 even-sized balls, each weighing 15g (½oz). Shape them into pointed cones and place them on the prepared baking tray (sheet).

4 Bake in the oven for 12–15 minutes, until the tips colour. Remove from the oven and leave to cool.

5 Prepare a bowl of tempered chocolate as instructed on page 14. Dip the base of each cone into the chocolate and set on a clean baking tray (sheet) to set for 1 hour in a cool, dry area.

Store in an airtight container and consume within 1 week.

TURKISH DELIGHT

RASPBERRY & ROSE AND LEMON & ORANGE BLOSSOM

Turkish delight dates back hundreds of years, with honey, rosewater and lemon some of the original flavours used. Modern recipes often contain gelatine, although traditionally this was not the case. Cornflour (cornstarch) should be used to thicken the mixture instead. This is the method I have used, but it does require patience as the mixture must be cooked for a long time over a low heat and left to set overnight. Fry's Turkish Delight was always a big favourite in my family – growing up, I always liked the unique texture and when I felt brave enough I would sometimes nick one of my dads that he had hidden away..

Makes 30 pieces

200g (7oz/scant 2 cups)
  icing (powdered) sugar
85g (3oz/¾ cup)
  cornflour (cornstarch)
300ml (½ pint/1¼ cups) water
300g (10½oz) raspberry purée
450g (1lb 1oz/2 cups)
  caster (superfine) sugar
5g (1 teaspoon) cream of tartar
60g (2oz/¼ cup) honey
30ml (1fl oz/2 tablespoons) rosewater

To coat:

250g (9oz/2 cups)
  icing (powdered) sugar
250g (9oz/2 cups)
  cornflour (cornstarch)

You will also need:
• 37 x 11 x 2.5cm (14¾ x 4¼ x 1 inch)
  metal frame

1 Line a baking tray (sheet) with a non-stick baking mat or silicone (baking) paper and place the metal frame on top.

2 Mix the icing (powdered) sugar, cornflour (cornstarch) and 100ml (3½fl oz/scant ½ cup) of the water together in a bowl.

3 Put the raspberry purée in a pan, bring to the boil, then pour over the cornflour (cornstarch) mixture. Whisk thoroughly and return to the saucepan. Begin to cook over a low heat, stirring regularly, to ensure it doesn't stick.

4 Put the remaining water in a saucepan with the caster (superfine) sugar and heat to 120°C (248°F). Remove from the heat, add the cream of tartar, then pour this into the cornflour mixture. Continue to cook over a low heat for 30–40 minutes, stirring frequently to ensure the mixture is not sticking to the saucepan.

5 Add the honey and rosewater, cook for a further 5 minutes, then pour into the prepared metal frame. Leave to set in a cool, dry area for 24 hours.

6 When fully set, de-mould onto a chopping board and cut into 2.5cm (1 inch) cubes. At this stage the Turkish delight will still feel slightly soft.

7 Sift the icing (powdered) sugar and cornflour (cornstarch) together and then tip into a shallow tray or dish. Coat each Turkish delight cube in the mixture and leave to dry in this mixture for 2–3 hours.

Store in an airtight container and consume within 2 weeks.

FLAVOUR VARIATION

LEMON & ORANGE BLOSSOM

Replace the raspberry purée with 150ml (5fl oz/⅔ cup) lemon juice and 150ml (5fl oz/⅔ cup) orange juice and the rosewater with orange blossom water.

NOUGAT

MONTÉLIMAR, PROVENCAL, CHOCOLATE, CASSIS

*Although there are different versions all over Europe, notably the Italian Torrone,
the exact origins of nougat are not fully known. What is known is that nougat has been made in
the Provence region of France since the 16th century. There are two main types: nougat noir, which
is crunchy and made without eggs; and the soft nougat blanc, the most famous being Nougat de
Montélimar. Provence is famous for its lavender fields and traditionally nougat from the region
is made with their lavender honey. It adds a unique aroma when used in cooking, which always
brings back memories of this part of France for me.*

NOUGAT MONTÉLIMAR

Makes 50 pieces

Oil, for greasing
Icing (powdered) sugar, for dusting
185g (6½oz/⅔ cup) honey
335g (11¼oz/1⅔ cups) caster
  (superfine) sugar
110ml (3½fl oz/scant ½ cup) water
105g (3½oz) liquid glucose
75g (2¾oz) egg whites (about 2–3 eggs)
100g (3½oz/¾ cup) pistachio nuts
40g (1½oz/½ cup) flaked almonds,
  roasted
65g (2oz/½ cup) whole almonds,
  roasted
85g (3oz/⅔ cup) whole hazelnuts,
  roasted

You will also need:
• *rice paper*
• *37 x 11 x 2.5cm (14¾ x 4¼ x 1 inch)
  rectangle frame*

1 Line a baking tray (sheet) with silicone
(baking) paper and place a piece of
rice paper on the tray. Place a 37 x 11
x 2.5cm (14¾ x 4¼ x 1 inch) rectangle
frame on top of the rice paper.

2 Brush the frame with oil and
dust the mat and frame with icing
(powdered) sugar to prevent sticking.

3 Put the honey in a saucepan. Put
the caster (superfine) sugar, water and
glucose in a separate saucepan. Put the
egg whites in the bowl of an electric
mixer fitted with a whisk attachment
and whisk on a slow speed.

4 Bring the honey to the boil and
cook to 121°C (250°F). Pour into
the whisking egg whites and continue
whisking on a medium speed.

5 Place the saucepan with the sugar
over a medium heat and cook to
145°C (293°F), then gently pour this
into the egg white mixture. Continue
to whisk on a medium speed for
about 8–10 minutes until the meringue
becomes firm.

6 Remove the bowl from the machine.
Mix in all the nuts. Spread the mixture
into the prepared frame, cover with a
second sheet of rice paper, then roll
out to fit the frame using a rolling pin.
Leave to set in a cool, dry area for
2 hours.

7 Use a sharp serrated knife to cut
the nougat into 2 x 3.5cm (¾ x 1¼
inch) pieces.

*Store in an airtight container and
consume within 1 month.*

CASSIS NOUGAT

CHOCOLATE NOUGAT

NOUGAT MONTELIMAR

NOUGAT PROVENCAL

NOUGAT PROVENCAL

Makes 50 pieces

375g (13oz/3 cups)
  roasted whole almonds
40g (1½oz/⅓ cup) pistachios
180g (6oz) **Confit Cherries**
  (see page 244)
225g (8oz/generous 1 cup)
  caster (superfine) sugar
150g (5½oz/½ cup) lavender honey
60ml (2fl oz/¼ cup) water
10g (¼oz) invert sugar

You will also need:
• *rice paper*
• *37 x 11 x 2.5cm (14¾ x 4¼ x 1 inch)
  rectangle frame*

I Line a baking tray (sheet) with silicone
(baking) paper and place a piece of rice
paper on the tray. Place a 37 x 11 x
2.5cm (14¾ x 4¼ x 1 inch) rectangle
frame and on top of the rice paper.
Brush the frame with oil. Preheat the
oven to 120°C (240°F/gas¼).

2 Warm the nuts in the oven for
10 minutes. Strain the Confit Cherries.
Put the sugar, honey, water and invert
sugar in a saucepan and cook over a
low heat until all of the sugar dissolves.
Turn up the heat and cook until it
reaches 150°C (302°F).

3 Remove from the heat and add
the nuts and Confit Cherries. Mix to
ensure the nuts and cherries are evenly
dispersed, then pour into the prepared
frame. Place a second sheet of rice
paper on top, then roll out using a rolling
pin. Leave to set in a cool, dry area for
2 hours. Use a sharp serrated knife to
cut the nougat into 2 x 3.5cm (¾ x 1¼
inch) pieces.

*Store in an airtight container and
consume within 1 month.*

CHOCOLATE NOUGAT

Makes 50 pieces

165g (5¾oz/½ cup) honey
330g (11¼oz/generous 1½ cups)
  caster (superfine) sugar
125ml (4fl oz/½ cup) water
60g (2oz) liquid glucose
50g (1¾oz) egg whites (about 2 eggs)
100g (3½oz) chocolate
  (100% cocoa solids)
25g (1oz) pistachio nuts
115g (3¾oz/scant 1 cup) almonds
65g (2¼oz/½ cup) hazelnuts

You will also need:
• *rice paper*
• *37 x 11 x 2.5cm (14¾ x 4¼ x 1 inch)
  rectangle frame*

I Follow the instructions for the
Nougat Montélimar, but melt the
chocolate to 45°C (113°F) and add it to
the nougat mixture after 8–10 minutes
when the meringue has become firm.
Make sure it is thoroughly whisked in
before adding the nuts.

CASSIS NOUGAT

Makes 50 pieces

10g (¼oz) egg white powder
15g (½oz) egg whites (about ½ an egg)
60g (2oz) cassis purée
290g (10oz/1½ cups)
  caster (superfine) sugar
200g (7oz/¾ cup) honey
300g (10½oz) liquid glucose
115ml (4fl oz/scant ½ cup) water
150g (5½oz/1¼ cups) almonds
150g (5½oz/1¼ cups) hazelnuts
15g (½oz) pistachio nuts
55g (2oz) shop-bought confit grapefruit,
  chopped

You will also need:
• *rice paper*
• *37 x 11 x 2.5cm (14¾ x 4¼ x 1 inch)
  rectangle frame*

I Follow the instructions for the
Nougat Montélimar, but begin by
mixing the egg white, egg white
powder, cassis purée and 175g
(6oz/1⅓ cups) of the sugar in the
bowl of an electric mixer fitted with
a whisk attachment. Then continue
with the same method but with the
addtition of the confit grapefruit.

4

MARSHMALLOW

BLACKCURRANT & LAVENDER, LEMON & ELDERFLOWER, APRICOT & GINGER,
RASPBERRY & ROSE, STRAWBERRY & RHUBARB

The ultimate childhood memory of marshmallow has to be toasting them on an open fire. This confection is named 'marshmallow' because of the plant used in the original recipe, which was developed by the Ancient Egyptians as a throat remedy for their nobility. The sap of the marshmallow plant was also used by the Romans and Greeks as a remedy for many ailments. It wasn't until the early 1800s that it was adapted by the French to become confectionery rather than a medicine. It was the innovative confectioners of small French boutiques who evolved the recipe to become what we know and love today.

Makes 40 marshmallows

10g (¼oz) leaf gelatine
100g (3½oz/¾ cup)
  icing (powdered) sugar
100g (3½oz/¾ cup)
  cornflour (cornstarch)
100ml (3½fl oz) blackcurrant purée
20ml (4 teaspoons) **Lavender Infusion**
(see page 239)
225g (8oz/1 cup) caster (superfine)
  sugar plus 10g (¼oz)
135ml (4¾fl oz/½ cup) water
38g (1½oz) egg whites (about 2 eggs)
1g (a pinch) cream of tartar
oil, for greasing

You will also need:
• 37 x 11 x 2.5cm (14¾ x 4¼ x 1 inch)
  rectangle metal frame

1 Soak the gelatine in a bowl of ice-cold water for a few minutes. Squeeze the gelatine to remove the excess water. Sift the icing (powdered) sugar and cornflour (cornstarch) into a bowl.

2 Put the fruit purée in a saucepan over a medium heat and bring to the boil. Remove from the heat and stir in the soaked gelatine until dissolved. Add the Lavender Infusion.

3 Put 225g (8oz/1 cup) of caster (superfine) sugar and water in a saucepan over a medium heat and heat to 130°C (266°F). Whisk the egg whites with the cream of tartar and the additional 10g (¼oz) of sugar in a clean bowl to a soft peak. Simultaneously pour the sugar syrup into the whisking egg. Add the fruit purée mixture and increase the speed. Continue to whisk until the meringue reaches a full peak and cools in temperature.

4 Brush the frame with oil and dust the mat and frame with the icing (powdered) sugar mix to prevent sticking. Pour and spread the mixture into the frame. Cover the surface with more of the icing (powdered) sugar mix, reserving some for dusting. Leave to set for at least 2–3 hours. De-mould onto a chopping board and cut into 2.5cm (1 inch) cubes. Roll in the icing (powdered) sugar mixture to finish.

Store in an airtight container and consume within 2 weeks.

FLAVOUR VARIATIONS

LEMON & ELDERFLOWER

Use 90ml (3¼fl oz) lemon juice and 20ml (¾fl oz) elderflower cordial.

APRICOT & GINGER

Use apricot purée with the addition of 1g (a pinch) ground ginger.

RASPBERRY & ROSE

Use raspberry purée with the addition of 10ml (2 teaspoons) Rose Infusion (see variation page 239).

STRAWBERRY & RHUBARB

Use half strawberry purée and half rhubarb purée.

PÂTE DE FRUITS

RASPBERRY, STRAWBERRY, BLACKCURRANT, LIME, LEMON, ORANGE

I have used a classic pâte de fruits recipe to recreate Rowntree's iconic confection, which was launched in 1881 – the different colours and the sugar coatings used to fascinate me as a young laddie. The Auvergne region, in south-west France, is renowned for its pâte de fruits as it was created there by a French pâtissier called Gillierus during the 17th century.

Makes 24 of each flavour

240g (8½oz) **fruit juice or purée**
  (either lemon, orange or lime juice
  or raspberry, strawberry or
  blackcurrant purée)
225g (8oz/1 cup)
  caster (superfine) sugar
95g (3¼oz) liquid glucose
10g (¼oz) pectin
2.5ml (½ teaspoon) lemon juice
250g (9oz/1¼ cups) granulated sugar,
  for rolling

You will also need:
• one 24-hole silicone pomponette
  mould, with 3 x 2cm (1¼ x ¾ inch)
  cavities

1 Put the fruit purée, 150g (5½oz/
¾ cup) of the sugar and the liquid
glucose in a saucepan and bring to
the boil.

2 Mix the remaining sugar with the
pectin in a small bowl, then whisk this
into the boiling fruit purée.

3 Continue to cook over a low heat,
stirring continuously, until the mixture
reaches 104°C (219°F) on a sugar
(candy) thermometer.

4 Mix in the lemon juice and continue
to cook for 3–4 minutes.

5 Pour the mixture into the silicone
mould and leave to set for 2–3 hours
in a cool, dry area.

6 De-mould the pâte de fruits and
roll in the granulated sugar.

*Store in an airtight container and
consume with 1 month.*

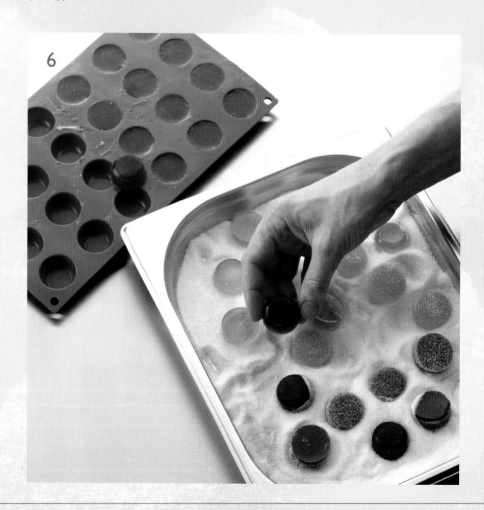

WHISKY TABLET

Tablet is a real Scottish tradition and something my granny used to take great pride in. The recipe I have used dates back a long way – it uses fresh milk rather than evaporated milk, unlike most modern recipes. A recipe using fresh milk takes far longer to cook, but is worth it as the flavour is so much better. As a true Scotsman, I have added a wee whisky to give it an extra dimension.

Makes 60 pieces

450g (1lb 1oz/2 cups)
  caster (superfine) sugar
30g (1¼oz/2 tablespoons)
  golden syrup (light corn syrup)
80g (3oz/⅓ cup/¾ stick)
  sea salt butter
240ml (8½fl oz/1 cup) milk
30ml (1fl oz) Scotch whisky

You will also need:
• *15cm (6 inch) square metal frame*

1 Line a baking tray (sheet) with a non-stick baking mat or silicone (baking) paper and place the 15cm (6 inch) square metal frame on top.

2 Put the sugar, syrup, butter and milk in a large heavy-based saucepan and heat over a low heat until all the sugar has dissolved. Continue to cook over a low heat until the mixture reduces in weight to 600g (1lb 5oz).

3 When the mixture has reduced, add the whisky and turn up the heat to medium. Cook the mixture to 115°C (239°F).

4 Remove the saucepan from the heat and beat the mixture with a spatula or wooden spoon. The mixture on the sides of the saucepan will start to become grainy. The more you mix, the more granular the final product will become. Pour into the prepared mould and leave to cool and set for about 4 hours.

5 When the mixture is fully set, cut into 2cm (¾ inch) pieces.

Store in an airtight container and consume within 1 month.

MOU

SEA SALT, ORANGE & ALMOND, CHOCOLATE, HAZELNUT, PISTACHIO, RASPBERRY

Mou means 'soft' in French. The earliest known salted caramel was created by the Arabs, who called it kurat al milh, *which translates as 'sweet ball of salt'. It has remained popular in Brittany, where fleur de sel is produced, but in recent years has become a favourite everywhere.*

SEA SALT MOU

Makes 50 pieces

150ml (5fl oz/⅔ cup)
  whipping (pouring) cream
1 vanilla pod (bean), split lengthways
340g (11½oz/1¾ cups)
  caster (superfine) sugar
35g (1¼oz) liquid glucose
140g (5oz/⅔ cup/1¼ sticks)
  sea salt butter, cubed

1 Put an 18cm (7 inch) square deep-sided silicone mould on a baking tray (sheet).

2 Put the cream in a saucepan. Scrape the vanilla seeds into the saucepan and drop in the empty pod (bean) too. Bring the cream to the boil. Remove from the heat and leave to infuse for 30 minutes, then discard the pod (bean).

3 Place a heavy-based saucepan over a medium heat, gradually add the sugar and glucose and stir occasionally. Cook until it forms an amber caramel.

4 Slowly add the infused cream, mix well and cook the caramel to 110°C (230°F). Add the butter, piece by piece. Mix well and continue to cook until it reaches 125°C (257°F). Pour into the prepared mould and leave to set overnight in a cool, dry area. Cut into 2 x 3cm (¾ x 1¼ inch) pieces.

Store in an airtight container and consume within 2 weeks.

ORANGE & ALMOND MOU

Makes 50 pieces

50ml (2fl oz/scant ¼ cup) orange juice
165ml (5½fl oz/⅔ cup)
  whipping (pouring) cream
5g (1 teaspoon) grated orange zest
205g (7oz/1 cup)
  caster (superfine) sugar
80ml (3fl oz/⅓ cup) water
105g (3½oz/½ cup/1 stick)
  unsalted butter, cubed
80g (3oz/1 cup) toasted flaked almonds

1 Put the orange juice in a saucepan, bring to the boil and cook until the quantity reduces by half.

2 Put the cream and orange zest in a separate saucepan. Bring to the boil, then remove from the heat and leave to infuse for 10 minutes, before straining.

3 Put the sugar, water and orange juice reduction together in a heavy-based saucepan over a medium heat. Cook to 145°C (293°F), then remove from the heat and add the infused cream and mix well.

4 Add the butter piece by piece. Return to the heat and cook to 124°C (255°F). Remove from the heat and add the flaked almonds, then pour into the prepared mould and leave to set overnight in a cool, dry area. Cut into 2 x 3cm (¾ x 1¼ inch) pieces.

Store in an airtight container and consume within 2 weeks.

CHOCOLATE MOU

Makes 50 pieces

220ml (8fl oz/scant 1 cup)
  whipping (pouring) cream
½ vanilla pod (bean), split lengthways
290g (10oz/1⅓ cups) caster (superfine) sugar
40g (1½oz) liquid glucose
20g (¾oz) unsalted butter, cubed
100g (3½oz) dark (bittersweet) chocolate
  (63% cocoa solids), finely chopped

1 Use the same method as the Sea Salt Mou but add the chocolate after the butter; mix until fully melted before pouring into the mould.

FLAVOUR VARIATIONS:

HAZELNUT
Use the same ingredients and method as the Sea Salt Mou and add 70g (2¾oz/½ cup) roasted hazelnuts and 50g (1¾oz) Hazelnut Praline (see page 242).

PISTACHIO
Use the same ingredients and method as the Hazelnut Mou, but replace the hazelnuts with pistachios and the praline with Pistachio Paste (see page 242).

RASPBERRY
Follow the same method as Orange & Almond Mou, but replace the orange juice with 85ml (3fl oz) raspberry purée (do not reduce), reduce the cream to 85ml (3fl oz/⅓ cup), increase the butter to 150g (5½oz) and omit the almonds and orange zest.

Basics

PÂTE SUCRÉE

Literally translated, pâte sucrée *means 'sugared dough'. It is a versatile pastry and used in a variety of large and small tarts.*

....

Makes 1kg (2¼lb)

250g (9oz/generous 1 cup/2¼ sticks)
  room temperature unsalted butter, cubed
200g (7oz/1½ cups) icing (powdered) sugar, sifted
100g (3½oz) whole eggs (about 2 eggs)
500g (1lb 2oz/3¾ cups) plain (all-purpose) flour, sifted
3g (½ teaspoon) salt

1 Put the butter in a mixing bowl and beat until soft and smooth. Add the icing (powdered) sugar and beat together until smooth.

2 Gradually incorporate the eggs, making sure the mixture becomes fully emulsified.

3 Add the flour and salt and mix to a smooth, homogeneous mass.

4 Turn the dough out onto the work surface, shape it into a block and wrap it in cling film (plastic wrap). Put the dough in the fridge to rest for 2–3 hours.

This pastry can be kept refrigerated for 3 days and frozen for up to 1 month.

FLAVOUR VARIATION

Chocolate Pâte Sucrée: *make as above but change the amount of flour to 420g (14½oz/3 cups) and add 80g (3oz/¾ cup) cocoa powder, sieved with the flour.*

HAZELNUT AND ALMOND PASTRY

This recipe is a derivative of the pâte sucrée, *but with ground nuts added to enhance richness and flavour.*

....

Makes 1.3kg (2lb 8oz)

375g (13oz/1¾ cups/3½ sticks)
  room temperature unsalted butter, cubed
155g (5½oz/generous 1 cup) icing (powdered) sugar, sifted
125g (4½oz) whole eggs (about 2–3 eggs)
500g (1lb 2oz/3¾ cups) plain (all-purpose) flour, sifted
85g (3oz/¾ cup) ground hazelnuts
85g (3oz/¾ cup) ground almonds
2g (½ teaspoon) salt

1 Put the butter in a mixing bowl and beat until soft and smooth. Add the icing (powdered) sugar and beat together until smooth.

2 Gradually incorporate the eggs, making sure the mixture becomes fully emulsified.

3 Mix in the flour, ground nuts and salt and mix to a smooth, homogeneous mass.

4 Turn the dough out onto the work surface, shape it into a block and wrap it in cling film (plastic wrap). Put the dough in the fridge to rest for 2–3 hours.

This pastry can be kept refrigerated for 3 days and frozen for up to 1 month.

FLAVOUR VARIATION

Almond Pastry: *this can simply be made into an almond pastry by replacing the ground hazelnuts with the same amount of ground almonds.*

MARIGNON DOUGH AND ROUGH PUFF PASTRY APPEAR ON PAGES 66 AND 67.

PÂTE SABLÉE

When translated from French, pâte sablée means 'sandy dough'. The texture is light and crumbly so is ideal for sweet tarts and biscuits.

....

Makes 1kg (2¼lb)

500g (1lb 2oz/3¾ cups) plain (all-purpose) flour, sifted
1g (a pinch) salt
200g (7oz/1½ cups) icing (powdered) sugar, sifted
350g (12oz/1½ cups/3 sticks) cold unsalted butter, cubed
30g (1¼oz) egg yolks (about 1½ eggs)
½ vanilla pod (bean), split lengthways

1 Put the dry ingredients directly on the work surface. Add the cubed butter and the seeds scraped from the split vanilla pod (bean) and rub together until no lumps of butter remain.

2 Make a well in the centre, add the wet ingredients and mix to form a smooth, homogeneous mass.

3 Shape the dough into a block and wrap it in cling film (plastic wrap). Put the dough in the fridge to rest for 2–3 hours.

This pastry can be kept refrigerated for 3 days and frozen for up to 1 month.

FLAVOUR VARIATION

Matcha Pâte Sablée: *make as above but without the vanilla and add 10g (¼oz) matcha powder with the flour and sieve together.*

FILO PASTRY

This isn't the easiest or quickest recipe to make, but the results are well worth the effort. Homemade filo pastry is lighter and crispier than any shop-bought version. It is a fun recipe to make. You will know when it is the right thickness when you can see through the filo pastry and it becomes transparent.

....

Makes 900g (2lb 2oz)

500g (1lb 2oz/3¾ cups)
  very fine flour (type 00 pasta flour), sifted
2g (a pinch) salt
80g (3oz) egg yolks (about 4 eggs)
200ml (7fl oz/generous ¾ cup)
  warm water (about 37°C/99°F)
120g (4oz) egg whites (about 4 eggs)
20g (¾oz/1½ tablespoons) caster (superfine) sugar
15ml (1 tablespoon) rapeseed oil, plus extra for coating

1 Mix the sifted flour and salt together in a mixing bowl. Whisk the egg yolks in a bowl until light in colour, then mix with the warm water.

2 Put the egg whites in a clean bowl with the sugar and mix to a light meringue.

3 Add the egg yolk mixture to the light meringue and mix until combined.

4 Make a well with the flour and salt and add the egg mixture, then work to form a dough.

5 Work the dough on the work surface for 15–20 minutes until the dough becomes elastic.

6 Make a slight well in the dough and pour in the oil. Continue to work the dough until the oil is completely absorbed and will release from the work surface.

7 Split the finished dough into 2 pieces. Coat with a little extra oil, wrap in cling film (plastic wrap) and put in the fridge to rest for at least 2–3 hours.

This pastry can be kept refrigerated for 1 day and frozen for up to 1 month.

CHOUX PASTRY

Catherine de' Medici's chef created the first version of choux pastry in around 1540. Originally it was known as pâte à panterelli *after the chef. Later it became known as* pâte à popelini, *then* pâte à popelin. *Popelins were cakes made in the Middle Ages in the shape of a woman's breasts. A pâtissier called Avice developed the paste during the 18th century and created choux buns. Marie-Antoine Carême went on to perfect the recipe in the 19th century, and that is what we know today as choux pastry.*

Makes 800g (1lb 12oz)

125ml (4½fl oz/½ cup) water
125ml (4½fl oz/½ cup) milk
125g (4½oz/½ cup/generous 1 stick) unsalted butter, cubed
12g (¼oz/1 tablespoon) caster (superfine) sugar
160g (5¾oz/scant 1¼ cups) plain (all-purpose) flour, sifted
2g (a pinch) salt
250g (9oz) whole eggs (about 5 eggs), beaten

1 Heat the water, milk, butter and sugar in a saucepan. Bring up to the boil. Take the saucepan off the heat and add the sifted flour and salt. Use a spatula to stir until completely combined.

2 Return the saucepan to the hob, reduce the heat to low and continue stirring with a spatula until the dough leaves the sides of the saucepan.

3 Take off the heat, transfer the dough to a mixing bowl and leave to cool for 2–3 minutes, stirring occasionally.

4 Gradually add the beaten eggs into the dough. Beat with a spatula until the mixture is smooth. The consistency should be neither too soft nor too hard; it should drop off the spoon leaving a smooth 'V' shape.

5 The choux dough is now ready to be piped into shapes.

Use immediately.

Note: *when cooking choux pastry it is vital that you do not open the oven for 12–15 minutes after placing the choux into the oven. Choux pastry rises when the moisture in the dough heats and creates steam; if the oven is opened before the outside of the dough has had time to cook, the steam comes out of the paste and the pastry collapses.*

GENOISE

Genoise is a sponge cake named after the city of Genoa. It is the most widely used sponge recipe in pâtisserie, as it is simple yet versatile. It can be thinly spread onto a mat but is traditionally baked in a tin.

Makes two 30 x 40cm (12 x 16 inch) baking trays (sheets)

300g (10½oz) whole eggs (about 6 eggs)
300g (10½oz/1½ cups) caster (superfine) sugar
300g (10½oz/2¼ cups) plain (all-purpose) flour, sifted
125g (4½oz/½ cup/generous 1 stick) unsalted butter, melted

1 Preheat the oven to 190°C (375°F/gas 5) and line two 30 x 40cm (12 x 16 inch) baking trays (sheets) with silicone (baking) paper (you could also use a non-stick baking mat of the same size).

2 Put the eggs and sugar in a clean, sterilized bowl. Whisk over a bain-marie (water bath) to 37°C (99°F). Remove the bowl from the saucepan of water and continue to whisk to the ribbon stage.

3 Carefully begin to fold the flour through the whisked sabayon mixture using a spatula. When the flour is three-quarters folded through, take 2 large scoops of the mixture and add it to the melted butter.

4 Add the butter mixture to the base sabayon mixture and continue to fold through. Fold in until the mixture is incorporated and smooth.

5 Pour into the prepared baking trays (sheets) or non-stick baking mat and spread out evenly with a step-palette knife.

6 Bake in the preheated oven for about 15 minutes until golden brown and the sponge springs back when pressed gently. Leave to cool.

Ideally use immediately or freeze for up to 1 month.

> ### FLAVOUR VARIATION
> **Chocolate Genoise:** *make as above but use 230g (8oz/1¾ cups) flour and add 60g (2oz/⅔ cup) cocoa powder and sieve together.*

ALHAMBRA SPONGE

This Spanish sponge is rich and buttery, and a favourite of mine for layering inside pâtisserie.

....

Makes two 30 x 40cm (12 x 16 inch) baking trays (sheets)

200g (7oz) whole eggs (about 4 eggs)
50g (1¾oz) egg yolks (about 2–3 eggs)
80g (3oz/⅓ cup) caster (superfine) sugar
25g (1oz/1¾ tablespoons) plain (all-purpose) flour, sifted
25g (1oz/1¾ tablespoons) cornflour (cornstarch), sifted
30g (1¼oz/2 tablespoons) cocoa powder, sifted
100g (3½oz/½ cup/1 stick) unsalted butter

1 Make the sponge following the Genoise method opposite, adding the egg yolks with the whole eggs and sugar, and adding the cornflour (cornstarch) and cocoa powder with the flour.

Use immediately or freeze for up to 1 month.

SWISS ROLL SPONGE

A light sponge, mainly consisting of eggs and sugar, used for making Swiss roll cake.

....

Makes one 30 x 40cm (12 x 16 inch) baking tray (sheet)

150g (5½oz) whole eggs (about 5 eggs)
125g (4½oz/scant ⅔ cup) caster (superfine) sugar
20ml (¾fl oz) *Simple Syrup* (see page 238)
125g (4½oz/1 cup) plain (all-purpose) flour, sifted

1 Preheat the oven to 190°C (375°F/gas 5) and line a baking tray (sheet) with a non-stick baking mat.

2 Put the eggs, sugar and Simple Syrup in a clean, sterilized mixing bowl and whisk together over a bain-marie (water bath) to 37°C (99°F). Remove the bowl from the bain-marie and continue to whisk until it reaches ribbon stage. Carefully fold the sieved flour through the whisked sabayon.

3 Use a step-palette knife to spread the mixture evenly onto the prepared baking tray (sheet). Bake for 12–15 minutes until it begins to colour and the sponge springs back when gently pressed. Cover with a sheet of silicone (baking) paper and leave to cool.

Use immediately.

PAIN DE GÈNE

Pain de Gène or Genoa cake is named after the Italian port town of Genoa. It was created by a French pâtissier during the 1800s. The town lay siege to a French marshal and the people of the city were starving, their only food being rice and almonds. During the siege they consumed more than 50 tonnes of almonds.

....

Makes two 30 x 40cm (12 x 16 inch) baking trays (sheets)

75g (2¾oz) whole eggs (about 1–2 eggs)
60g (2oz) egg yolks (about 3 eggs)
110g (4oz/generous 1 cup) ground almonds
110g (4oz/¾ cup) icing (powdered) sugar
75g (2¾oz/⅓ cup/¾ stick) unsalted butter
60g (2oz/½ cup) plain (all-purpose) flour, sifted
90g (3¼oz) egg whites (about 3 eggs)
50g (1¾oz/¼ cup) caster (superfine) sugar

1 Preheat the oven to 190°C (375°F/gas 5) and line two 30 x 40cm (12 x 16 inch) baking trays (sheets) with silicone (baking) paper (you could also use a non-stick baking mat of the same size).

2 Put the whole eggs and egg yolks, ground almonds and icing (powdered) sugar together in a mixing bowl and beat together for 10–12 minutes until the mixture is light and aerated.

3 Melt the butter (ensuring it is not too warm). Fold the flour into the egg mixture and mix. Put the egg whites and caster (superfine) sugar in a clean, sterilized bowl and whisk to a firm meringue. Alternatively, whisk in an electric mixer fitted with a whisk attachment.

4 When the flour is three-quarters folded through, take 2 large scoops of the mixture and add it to the melted butter. Add the butter mixture back into the base mixture and continue to fold through. Fold in until the mixture is incorporated and smooth.

5 Fold the meringue into the base mixture and mix until combined. Spread onto the prepared baking trays (sheets). Bake in the preheated oven for 12–15 minutes until golden. Leave to cool.

Use immediately or freeze for up to 1 month.

ITALIAN MERINGUE

This is the original method of making meringue. The egg whites are not cooked during the process, but whisked while the sugar is gradually added in stages. It is the least stable of the three meringues, but also the lightest.

180g (6oz) egg whites (about 6 eggs)
300g (10½oz/1½ cups)
   caster (superfine) sugar
25g (1oz/2 tablespoons) liquid glucose
85ml (3fl oz/⅓ cup) water

1 Whisk the egg whites in the clean bowl of an electric mixer fitted with the whisk attachment. Alternatively, use an electric hand-held whisk or whisk by hand.

2 Combine the sugar, glucose and water in a saucepan over a medium heat and boil to a temperature of 121°C (250°F).

3 Gently pour the boiling syrup very slowly into the meringue – have the machine on a slow speed while this is in process.

4 When all the syrup is incorporated, return the machine to full speed and whisk to a stiff meringue and until the mixture is cold in temperature.

Use immediately.

FRENCH MERINGUE

This is made with a boiled sugar syrup that is added to the egg whites, then whisked until cold. It is the most stable of the three and glossy in appearance.

150g (5½oz) egg whites (about 5 eggs)
200g (7oz/1 cup)
   caster (superfine) sugar
100g (3½oz/scant ¾ cup)
   icing (powdered) sugar, sifted

1 Place the egg whites in the clean mixing bowl of an electric mixer fitted with a whisk attachment. Alternatively, use an electric hand-held whisk or whisk by hand. Whisk until it begins to foam.

2 Add half the caster (superfine) sugar and continue to whisk to form soft peaks.

3 Continue to whisk again and add the remaining caster (superfine) sugar. Whisk to form a stiff meringue.

4 Fold in the icing (powdered) sugar.

Use immediately.

SWISS MERINGUE

This type of meringue was the last to be created, during the middle of the 19th century. It is made by whisking egg whites and sugar together over hot water in a bain-marie (water bath). It is used in our macaron recipes.

150g (5½oz) egg whites (about 5 eggs)
300g (10½oz/1½ cups)
   caster (superfine) sugar

1 Combine the egg whites and sugar in a mixing bowl until light and fluffy.

2 Place the bowl over the bain-marie (water bath) and whisk together.

3 Continue to whisk until the mixture reaches 45–50°C (113–122°F) on a thermometer.

4 Remove the bowl from the heat and continue to whisk in an electric mixer fitted with the whisk attachment until the meringue is cool.

Use immediately.

DARK CHOCOLATE MACARONS

Understanding your oven is key to perfecting these Parisien macarons.

....

Makes 18–20 macarons

240g (8½oz) egg whites (about 8 eggs)
250g (9oz/2½ cups) ground almonds, sifted
250g (9oz/2 cups) icing (powdered) sugar, sifted
50g (1¾oz/½ cup) cocoa powder
250g (9oz/1¼ cups) caster (superfine) sugar

1 Preheat the oven to 150°C (300°F/gas 2). Put half the egg whites in a mixing bowl with the ground almonds, icing (powdered) sugar and cocoa powder. Beat to a paste.

2 Put the remaining egg whites and the caster (superfine) sugar in a separate bowl and beat with a whisk until smooth. Place the bowl over a bain-marie (water bath) and whisk until the meringue is 65°C (149°F). Transfer to the bowl of an electric mixer (or continue by hand) and whisk until a stiff meringue forms and it returns to room temperature.

3 Using a spatula, fold the meringue into the cocoa paste until it is smooth. Spoon the mixture into a piping (pastry) bag fitted with the size of plain nozzle (tip) required by the recipe and pipe your required size diameter bulbs onto a baking tray (sheet) lined with a non-stick baking mat. Leave to dry out for 30 minutes. Bake for 20–25 minutes. Leave to cool.

Ideally use the same day, but can be stored in an airtight container for 3 days.

FLAVOUR VARIATIONS

Milk Chocolate Macarons: *make as above but reduce the cocoa powder to 25g (1oz/¼ cup).*
Coffee Macarons: *make as above but omit the cocoa powder and add 16g (½oz) of instant coffee to the egg, almond and icing (powdered) sugar base.*

FLAVOUR VARIATIONS

Almond or Hazelnut Dacquoise: *make as above but use either all ground almonds or all hazelnuts.*
Coconut Dacquoise: *make as above but use desiccated coconut instead of hazelnuts and almonds.*

HAZELNUT AND ALMOND DACQUOISE

Dacquoise is a meringue enriched with ground nuts and sometimes butter. It is great to use in pâtisserie for added texture as it is both crisp and chewy.

....

Makes two 30 x 40cm (12 x 16 inch) baking trays (sheets)

110g (4oz/generous 1 cup) ground hazelnuts
75g (2¾oz/¾ cup) ground almonds
60g (2oz/½ stick) unsalted butter
300g (10½oz/1½ cups) caster (superfine) sugar
40g (1½oz/2½ tablespoons) cornflour (cornstarch)
200g (7oz) egg whites (about 6–7 eggs)
icing (powdered) sugar, for dusting

1 Preheat the oven to 170°C (325°F/gas 3). Spread the ground hazelnuts and almonds out on a baking tray (sheet) and roast for 8–10 minutes. Set aside to cool. Increase the oven temperature to 180°C (350°F/gas 4).

2 Melt the butter, making sure not to over heat. Mix the roasted nuts, half the caster (superfine) sugar and the cornflour (cornstarch) together thoroughly and place on a sheet of silicone (baking) paper.

3 Whisk the egg whites and remaining caster (superfine) sugar in the clean bowl of an electric mixer fitted with a whisk attachment to make a stiff meringue. Alternatively, use an electric hand-held whisk or whisk by hand.

4 When the meringue is three-quarters whisked, fold the dry ingredients into the meringue. Add a spoonful of the meringue mix to the melted butter and fold together. Pour the butter mix into the rest of the meringue. Mix with the spatula until you have a smooth, homogeneous mixture.

5 Pipe or spread onto a non-stick baking mat or a baking tray (sheet) lined with silicone (baking) paper. Liberally dust with icing (powdered) sugar. Bake in the preheated oven for 18–20 minutes. Leave to cool.

Use immediately or wrap in cling film (plastic wrap) and store in the freezer for up to 1 month.

CRÈME PÂTISSIÈRE

This is a main staple in any pastry kitchen as its uses are very diverse. It is not only a crème in itself, and can be made in many different flavours, but it is also the base for other recipes, such as Crème Mousseline *and* Crème Diplomat *(see opposite).*

Makes 750g (1lb 10oz)

500ml (18fl oz/generous 2 cups) milk
1 vanilla pod (bean), split lengthways
120g (4oz) egg yolks (about 6 eggs)
100g (3½oz/½ cup)
  caster (superfine) sugar
50g (1¾oz/⅓ cup)
  plain (all-purpose) flour, sifted

1 Put the milk in a saucepan. Scrape the seeds from the split vanilla pod (bean) into the milk and drop in the split pod (bean) too. Bring to the boil.

2 In a mixing bowl, whisk together the egg yolks and sugar. Continue whisking until the mixture slightly thickens and turns light in colour, 2–3 minutes. Add the sifted flour and whisk again until smooth.

3 Pour half the infused milk into the mixing bowl and whisk again until there are no lumps.

4 Pass this mixture through a fine sieve (strainer), then return the mixture back to the remaining milk in the saucepan.

5 Continuously whisk the mixture until it comes to the boil. Reduce the temperature to a simmer and continue to stir and cook for 5–6 minutes.

6 Take the saucepan off the heat and pour the crème pâtissière into a shallow dish or tray. Cover with cling film (plastic wrap) and cool rapidly.

Store, covered, in the fridge for up to 2 days.

FLAVOUR VARIATION

CHOCOLATE CRÈME PÂTISSIÈRE

Makes 825g (1lb 12oz)

500ml (18fl oz/generous 2 cups) milk
½ vanilla pod (bean), split lengthways
120g (4oz) egg yolks (about 6 eggs)
100g (3½oz/½ cup) caster (superfine) sugar
40g (1½oz/¼ cup) plain (all-purpose) flour, sifted
40g (1½oz/scant ½ cup) cocoa powder, sifted
50g (1¾oz) dark (bittersweet) chocolate (70% cocoa solids), chopped

Follow the recipe opposite, but add the cocoa powder with the flour in **step 2**. Also add the chopped chocolate at the end of **step 5**, mix until the chocolate has been fully incorporated before pouring into the dish or tray.

Store, covered, in the fridge for up to 2 days.

MORE FLAVOUR VARIATIONS

Raspberry Crème Pâtissière: *make as for the main recipe opposite, but whisk 20g (¾oz) freeze-dried raspberry powder into the cooked crème pâtissière.*
Pistachio Crème Pâtissière: *make as for the main recipe opposite, but whisk 40g (1½oz) Pistachio Paste (see page 242) into the cooked crème pâtissière.*
Coffee Crème Pâtissière: *make as for the main recipe opposite, but infuse 10g (¼oz) fresh coffee in the milk and leave to infuse for 30 minutes, before straining and using as instructed.*
Grand Marnier Crème Pâtissière: *make as for the main recipe opposite, but mix in 50ml (2fl oz/scant ¼ cup) Grand Marnier once cooled.*

CRÈME DIPLOMAT

Essentially a lightened Crème Pâtissière (see page 234) with the addition of whipped cream.

Makes 500g (1lb 2oz)

2g (⅛oz) leaf gelatine
½ quantity of **Crème Pâtissière**
  (see page 234)
150ml (5fl oz/⅔ cup)
  double (heavy) cream

1 Soak the gelatine in a bowl of ice-cold water for a few minutes until soft. Squeeze the gelatine to remove excess water.

2 Prepare the Crème Pâtissière, remove from the heat and add the pre-soaked gelatine.

3 Pour into a mixing bowl and leave to cool, stirring occasionally.

4 Semi-whip the cream and fold into the cooled Crème Pâtissière.

Put in the fridge for at least 30 minutes before use.

FLAVOUR VARIATION

White Chocolate and Grand Marnier Crème Diplomat:
make as above but after the gelatin is added, mix in 200g (7oz) finely chopped white chocolate to the Crème Pâtissière, ensuring all the white chocolate melts into the mixture. Once cooled, add 30ml (2 tablespoons) Grand Marnier, mix well, then fold in the cream.

CRÈME MOUSSELINE

Mousseline is a Crème Pâtissière (see page 234) that is enriched with butter and beaten to make it light in texture.

Makes 550g (1lb 4oz)

½ quantity of **Crème Pâtissière**
  (see page 234)
200g (7oz/scant ¾ cup/1¾ sticks)
  room temperature unsalted butter,
  cubed

1 Prepare the Crème Pâtissière, remove from the heat and pour into the bowl of an electric mixer.

2 Beat on a low speed until it reaches room temperature, ensuring you scrape the sides of the bowl as it mixes.

3 Increase the speed, then gradually add the butter cube by cube, until it is fully combined.

Use immediately.

FLAVOUR VARIATIONS

Honey Crème Mousseline:
make as above with the addition of 30g (1¼oz) honey.
Praline Crème Mousseline:
make as above with the addition of 40g (1½oz) Praline Paste (see page 242).
Chocolate Crème Mousseline:
make as above but use the Chocolate Crème Pâtissière (see variation page 234).

CRÈME CHANTILLY

Crème Chantilly is mainly used as decoration or as an accompaniment. It is simply sweetened cream with the addition of vanilla. It is very important to always use real vanilla.

Makes 375g (13oz)

180ml (6fl oz/¾ cup)
  whipping (pouring) cream
180ml (6fl oz/¾ cup)
  double (heavy) cream
½ vanilla pod (bean), split lengthways
18g (1 tablespoon)
  caster (superfine) sugar

1 Whisk both creams, the vanilla seeds from the pod (bean) and the sugar together until soft peaks form.

Use immediately.

Note: *ensure that all of your equipment is cool and immediately whip the cream. Use straight away or return to the fridge – this is to ensure that the cream does not separate.*

BUTTERCREAM

There are many recipes and methods to make buttercream, but this technique is the same as the original recipe. Syrup is poured into whisking egg yolks and butter is added when it has cooled.

....

Makes 385g (13½oz)

100g (3½oz/½ cup)
  caster (superfine) sugar
30ml (1fl oz/2 tablespoons) water
60g (2oz) egg yolks (about 3 eggs)
225g (8oz/1 cup) unsalted butter,
  softened

1 Put the sugar and water in a saucepan, bring to the boil and heat to 121°C (250°F).

2 Put the egg yolks in the bowl of an electric mixer and whisk. Slowly pour the hot syrup into the sabayon and whisk until it is thick and cool.

3 Gradually add the softened butter while still whisking. When all the butter has been incorporated, continue to beat until light and aerated.

Use immediately.

FLAVOUR VARIATIONS

Sesame Buttercream: make as above but with the addition of 20g (¾oz) shop-bought sesame paste.
Lemon Buttercream: make as above but with the addition of the grated zest of 1 lemon added after the butter.

ALMOND CREAM

A baked almond sponge, traditionally used in Bakewell Tarts and fruits tarts. It's great for soaking with a boozy syrup.

....

Makes 1kg (2¼lb)

250g (9oz/generous 1 cup/2¼ sticks)
  unsalted butter, softened
250g (9oz/1¼ cups)
  caster (superfine) sugar
250g (9oz) whole eggs
  (about 5 eggs), beaten
250g (9oz/2½ cups) ground almonds
50g (1¾oz/⅓ cup)
  plain (all-purpose) flour, sifted

1 Put the butter and sugar in a mixing bowl and beat until light in colour.

2 Gradually beat in the eggs and mix until combined.

3 Fold in the ground almonds and the flour and mix until smooth.

Use immediately.

FLAVOUR VARIATIONS

Chocolate Almond Cream: make as above but with 40g (1½oz) flour and 20g (¾oz) cocoa powder.
Hazelnut Cream: make as above but replace the ground almonds with ground hazelnuts.
Orange Almond Cream: make as above but with the addition of the grated orange zest of 1 orange added with the butter.

FRANGIPANE

This is an enriched Almond Cream (see left), with the addition of Crème Pâtissière and rum.

....

Makes 900g (2lb 2oz)

½ quantity of **Crème Pâtissière**
  (see page 234)
½ quantity of **Almond Cream** (see left)
40ml (1½fl oz/2½ tablespoons)
  dark rum

1 Beat the Crème Pâtissière in a mixing bowl until smooth.

2 Fold this into the prepared Almond Cream.

4 Stir through the rum.

Use immediately.

FLAVOUR VARIATION

Pistachio and Kirsch Frangipane: make as above but use kirsch instead of rum. Then mix in 50g (1¾oz) Pistachio Paste (see page 242) to finish.

CRÈME BRÛLÉE

Translated into English, 'creme brulée' simply means 'burnt cream'. It is essentially a slow-baked custard that can be eaten on its own or be used as a component within pâtisserie.

....

Makes 1kg (2¼lb)

250ml (9fl oz/1 cup)
  whipping (pouring) cream
250ml (9fl oz/1 cup)
  double (heavy) cream
1 vanilla pod (bean), split lengthways
1g (a pinch) freshly grated nutmeg
120g (4oz) egg yolks (about 6 eggs)
100g (3½oz/½ cup)
  caster (superfine) sugar

1 Put both creams in a saucepan. Scrape the seeds from the split vanilla pod (bean) into the saucepan and drop in the split pod (bean) too. Add the grated nutmeg and bring to the boil. Remove from the heat, cover and leave to infuse for 30 minutes.

2 Whisk together the egg yolks and sugar in a bowl until light in colour.

3 Mix the boiled, infused cream into the egg yolk and sugar mixture and mix until smooth.

4 Pass the custard through a fine sieve (strainer). Place the vanilla pod (bean) back into the sieved mixture, cover and leave to cool.

Store in airtight container in the fridge overnight to increase the flavour. Use within 2 days.

LEMON CURD

Fruit curd is often used within pâtisserie to create a tangy texture and smooth flavour.

....

Makes 925g (2lb 3oz)

200ml (7fl oz/generous ¾ cup)
  lemon juice
grated zest of 4 lemons
450g (1lb) whole eggs (about 9 eggs)
160g (5½oz/¾ cup)
  caster (superfine) sugar
170g (6oz/¾ cup/1½ sticks)
  unsalted butter, cubed

1 Put the lemon juice and zest in a saucepan and bring to the boil.

2 In a mixing bowl, whisk together the eggs and sugar until light in colour. Add half the lemon juice to the egg mixture and whisk until fully incorporated.

3 Return this mixture to the saucepan and continue to cook the curd over a low heat for a further 5 minutes. Take the saucepan off the heat and pass the mixture through a fine sieve (strainer) into a mixing bowl.

4 Mix in the butter, piece by piece, until fully incorporated. Pour into a shallow dish or tray and cover with cling film (plastic wrap).

Use immediately.

FLAVOURED JELLY

Jelly dates back to the 1800s and was originally considered a decadent dessert.

....

Makes about 250g (9oz)

For the Champagne Jelly:
6g (⅛oz) leaf gelatine
60g (2oz/scant ⅓ cup)
  caster (superfine) sugar
40ml (1½fl oz) water
1 vanilla pod (bean), split lengthways
150ml (5fl oz/⅔ cup) Champagne

For the Kir Royal Jelly:
6g (⅛oz) leaf gelatine
60g (2oz/scant ⅓ cup) caster
  (superfine) sugar
40ml (1½fl oz) water
1 vanilla pod (bean), split lengthways
120ml (4¼fl oz/½ cup) Champagne
30ml (1fl oz/2 tablespoons) crème de
  cassis

1 Soak the gelatine in ice-cold water for a few minutes until soft. Squeeze the gelatine to remove excess water.

2 Put the sugar, water and vanilla in a saucepan and bring to the boil. Add the softened gelatine, then strain into a jug. Add the champagne (and crème de cassis for the Kir Royal Jelly) and leave to semi-set for 20 minutes. Leave to cool.

Use immediately.

FLAVOUR VARIATIONS

Passion Fruit Curd: *make as above but replace the lemon juice with passion fruit purée and omit the zest. Add the seeds of 2 passion fruit at the end.*
Peach Curd: *make as above using the following ingredients – 300g (10½oz) peach purée, 50ml (2fl oz) lemon juice, 300g (10½oz) whole eggs, 120g (4½oz/ scant ⅔ cup) caster (superfine) sugar and 125g (4½oz/½ cup/1⅛ sticks) cubed room temperature unsalted butter. Add 2g (⅛oz) pre-soaked gelatine just prior to adding the butter.*

PANNA COTTA

A traditional Italian dessert, which is essentially a set cream. Its versatile and can be used as a component in various desserts.

....

Makes 300g (10½oz)

150ml (5fl oz/⅔ cup)
  double (heavy) cream
150ml (5fl oz/⅔ cup) milk
1 vanilla pod (bean), split lengthways
2.5g (½ teaspoon) leaf gelatine
15g (½oz) caster (superfine) sugar

1 Put the cream and milk in a saucepan. Scrape the seeds from the vanilla pod (bean) into the saucepan and drop in the empty pod (bean) too. Bring to the boil, then take off the heat. Cover with cling film (plastic wrap) and leave to infuse for 1 hour.

2 Soak the gelatine in a bowl of ice-cold water for a few minutes until soft. Squeeze the gelatine to remove excess water. Add the sugar to the saucepan of cream and vanilla, return to the heat and bring to the boil. Take off the heat and add the soaked gelatine. Pour the mixture through a sieve (strainer) into a bowl or ice bain-marie (water bath) and leave to cool for about 20 minutes. Once the panna cotta has semi-set, whisk the mixture to ensure the vanilla seeds are evenly dispersed.

Use immediately and store in the fridge.

FRUIT COMPOTE

Compotes bring a freshness and intensity of flavour with fresh fruit used. The acidity of the compote can cut through the sweetness or creaminess of a dish to create a more balanced flavour.

....

Makes 200g (7oz)

15g (1 tablespoon)
  caster (superfine) sugar
5g (1 teaspoon) pectin
100g (3½oz) raspberry purée
  (or other fruit purée)
100g (3½oz) raspberries (or other fruit)

1 Mix together the sugar and pectin in a small bowl. Put the raspberry purée and raspberries in a saucepan and bring to the boil. Add the sugar and pectin and cook for 2–3 minutes.

2 Pour into a shallow tray. Leave to cool, then put in an airtight container and transfer to the fridge.

Store in an airtight container in the fridge for up to 3–4 days.

SIMPLE SYRUP

This is a basic recipe used mostly for soaking sponges and cakes.

....

Makes 400ml (14fl oz/1¾ cups)

225ml (8fl oz/scant 1 cup) water
190g (6½oz/scant 1 cup)
  caster (superfine) sugar
1½ peels of lemon zest
½ vanilla pod (bean), split lengthways

1 Put the water, sugar and lemon zest in a saucepan. Scrape the seeds from the split vanilla pod (bean) into the water and drop in the empty pod (bean) too. Bring to the boil and cook for 2–3 minutes. Take off the heat and leave to cool.

Store in an airtight container in the fridge for up to 1 month.

FLAVOUR VARIATIONS

Grand Marnier, Kirsch or Rum Syrup: *add 200ml (7fl oz/ generous ¾ cup) alcohol of your choice once the syrup has cooled.*
Light Syrup: *make a syrup as above using 600ml (1 pint/2½ cups) water, 300g (10½oz/1½ cups) caster (superfine) sugar and the 1 split and scraped vanilla pod (bean). Makes 800ml (28fl oz/3⅓ cups).*

LIGHT FRUIT NAPPAGE

This is a very light glaze generally used for glazing fruits used for decorations.

....

Makes 625g (1lb 4oz)

300ml (10fl oz/scant 1¼ cups) water
300g (10½oz) liquid glucose
40g (1½oz) caster (superfine) sugar
18g (¼oz) pectin

1 Place the water and glucose in a saucepan and bring to the boil. Mix together the sugar and pectin in a small bowl, whisk into the boiling mixture and cook for about 2–3 minutes. Transfer to an airtight container and leave to cool before transferring to the fridge.

Store in an airtight container in the fridge for up to 1 week.

LAVENDER (OR ROSE) INFUSION

A natural infusion used for adding intense flavour to confectionery.

....

Makes 100ml (3½fl oz)

60g (2oz/generous ½ cup) caster (superfine) sugar
100ml (3½fl oz/scant ½ cup) water
20g (¾oz) fresh or dried lavender flowers (or rose petals)

1 Boil together the sugar and water to make a syrup. Add the lavender, remove from the heat and cover with cling film (plastic wrap). Leave to infuse for 2 hours.

2 Strain the syrup through a fine sieve and store in an airtight container in the fridge until ready to use.

Store in an airtight container in the fridge for up to 2 weeks.

APRICOT NAPPAGE

This is a traditional glaze used for a variety of pâtisserie and cakes.

....

Makes 850g (1lb 13oz)

200g (7oz) Cox apples, washed and roughly chopped
200g (7oz) fresh apricots, stoned and roughly chopped
400g (14oz/2 cups) caster (superfine) sugar
100ml (3½fl oz/scant ½ cup) water
12g (¼oz) pectin
5ml (1 teaspoon) lemon juice

1 Put the apples and apricots in a saucepan with half the sugar and the water. Cook over a low heat for about 15–20 minutes until the apples become soft. Remove from the heat, then leave to cool slightly.

2 Transfer to a food processor and blend until smooth.

3 Put the puréed fruit in a clean saucepan, return to the heat and bring to the boil.

4 Mix together the remaining sugar with the pectin in a bowl. Take the boiling purée off the heat, add the pectin and sugar, return to the heat and cook over a low heat for 5 minutes.

5 Add the lemon juice, bring back to the boil, then remove from the heat and leave to cool slightly.

6 Pass though a fine sieve (strainer) into an airtight container and leave to cool before transferring to the fridge.

Store in an airtight container in the fridge and use within 1 week.

FRUIT GLAZE

This glaze is ideal for glazing the tops of entremets and small pâtisserie. It is often called mirror glaze as it is so shiny.

....

Makes 275g (9¾oz)

8g (¼oz) leaf gelatine
175g (6oz) strawberry purée (or other fruit purée)
100g (3½oz) **Simple Syrup** *(see page 238)*
½ vanilla pod (bean), split lengthways

1 Soak the gelatine in a bowl of ice-cold water for a few minutes until soft. Squeeze to remove any excess water. Put the strawberry purée and Simple Syrup in a saucepan.

2 Scrape the seeds from the split vanilla pod (bean) into the saucepan and drop in the empty pod (bean) too. Bring to the boil.

3 Take off the heat, add the soaked gelatine, mix well, then strain into an airtight container. Leave to cool.

Store in an airtight container in the fridge and use within 1 week.

FLAVOUR VARIATIONS

Various: *you can use different flavoured fruit purées to make this fruit glaze, such as raspberry, cherry, blackcurrant and orange.*

DARK (BITTERSWEET) CHOCOLATE GLAZE

This glaze is simple to make, but looks very impressive. It is exceptionally shiny, when made well and glazed at the right temperature. Too hot will create bubbles; and too cold will make it thick.

....

Makes 750g (1lb 10oz)

18g (¾oz) leaf gelatine
235ml (8¼fl oz/1 cup) water
300g (10½oz/1½ cups)
  caster (superfine) sugar
100g (3½oz/1 cup)
  cocoa powder, sifted
170ml (6fl oz/¾ cup)
  whipping (pouring) cream

1 Soak the gelatine in a bowl of ice-cold water for a few minutes until soft. Squeeze to remove any excess water.

2 Put the water and sugar in a saucepan, bring to the boil, then continue to simmer over a low heat for 2–3 minutes.

3 Add the sifted cocoa powder and the cream.

4 Bring back to the boil and simmer for 4–5 minutes.

5 Take the saucepan off the heat, add the gelatine and stir until dissolved.

6 Strain, then leave to cool.

Store in an airtight container in the fridge and use within 4 days.

MILK CHOCOLATE GLAZE

This glaze is similar to a ganache, so it is very rich in flavour.

....

Makes 650g (1lb 7oz)

400g (14oz) milk chocolate
  (35% cocoa solids), finely chopped
260ml (9fl oz/1 generous cup)
  whipping (pouring) cream
40g (1½oz) liquid glucose

1 Put the chopped chocolate in a mixing bowl. Put the cream and liquid glucose in a saucepan and bring to the boil.

2 Pour the boiled cream over the chocolate and mix well until emulsified.

3 Transfer to a container and leave to cool.

Store in an airtight container in the fridge and use within 4 days.

WHITE CHOCOLATE GLAZE

A versatile glaze that gives a glossy finish and can be adapted with the addition of different coloured ingredients.

....

Makes 850g (1lb 13oz)

15g (½oz) leaf gelatine
210ml (7¼fl oz/generous ¾ cup) water
105g (3½oz/½ cup)
  caster (superfine) sugar
210g (7½oz) liquid glucose
140ml (5fl oz/⅔ cup)
  double (heavy) cream
210g (7½oz) white chocolate,
  finely chopped

1 Soak the gelatine in a bowl of ice-cold water for a few minutes until soft. Squeeze to remove any excess water.

2 Put the water, sugar and liquid glucose in a saucepan, bring to the boil and heat to 103°C (218°F).

3 Add the cream and soaked gelatine to the saucepan. Pour the hot cream over the white chocolate in another bowl, then blitz with a hand-held electric blender until smooth.

Store in an airtight container in the fridge and use within 4 days.

RASPBERRY JAM

The name 'jam' came into the English language in the 18th century; prior to that it was referred to as preserve or conserve. Methods of preserving fruit are ancient in history, and recipes were published in France as early as the 14th century. Jams are still an essential element of a great deal of baking.

....

Makes 2 x 200g (7oz) jars

150g (5½oz) raspberry purée
150g (5½oz/1¼ cups) raspberries
120g (4oz/scant ½ cup) caster (superfine) sugar
20g (¾oz) pectin
10ml (2 teaspoons) lemon juice

1 Put the raspberry purée, raspberries and 75g (2¾oz/ ⅓ cup) of the sugar in a heavy-based saucepan and bring to the boil.

2 Mix the remaining sugar with the pectin in a small bowl. Whisk the pectin mixture into the boiling raspberry liquid.

3 Continue to cook over a low heat, stirring continuously until the mixture reaches 104°C (219°F). Add the lemon juice and continue to cook for a further 2–3 minutes.

4 Test to see if the jam has reached setting point. Spoon a small amount of jam onto a cold plate or saucer, then put in the fridge for 2 minutes. Gently press the edge of the jam with a spoon. It is set if a skin has formed and the edges wrinkle. If it doesn't, continue to cook the jam for another 2 minutes, then check again.

5 Pour the jam into a sterilized jam jar and leave to cool before closing the lid.

Store in the fridge for up to 1 month.

FLAVOUR VARIATIONS

Various: *you can change the flavour of jam by just using the same amounts of your chosen fruit and purée. Good flavours are: apricot, redcurrant, cherry, strawberry and blackcurrant.*

REDCURRANT JELLY

A very traditional British preserve. It is often served with savoury food but can be equally tasty in pâtisserie.

....

Makes 3 x 200g (7oz) jars

800g (1lb 12oz) redcurrants
125ml (4½fl oz/½ cup) water
500g (1lb 2oz/2½ cups) caster (superfine) sugar
 (this may vary depending on quantity of redcurrant liquid)
25ml (1fl oz) lemon juice

1 Put the redcurrants and water in a saucepan and cook over a medium heat until the redcurrants begin to break down and release liquid. This will take about 20 minutes.

2 Put a sieve or colander over a clean saucepan and strain the cooked redcurrants through a fine sieve or muslin cloth for at least 3 hours, ideally overnight.

3 When the liquid has drained into the saucepan below, you should be left with about 500ml (18fl oz/2 cups). Discard the drained berries.

4 Add an equal quantity of sugar to the pan of redcurrant liquid. Cook over a medium heat, stirring frequently, until the mixture reaches 104°C (219°F). Add the lemon juice and continue to cook for a further 2–3 minutes.

5 Test to see if the jam has reached setting point. Spoon a small amount of jam onto a cold plate or saucer, then put in the fridge for 2 minutes. Gently press the edge of the jam with a spoon. It is set if a skin has formed and the edges wrinkle. If it doesn't, continue to cook the jam for another 2 minutes, then check again. Pour into sterilized jam jars and leave to cool before closing the lid.

Store in the fridge for up to 1 month.

FLAVOUR VARIATION

Apricot: *use the above recipe but set aside 50g (1¾oz) sugar in a small bowl and mix well with 40g (1½oz) pectin. Whisk this into the mixture when it begins to boil and continue to cook until it reaches 104°C (219°F).*

MARMALADE

In Scottish folklore, there is a story of the origin of marmalade. A cargo of Seville oranges arrived in the port of Dundee. A local grocer bought the oranges believing they could be sold as eating oranges. On tasting the sour fruit, he realized that no one would buy them. Not wanting to waste them, his clever wife cooked them with sugar to make a preserve. It proved popular and the public love it to this day.

Makes 600g (1lb 6oz)

2 Seville oranges (weighing about 225g/8oz in total)
½ a lemon
500ml (18fl oz/generous 2 cups) water
400g (14oz/2 cups) jam sugar
25g (1oz/2 tablespoons) dark soft brown sugar

1 Remove the orange peel in long strips using a peeler, trim any white pith from the peel, then finely slice and place in a muslin (cheesecloth) bag.

2 Roughly chop the oranges and lemon, put in a saucepan with the water, both sugars and the peel in the muslin (cheesecloth) bag. Simmer over a low heat, uncovered, for about 2 hours until the fruit is tender. Remove the muslin (cheesecloth) bag and set aside to drain. Line a colander with layers of muslin (cheesecloth) and set over a bowl. Strain the contents of the saucepan through the muslin, leave to drain for 30 minutes, then squeeze the remaining liquid by twisting the cloth.

3 Return the strained liquid and the peel from the muslin (cheesecloth) to a clean saucepan, bring to the boil and cook until it reaches 104°C (219°F), stirring continuously. Test the marmalade is setting: spoon a small amount onto a cold plate and leave to cool. If it sets, take the marmalade off the heat and place in a sterilized jar, then seal. If it does not set, try again after a few more minutes.

Store in an airtight container in the fridge for up to 1 month.

FLAVOUR VARIATIONS

Yuzu Marmalade: *make as above but use the same weight of yuzu instead of oranges.*
Lemon Marmalade: *make as above but use lemons not oranges.*

PRALINE PASTE

This can be bought, but the flavour of homemade praline paste is much better. Praline paste is a mixture of sugar and nuts cooked over a high heat until it caramelizes, then blended in a machine to form a paste. Please ensure that your mixer is robust enough, as the caramelized sugar can be very hard.

Makes 2 x 200g (7oz) jars

150g (5½oz/generous 1 cup) hazelnuts
150g (5½oz/generous 1 cup) almonds
300g (10½oz/1½ cups) caster (superfine) sugar
10ml (2 teaspoons) hazelnut oil

1 Preheat the oven to 200°C (400°F/gas 6). Spread the nuts out on a baking tray (sheet) lined with a non-stick baking mat. Roast in the preheated oven for 8–10 minutes until lightly golden and then transfer to a heavy-based saucepan.

2 Cook over a medium heat while gradually adding the sugar and stirring continuously. Continue to cook and stir until the sugar turns an amber caramel, about 15–18 minutes.

3 Pour the caramelized nuts onto a baking tray (sheet) lined with a non-stick baking mat and leave to cool.

4 When the nuts have cooled, break up the praline and transfer it to a good food processor or blender. Add the hazelnut oil and blitz until you have a smooth paste.

Store in an airtight container for up to 2 months.

FLAVOUR VARIATIONS

Various: *you can make any flavour of nut paste by changing the nuts and oil used. Good flavours are walnut, hazelnut or peanut.*

PISTACHIO PASTE

100g (3½oz/⅔ cup) pistachios
15ml (1 tablespoon) pistachio oil (or a flavourless nut oil instead)

Put the pistachios and oil in a food processor or blender and blitz together until it becomes a smooth paste.

CRYSTALLIZED HAZELNUTS (OR ALMONDS)

Crystallized nuts make a lovely decoration and also add texture.

....

Makes 300g (10½oz)

250g (9oz/scant 2 cups) hazelnuts
  (or almonds), lightly roasted
100g (3½oz/½ cup)
  caster (superfine) sugar
40ml (1½fl oz) water

1 Put the hazelnuts in a saucepan and lightly warm on the stove.

2 At the same time, put the sugar and water in another saucepan and cook to 118°C (244°F).

3 Pour the cooked sugar onto the hazelnuts and mix well.

4 Place the saucepan onto the stove and, stirring continuously, cook over a medium heat until the sugar crystallizes.

5 Remove from the heat, spread and separate out the nuts on a non-stick baking mat and leave to cool.

Store in an airtight container and use within 2 weeks.

CARAMELIZED ALMOND BATONS

Caramelized nuts are very nostalgic, especially the smell while cooking them. The cooked sugar and added butter gives a golden appearance and rich flavour.

....

Makes 350g (12oz)

250g (9oz/2 cups) almond batons,
  lightly roasted
40ml (1½fl oz) water
100g (3½oz/½ cup)
  caster (superfine) sugar
12g (1 tablespoon) unsalted butter

1 Put the almond batons in a saucepan and lightly warm on the stove. At the same time, put the water and sugar in another small saucepan and cook to 118°C (244°F).

2 Pour this syrup over the almonds, then set over a medium heat and cook until the almond batons crystallize and then gradually caramelize, stirring continuously. Take off the heat, then add the butter.

3 Spread and separate the nuts out on a baking tray (sheet) lined with a non-stick baking mat and leave to cool.

Store in an airtight container and use within 2 weeks.

CRYSTALLIZED PISTACHIOS

A great way of adding colour and texture to dishes.

....

Makes 100g (3½oz)

100g (3½oz/¾ cup) pistachios
10ml (2 teaspoons) kirsch
30g (1¼oz/2 tablespoons)
  caster (superfine) sugar

1 Preheat the oven to 200°C (400°F/ gas 6). Mix the pistachios and kirsch together in a bowl, add the sugar and mix well.

2 Spread the nuts out on a non-stick baking mat. Bake in the preheated oven for 4–5 minutes, turning regularly, until crystallized. Separate the nuts and leave to cool.

Store in an airtight container and use within 2 weeks.

FLAVOUR VARIATIONS

Caramelized Almond nibs:
make as above but replace the almond batons with the same amount of almond nibs.
Caramelized Walnuts:
make as above but replace the almond batons with 150g (5½oz) walnut halves.
Caramelized Hazelnuts: *make as above but use halved hazelnuts.*

ARMAGNAC-MARINATED PRUNES

Prunes marinated in Armagnac are a favourite from South West France. The best way to eat these is after they have been marinating for at least a month. I would happily eat them on their own, although there are many wonderful dishes that they could be used in.

....

Makes 2 x 200g (7oz) jars

425ml (15fl oz/generous 1¾ cups) water
90g (3¼oz/scant ½ cup)
  caster (superfine) sugar
5g (1 teaspoon) Earl Grey tea leaves
250g (9oz/2 cups) prunes
  (ideally prunes d'agen) pitted
125ml (4½fl oz/½ cup) Armagnac

1 Put the water and sugar in a saucepan and bring to the boil. Put the tea leaves in an infuser bag.

2 Put the tea bag in the saucepan of syrup. Take the saucepan off the heat and leave to infuse for 2 minutes.

3 Add the prunes to the tea-infused syrup. Leave to marinate for 1 hour.

4 Remove the tea bag and add the Armagnac.

5 Spoon the prunes into 2 sterilized jars and pour over the marinating syrup. Cover the jars and leave to cool. Once completely cool, close the lids and leave to marinate overnight or preferably up to 1 month before use.

Store in the fridge for up to 3 months.

RUM-SOAKED SULTANAS

These are quick and easy to prepare. I like to keep a jar in my fridge to add to desserts to make them extra special.

....

Makes 350g (12oz)

250g (9oz/1¾ cups) sultanas
  (golden raisins)
100ml (3½fl oz/scant ½ cup) dark rum

1 Bring a saucepan of water to the boil and add the sultanas (golden raisins).

2 Simmer for 2–3 minutes, then strain.

3 Spoon the sultanas (golden raisins) into sterilized jars and pour over the dark rum.

4 Seal and leave to marinate for at least 24 hours.

Store in the fridge for up to 3 months.

FLAVOUR VARIATION

Rum-soaked Raisins: *make as above but replace the sultanas with the same amount of raisins.*

CONFIT CHERRIES

Glacé cherries are incredibly nostalgic to me, but far too sweet to eat. I experimented to find an alternative way to preserve cherries, while still capturing that nostalgic taste.

....

Makes 600g (1lb 6oz)

200g (7oz/1 cup)
  caster (superfine) sugar
50ml (2fl oz/scant ¼ cup) water
200g (7oz/1 cups) cherries, pitted
½ a lemon
100ml (3½fl oz/scant ½ cup)
  apple juice

1 Put the sugar and water in a saucepan and bring to the boil. When all of the sugar has dissolved, add the cherries and the lemon half. Reduce to a low heat and simmer for about 20–30 minutes, until the syrup thickens. Remove from the heat and leave for at least 2–3 hours (overnight ideally) for the cherries to marinate in the syrup. Strain the cherries and reserve the excess syrup.

2 Put the reserved syrup in a saucepan and add the apple juice. Bring to the boil and cook for 5 minutes. Reduce the heat and add the strained cherries. Cook slowly to 104°C (219°F). Remove from the heat and leave to cool.

Store in an airtight container in the fridge for up to 3 months

FONDANT

Before working for Pierre Koffmann, I had only ever used bought fondant. On being told by Pierre to make it myself, I researched the best recipes and learned how to perfect it. Homemade fondant is always glossier and smoother when made right.

....

Makes 1.2kg (2lb 12oz)

1g (a pinch) cream of tartar
240ml (8½fl oz/1 cup) water
980g (2¼lb/scant 5 cups)
  caster (superfine) sugar
120g (4oz) liquid glucose

1 Make a paste with the cream of tartar and 30ml (1fl oz/2 tablespoons) of the water, mix until smooth.

2 Put the sugar and rest of the water in a saucepan and mix together. Bring to the boil. Use a pastry brush dipped in water to remove any sugar crystals from the sides of the saucepan as the syrup boils. Continue to heat the syrup until it reaches 106°C (222°F). Add the cream of tartar paste and then add the liquid glucose.

3 Continue to cook until the syrup reaches 117°C (242°F). Remove from the heat and pour onto a marble slab. Use a scraper to work the fondant by moving it from the outside into the centre and spreading back out again. Continue this process until it cools, then becomes white and thickens. Place in a plastic airtight container and cover with cling film (plastic wrap) to prevent a skin forming.

Preparing fondant for use:

4 To prepare the fondant for use, warm 600g (1lb 5oz) fondant to 32–35°C (89–95°F) with 40ml (1½fl oz) Simple Syrup)see page 238). If it is too thick, add small quantities of syrup until the right consistency is formed.

Store in an airtight container for up to 2 months.

FLAVOUR VARIATIONS

Chocolate Fondant: *melt 60g (2oz) chocolate and mix well with 600g (1lb 5oz) prepared fondant.*

Raspberry Fondant: *add 15g (½oz) freeze-dried raspberry powder to 600g (1lb 5oz) prepared fondant.*

Pistachio Fondant: *add 40g (1½oz) Pistachio Paste (see page 242) to 600g (1lb 5oz) prepared fondant.*

Caramel Fondant: *make a dark amber caramel by gradually adding 200g (7oz/1 cup) caster (superfine) sugar into a heavy-based pan, then add 75ml (2¾fl oz/⅓ cup)water and leave to cool. To prepare the fondant, mix about 75g (2¾oz) caramel with 600g (1lb 5oz) fondant. Any excess caramel can be stored in an airtight container for up to 2 months.*

Coffee Fondant: *mix 10g (¼oz) instant coffee with 15ml (1 tablespoon) warm water. Add to 600g (1lb 5oz) prepared fondant.*

Vanilla Fondant: *split and scrape the seeds from a vanilla pod and mix well with 600g (1lb 5oz) prepared fondant.*

Note: Alternatively, a food processer can be used to make fondant. Once cooked to 117°C (242°F), remove the syrup from the heat and cover with cling film (plastic wrap). Leave to cool to 50°C (122°F) before placing into a food processor and mixing until it cools, then becomes white and thickens.

ROYAL ICING

Royal icing is an opaque, white icing, which sets firm. It needs to be used quickly, as when it is exposed to air it sets very fast.

....

Makes 300g (10½oz)

40g (1½oz) egg whites (about 1½ eggs)
250g (9oz/1¾ cups)
  icing (powdered) sugar, sifted
10ml (2 teaspoons) lemon juice

1 Place the egg whites in a mixing bowl, beat at a low speed and gradually add the icing (powdered) sugar.

2 Once fully incorporated, beat at a high speed for 2 minutes.

3 Add the lemon juice and beat for a further minute.

4 When ready, the icing will fall in a fine, straight point whichever way you turn the beater. If the icing is too thick and does not form, add a touch more egg white. If it is too liquid and the point flops over when you hold it upwards, add a little more icing (powdered) sugar.

Store in an airtight container to avoid a crust forming for up to 1 week.

FLAVOUR VARIATION

Royal Icing for Piping: *make as above but beat by hand and use 15g (½oz) egg whites, 125g (4½oz/generous ¾ cup) icing (powdered) sugar and 5ml (1 teaspoon) lemon juice.*

WATER ICING

This icing recipe is perfect for creating a crisp and shiny coating on a variety of cakes and biscuits.

....

Makes 360g (12½oz)

300g (10½oz/2¼ cups) icing
  (powdered) sugar
60ml (2fl oz/¼ cup) lemon juice

I Sieve the sugar into a bowl and beat with the lemon juice until smooth.

Ideally use immediately, but can be stored in an airtight container for 2–3 days.

FLAVOUR VARIATION

Lemon Zest Water Icing: *make as above but add the grated zest of 1 lemon.*

DRIED ZEST

A simple yet effective decoration. It can add a splash of colour to a finished dish.

....

Makes 10g (¼oz)

I lime or lemon (or any citrus fruit)

I Preheat the oven to 60°C (140°F/gas ¼).

2 Grate the zest from the fruit onto a tray lined with silicone (baking) paper. Place in the oven for about 30 minutes. Once cooled, store in an airtight container.

Store in a jar for up to 2 weeks.

VANILLA SUGAR

Vanilla sugar adds a lovely flavour to dishes. This recipe uses a whole fresh vanilla pod (bean), but you could use up any empty pods (beans) by drying them out, adding them to a pot of sugar and leaving them to infuse.

....

Makes 300g (10½oz/1½ cups)

300g (10½oz/1½ cups) caster sugar
I vanilla pod (bean), split and scraped

I Mix the sugar and vanilla seeds together.

Store in a jar for up to 1 month.

FLAVOUR VARIATIONS

Cinnamon Sugar: *make as above but replace the vanilla seeds with 5g (⅛oz) ground cinnamon.*
Ginger Sugar: *make as above but replace the vanilla seeds with 5g (⅛oz) ground ginger.*

CLARIFIED BUTTER

Clarified butter is used for glazing fruits or pastry which is then baked. The clarifying process removes the milk solids from the butter, which means there are no small pieces that burn when cooked.

....

I Put cubes or slices of unsalted butter in a saucepan and melt gently over a low heat.

2 Let the butter gently simmer until the white foam rises to the top of the melted butter.

3 When no more foam seems to be rising to the surface, take the butter off the heat and skim off as much of the foam as you can with a ladle. Line a sieve (strainer) with a few layers of muslin (cheesecloth) and set over a bowl. Gently pour the butter through the lined sieve (strainer), which will remove any remaining white particles.

BEURRE NOISETTE

This is a classic French technique. It is made by cooking butter until the milk solids within it caramelize to create a nutty and rich flavour.

....

I Put cubes of unsalted butter in a saucepan over a medium heat. Let the butter melt, stirring frequently.

2 Once the butter has melted it will begin to foam a little then subside, continue to cook stirring frequently until the milk solids start to turn a light brown.

3 Remove from the heat and pour into a tray, then leave to cool.

CHOCOLATE DECORATIONS

FLAT SHEET TECHNIQUES

Preparing and spreading chocolate

1 Lightly stick a sheet of patterned or plain acetate to a plastic tray with a little oil, with the pattern facing up if applicable.

2 Use a palette knife to thinly and evenly spread the tempered chocolate (see page 14) over the top.

3 Leave to semi-set, then cut or score the chocolate using the required equipment as specified below. Place another sheet of acetate on top of the chocolate followed by a plastic tray to keep it flat while it sets.

Squares
Cut with the pastry wheels 2cm (¾ inch) apart to create squares.

Rectangles
Use a ruler and knife to cut rectangles to the required size.

Slivers
Spread the acetate with gold cocoa butter (as instructed in Preparing a Coloured Sheet opposite), then chocolate. Cut the semi-set chocolate into elongated 's' shapes across the length of the acetate.

Flat Chocolate Sticks
Use a small knife or pastry wheel to cut the chocolate sheet into thin lines.

Flat Wavy Sticks
See above but using fluted wheels.

Discs
Use a small pastry cutter or the tip of a plain metal piping nozzle to cut circles in the semi-set chocolate.

FLICKS AND WAVES

Waves

1 Thinly and evenly spread tempered chocolate (see page 14) over the top of a 10 x 12cm (4 x 4½ inch) sheet of acetate with a step-palette knife.

2 When semi-set, take a knife (or pastry wheels) and a ruler and score lines lengthways across the chocolate, about 1cm (½ inch) apart.

3 Place another sheet of acetate the same size on top. Quickly place between 2 sheets of corrugated plastic and gently push down. Remove from the plastic and trim the edges before serving.

Triangle Flicks

1 Cut out long thin triangles, 15 x 1cm (6 x ½ inch) in size, from a sheet of acetate. Spread each triangle with a thin layer of tempered chocolate (see page 14) using a step-palette knife. Leave to semi-set.

2 Use the tip of a small knife to carefully lift the triangle from the layer of chocolate. Place it in a curved tray at an angle and leave to set.

Curved Swiped Flick

1 Place a 12 x 3cm (4½ x 1¼ inch) sheet of acetate on a plastic tray. Dip the tip of your index finger in a small bowl of tempered chocolate (see page 14) and carefully swipe your finger on the acetate creating a delicate shape. Place on a curved tray and leave to set.

CHOCOLATE SHAVINGS

1 Hold a tempered block of chocolate at an angle and use a small knife to scrape the back of the block to create shavings. For smaller shavings, use just the tip of the knife.

2 Leave the shavings to stand for a few minutes to firm before moving.

PREPARING A COLOURED SHEET

1 Gently melt 50g (1¾oz) cocoa butter in a bain-marie (water bath) and mix in 5g (1 teaspoon) powdered colour for chocolate work. Heat to 45°C (113°F), then leave to cool to 32°C (90°F).

2 Lightly stick a sheet of acetate to a plastic tray with a little oil to stop it slipping and rub all over with cotton wool to remove any bubbles.

3 Use a clean, dry sponge or a fine-haired paintbrush to cover the acetate in the coloured cocoa butter. Use straight, fluid motions all in the same direction to create the desired effect, then create patterns or shapes as required.

A NOTE ON SETTING & STORING DECORATIONS

• All decorations should be left to fully set in a cool, dry area for 1–2 hours.

• All decorations must be kept, covered, in a cool, dry area for up to 2 months.

• Where applicable, decorations should be kept on the acetate until ready to use, then the acetate should be carefully peeled off.

Squares

Slivers

Waves

Curved Swiped Flicks

Triangle Flicks

PIPED TECHNIQUES

All piped techniques use a small paper piping cornet (see box below).

Curls

1 Cut a rectangle of acetate 4 x 18cm (1½ x 7 inches). Pipe thin straight lines of chocolate along the acetate, then leave to semi-set.

2 Carefully lift the chocolate-coated acetate and curl it around to create a spiral. Place it on a curved tray to set.

Joined-up Curls

See above but pipe the chocolate so that some of the lines overlap.

Single Curves

Large: Cut a 12 x 15cm (4½ x 6 inch) rectangle of acetate. Pipe thin straight lines of chocolate across the acetate, then leave to semi-set. Place into a curved tray to set.

Small: Follow the method above but use 5 x 12cm (2 x 4½ inch) rectangles of acetate.

Joined-up Curves

Follow the method above, but instead of piping straight lines, pipe the chocolate into an elongated oval shape, joining the lines as you do so.

Hoops

1 Cut out a rectangle of acetate to the required size. Pipe fine lines of chocolate across the length of the acetate, ensuring that you have a margin of 1cm (½ inch) on the left-hand side.

2 Create a hoop with the acetate ensuring that the right-hand side of the acetate pushes into the join on the chocolate lines. Place into a 5cm (2 inch) ring mould to set.

Cherry Stalks

1 Lightly stick a sheet of patterned or plain acetate to a plastic tray with a little oil and rub all over with cotton wool to remove any bubbles.

2 Pipe curved lines in the shape of cherry stalks and leave to set.

COPEAUX

Dark (Bittersweet) Chocolate

1 Spread a thin layer of tempered chocolate (see page 14) onto a marble or granite slab using a step-palette knife and leave to semi-set.

2 Use a metal scraper to push at an angle against the layer of chocolate to create thin cigar shapes (copeaux) – a short sharp movement to the side will cause the copeaux to stay on the marble. Leave the copeaux to set on the surface for a few minutes, then remove with the metal scraper.

Two-tone Copeaux

1 Spread a thin layer of tempered white chocolate onto a marble or granite slab using a step-palette knife and leave to semi-set. Use a comb scraper to drag vertically down, creating stripes.

2 On top of the white chocolate stripes spread dark chocolate to fill the newly made gaps and leave to semi-set.

3 Use a metal scraper to push at an angle against the layer of chocolate to create thin cigar shapes (copeaux) – a short sharp movement to the side will cause the two-tone copeaux to stay on the marble. Leave the two-tone copeaux to set on the surface for a few minutes, then remove with the metal scraper.

TO MAKE A PAPER CORNET

• Cut a sheet of silicone (baking) paper into triangles, making sure that you have one long side and two smaller sides.

• Curl the paper around to create a cone with the tip in the centre of the long side of the triangle.

• Tuck in the excess paper to hold it in place.

Piped Curls

Copeaux

Piped Curves

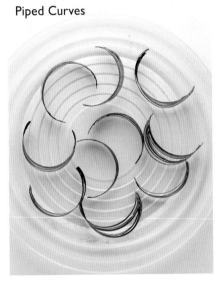

INDEX

INGREDIENTS

PÂTISSERIE & CHOCOLATE INGREDIENTS
Wild Harvest
www.wildharvestuk.com
Fresh As www.fresh-as.com
Keylink www.keylink.org

COUVERTURE CHOCOLATE
Amedei
www.kingsfinefood.co.uk
www.amedei-us.com
www.lario.com.au

OTHER COUVERTURE CHOCOLATE
Valrhona
www.chocolatetradingco.com
World Wide Chocolate
www.worldwidechocolate.com
Amano Artisan Chocolate
www.amanochocolate.com
Guittard Chocolate Company
www.guittard.com
Michel Cluizel
www.tcfinefoods.co.uk
www.chocosphere.com
Scharffen Berger
www.scharffenberger.com
Simon Johnson
www.simonjohnson.com
Aui Fine Foods
www.auiswisscatalogue.com

SPICES & SALTS
India Tree
www.indiatree.com
Steenbergs Organic
www.steenbergs.co.uk

FINE TEAS & QUALITY COFFEE
JING Tea
www.jingtea.com
Square Mile Coffee Roasters
www.shop.squaremilecoffee.com

JAPANESE INGREDIENTS
Atari-Ya Foods
www.atariya.co.uk
Japan Centre
www.japancentre.com

EQUIPMENT

KITCHEN EQUIPMENT
Russums www.russums-shop.co.uk
Nisbets www.nisbets.com
Mora www.mora.fr
Silikomart www.silikomart.com
Silicone Moulds
www.siliconemoulds.com
Sur la Table www.surlatable.com
Williams-Sonoma
www.williams-sonoma.com
Culinary Cookware
www.culinarycookware.com

CHOCOLATE EQUIPMENT & MOULDS
DécoRelief www.deco-relief.fr
Home Chocolate Factory
www.homechocolatefactory.com
Chef Rubber www.chefrubber.com
Chocoley www.chocoley.com
Savour Chocolate & Patisserie School
www.savourschool.com.au

STENCILS & DECORATIONS
PCB (France) www.pcb-creation.fr
Squires Kitchen
www.squires-shop.com
Sugarcraft www.sugarcraft.com

KITCHENWARE & GLASSES
David Mellor Design
www.davidmellordesign.com

ACKNOWLEDGEMENTS

Nostalgia plays an important part in my career, so it's been a pleasure to work again with a publisher who shares my vision. So many thanks to Jacqui Small and her hard-working team.

To Kevin Summers for his stunning photography and patience, to Robin Rout for his incredible design work and to Abi Waters, my editor, for her patience and dedication. Also, special thanks to Melissa Paul who has worked tirelessly in producing this book and whose support, dedication and creativity helped this book happen.

A huge thank you to all of the people who have inspired me over the years: Pierre Koffmann, Michel and Alain Roux, Pierre Hermé, Frédéric Cassel, Jean-Paul Hévin, Arnaud Larher, Laurent Duchêne, Raymond Blanc, Anton Edelmann, Marco Pierre White and Andreas Archerer. Also to all the team at Relais Desserts and to Cecilia Tessieri of Amedei for supplying the best couverture in the world.

A special mention for all the friends who have supported me: Scott Lyall, Willie Pike, Bruce Sangster, Tom Kitchin, Sara Jayne Stanes, Mike and Stella Nadell, Yolande Stanley, Neil Borthwick, Daniel Martelat, Craig Wilson, Éric Chavot, Gwen McIlroy, Frederick Mozart, Bruce Langlands, Arnold Isaacson, Scott Leonard, Ena Forsyth, Melanie Jappy and Ron McCabe. To the World Famous at Tannadice and to Methil, the wee East coast town in The Kingdom of Fife where my journey began.

Finally, my sister Karen, Neil and the bairns; to Suzue who has played a huge part in my story and of course to my beautiful daughter Amy Rose.

Lastly, to Jose Lasheras who is sadly no longer with us, but remains an endless source of artistic creativity.

William Curley

Dear William,
I know of your professionalism through Relais Desserts.
I am happy to see that you demonstrate your knowledge and your expertize in this work in order to share your passion for the benefit of others.
I perceive this book to be an act of sharing, of generosity. One can see the pleasure that you have in every photograph that shows the art of pâtisserie, which you know so well how to do.
Congratulations on this beautiful book.
Best wishes,

Cher William,
Je connais ton professionalisme à travers les Relais Desserts.
Je suis heureux de voir que tu mets tes connaissances, ton savoir faire dans cet ouvrage afin de partager ta passion aux services des autres.
Je perçois dans cette ouvrage, cette volonté de partage, de générosité. On voit le plaisir que tu as eu dans chaque photo de montrer l'art de la pâtisserie comme tu sais si bien le faire Bravo pour ce belle ouvrage
Sincères amitiés,

Arnaud Larher
MEILLEUR OUVRIER DE FRANCE, RELAIS DESSERTS

I am in awe of the way William has executed this pâtisserie – ranging from the classic to the most sophisticated – which undoubtedly recalls delicious childhood memories. Thanks to their clean and elegant finish these delicacies arouse a crazy desire for flavour. Once again, William proves that he knows how to challenge himself in order to awaken our senses.

Admiratif de la manière dont William traite ces pâtisseries; allant du classique au plus sophistiqué; et qui pour certains fait appel à nos souvenirs gourmands d'enfance.
De part leur finition sobre et élégants ces desserts suscitent une folle envie de gourmandise.
Une fois de plus William nous prouve qu'il sait se remettre en question, tout en mettant nos sens en éveil.

Laurent Duchêne
MEILLEUR OUVRIER DE FRANCE, RELAIS DESSERTS